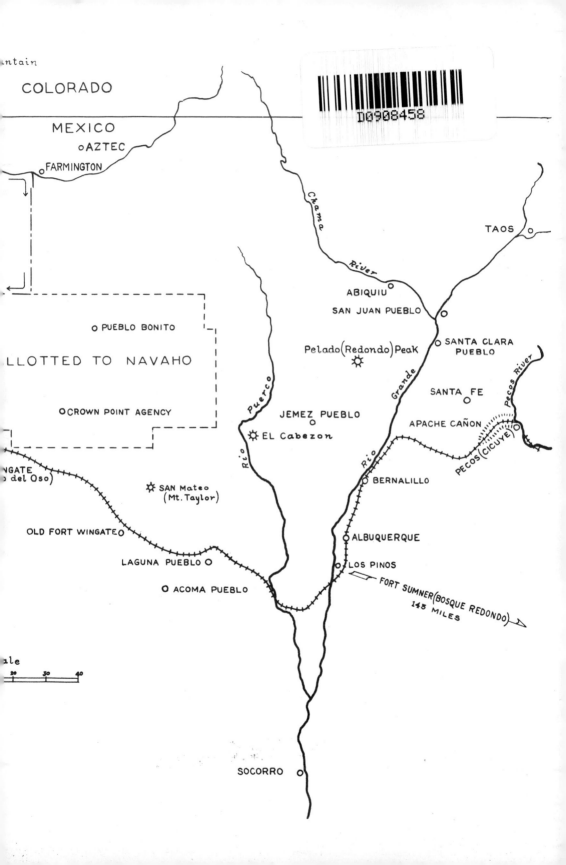

NAVAHO WEAVING

Navaho Weaving

ITS TECHNIC AND ITS HISTORY

Charles Avery Amsden

The Rio Grande Press Inc.,

1734 East 71st Place, Chicago 49, Illinois

First Edition
from which this
edition was reprinted
was supplied by
ERICH KOHLBERG
Kohlberg's
429—17th Street
Denver, Colorado

Reprinted with the cooperation
of the
SOUTHWEST MUSEUM
Highland Park, Los Angeles, Calif.

Color plates reprinted
through courtesy and cooperation of
THE UNIVERSITY OF NEW MEXICO PRESS
Albuquerque, New Mexico

A RIO GRANDE CLASSIC
First published in 1934.

LIBRARY OF CONGRESS CARD CATALOG NUMBER
64-20401

First Printing

1964

The Rio Grande Press Inc.,
1734 East 71st Place, Chicago 49, Illinois

NAVAHO WEAVING

ITS TECHNIC AND HISTORY

By

CHARLES AVERY AMSDEN

Foreword By

FREDERICK WEBB HODGE

THE FINE ARTS PRESS
SANTA ANA, CALIFORNIA

In Coöperation With
THE SOUTHWEST MUSEUM
1934

FOREWORD
By F. W. Hodge

IRILE and on-going, the Navaho, now the most populous of the tribes of the United States, are the only Indians who have prospered through defeat at arms. Raiders of the sedentary Pueblo Indians from as early as the latter part of the sixteenth century, and of Caucasian settlements of a later period, the Navaho and their Apache congeners kept the entire Southwest constantly astir, thereby directly affecting the lives and the culture of the inhabitants of milder mien until American forces put an end to their forays in the 1860's.

So far as knowledge extends, the Navaho, earlier known as one of a number of Apache bands—the "Apaches de Navajo,"—adopted the art of weaving from captive Pueblo women probably about the middle of the eighteenth century, following the acquirement of sheep through raids on the flocks of the pastoral Pueblo Indians and Mexicans. Substantial support of this is afforded by the fact that Pueblo women were early adopted into the Navaho tribe and assigned to specific clans; and it is known also that by the year 1780 they were officially reported as engaged in farming, raising herds, and weaving blankets and clothing of wool. Moreover, there is no evidence that any other tribe of Athapascan affinity, from the Tinneh or Déné of the Far North to the Apache of Arizona and New Mexico, ever engaged in loom-weaving, although the latter people, cousins of the Navaho, had an equal opportunity of doing so had they been so inclined. Defeated through the destruction of their flocks by American troops, sheep proved to be first the undoing and ultimately the stepping-stone to the success and wealth which the increasing Navaho tribe has achieved.

With its lowly beginning a century and a half or so ago, Navaho women gradually but surely developed the craft of weaving until ere very long they excelled their Pueblo teachers just as the Navaho priest-doctors have surpassed these village-dwellers in the elaboration of their dry-paintings until they have attained marvelous proficiency in design and execution—all borrowed, to be sure, but stamped with the individuality of the borrower, and a personal possession to the extent of personal coloring and shaping. It was thus that in time Pueblo weaving was almost lost to sight except to the specialist, for the product of the Navaho loom early found its way to far corners and now is famed almost everywhere. In-

deed almost any Southwestern blanket of Indian manufacture is labeled
"Navaho" in the popular mind, although it may have been woven at Zuñi
or in one of the Hopi villages, where the industry is still carried on.

Navaho weaving, judging by its descent from the textile art in cotton by the women of sedentary tribes of the Southwest many centuries
ago, may exemplify processes long lost, thus making its study a valuable
contribution to archeology and to ethnology alike. There is therefore no
ground for dismissing it as largely of modern or European inspiration,
regardless of the recency of the art among the Navaho. Indeed a fragment
from a remote horizon may prove to be a counterpart of Navaho weave
in which the whole process may become clear.

The place of the Navaho blanket as a cultural feature of the tribe has
been so well expressed by Dr. Edgar L. Hewett that we may well afford
to quote him at length:

"The Navaho made of blanket weaving not only a fine art but a profitable industry. The semi-nomadic pastoral life exactly suited their disposition. They rapidly acquired large flocks, discovered the plants that
would yield beautiful and lasting dyes, adopted the simple apparatus needed in weaving, developed marvelous sense of design and facility of hand
and eye. As a result the 'Navaho blanket' has become known far and
wide as a thing of beauty and utility. It has become the major resource of
the now most numerous of American Indian tribes, has dominated their
culture, and contributed more than any other one thing to their welfare
and virility. It has weathered the degenerating influence of commercializa-
tion and is an outstanding illustration of how an esthetic factor may shape
the destiny of a people.*

There have been numerous studies of primitive textiles, and several
on Navaho weaving have been published, but until now the subject has
usually been approached from the esthetic rather than from the technical
point of view. Born and reared on the selvage border of the Navaho
tribal range, so to speak, it was not unnatural for a student of such exceptional acumen as Mr. Charles Amsden early to acquire an interest in
these Indian neighbors, and especially in that phase of their culture which
was so constantly displayed before his eyes. Appreciating the need of a
comprehensive study of Navaho weaving from other than its purely
esthetic aspect, our author undertook his research into the technical side
of the subject in 1929, and devoted all of his available time and energy to

---

* Edgar L. Hewett, Ancient Life in the American Southwest, pp. 152-153, In-
dianpolis, 1930.

it during that and the following years. The results achieved are embodied in the present volume. Mr. Amsden's investigations have led him into many byways and hedges, considerably beyond the scope originally contemplated, for it has taken him far into the realm of Navaho history in an effort to trace the beginnings of the weaver's art, while his inquiry into the origin of the craft and its mutations, so far as the Navaho are concerned, has been fruitful of results which hitherto have been enveloped in the nebulæ of imperfect knowledge.

In addition to the technic of the weaver's craft, the volume presents a résumé of our archeological knowledge of the long career of the loom and its prototypes in the prehistoric Southwest, describes and illustrates in detail the various weaves used by the Navaho, and records the processes employed in making their native dyes. Following this will be found a discussion of Navaho weaving from the introduction of sheep by the first Spaniards, through its earliest historical references in old Spanish documents and its brilliant "bayeta period" to modern times when, as the author says, it was gradually transformed from a native craft of blanketry into a rug-making industry. The book closes with a chapter analyzing and tracing the growth of design and an account of the "revival" movement now in progress.

The illustrations are of great value in themselves. Instead of specializing in "pretty blankets," as previous writers have been prone to do, Mr. Amsden has made a special effort to obtain illustrations of old authentically-dated specimens; and through the generous coöperation of museums and private collectors the country over a group of excellent photographs of more than one hundred such blankets has been assembled. Many date back to the Civil War and even earlier. These with the historic old scenes and figures of early reservation days and the ample illustrations of every process in blanket-making far surpass any previous effort in that direction.

There is perhaps no greater problem in Indian affairs than that of adjusting the Indian to the American economic scheme. Education of the Indian has not been a great success, for few Indians can step out of school and take their place in the American community except as day-laborers. In the advancement of the Indian his native crafts thus far have been the most helpful, for they allow him to remain himself, to express himself, while at the same time they have an economic value. Of all these crafts that of Navaho weaving has been the most important factor in adjusting the Indian to our order of things. The white man can appreciate a good

sturdy rug and its simple Indian patterning, whereas basketry and pottery to him are mainly decorative. The Navaho rug is also useful, and the Indian will never be adjusted to us until a sufficient number of pursuits can be devised in ways useful or satisfying to both races.
Southwest Museum, Los Angeles

ACKNOWLEDGMENT

Scores of people helped me make this book: nearly every page of it records an obligation. I here express my thanks for the help and my deep appreciation of the courtesy with which it was given.

Especially am I grateful to the Trustees of Southwest Museum and to former Director James A. B. Scherer who secured their authorization of the study as a part of my Museum duties; to my wife and my associates of Southwest Museum who advised and assisted in many ways; to Dr. Frederick Webb Hodge who generously sponsored the work with a Foreword; and finally to Mr. Thomas E. Williams, director of the Fine Arts Press of Santa Ana Junior College, who had the courage to publish it.

CHARLES AVERY AMSDEN

DEDICATED
TO THE MEMORY OF

WASHINGTON MATTHEWS
Major, Medical Corps, U. S. Army

SYMPATHETIC OBSERVER, UNBIASED STUDENT,
FAITHFUL RECORDER, OF NAVAHO LIFE AND WAYS

CONTENTS

CHAPTER VII

PART II—THE HISTORY OF NAVAHO WEAVING

CHAPTER VIII

CHAPTER IX

CHAPTER X

CHAPTER XI

CHAPTER XII

CHAPTER XIII

CHAPTER XIV

CHAPTER XV

ILLUSTRATIONS

FIGURES

PLATES

PART I
THE TECHNIC OF
NAVAHO WEAVING

PLAITING

The simple criss-cross or overlap of strands of any material having
the slight flexibility needed to accomodate them to this over-and-under
ordering, is known as plaiting.[1] It has an important subdivision, which
is braiding.

BRAIDING

Schoolgirls who divide their hair into three ropes at the back of the
head and braid these into one—if any still do—are practising the simplest
form of weaving. Braiding it is called, and for the following reasons it
may be considered a branch of the general technic of plaiting. In all
plaiting the strands of material are interwoven by overlapping; but in
braiding these strips all start from a common point and tend in one direction (pl. 7a) while other forms of plaiting employ two sets of strips,
tending in opposite directions, as shown in plate 2b. An exception to this
statement must be noted, and it proves the close kinship of the two technics: in braiding, certain of the strands may be bent sharply inward until
they cross the others at approximately right angles, when braiding becomes plaiting in every sense of the term. An excellent illustration of this
merging of the two methods is given in Kidder and Guernsey (pl. 45, 1).

Three is the smallest number of strips with which braiding can be
done, but there is literally no greatest number. Hundreds of strings are
manipulated in this technic by some of the central and eastern tribes of
the United States. The Algonkian peoples in general, the Sauk and Fox in
particular, were adept at making very serviceable and attractive bags and
sashes of buffalo hair and apocynum (Indian hemp) by this method.

In the Southwest, braiding was known to the earliest people of whom
we have gained sufficient knowledge to venture upon giving them a
name—the Basketmakers. It therefore has some two thousand years of
antiquity in this instance, for these people quite probably were flourishing
and making the attractive braided sashes shown in plate 3 as early as the
time of Christ.[2]

---

[1] As our clothes tend to stretch at points of greatest strain, so does our
language; and many of our soundest words have been warped out of all form
through their constant misuse by persons too ignorant or too lazy to seek out the
word really expressive of their precise meaning. So I must offer the word plaiting
with an apology. It comes, says Webster, from the Latin plicare, to fold; and it is
involved with other derivatives, of meanings variant only in degree, such as plat,
pleat, ply. It has also been used interchangeably with the word braiding, but it will
be seen that they are first cousins, not twins.

[2] Such statements require justification to the average reader, but the explanation must be highly condensed: Basketmaker remains underlie those of the

a, Hopi ring basket of plaited yucca strips in diamond twill pattern, identical with those of the prehistoric Pueblos, detail of which is shown in b. Diameter 14 inches. Southwest Museum, cat. Q189.

b, Pattern of plaited yucca basket (see a), prehistoric Pueblo. This method of weaving in diagonal lines is known as twilling, the diamond twill being used here. After Kidder and Guernsey fig. 39.

c, Braided cotton sash, Hopi, in technic and function identical with the Basketmaker specimens of plate 3. Length, 8½ feet. Fred K. Hinchman coll. Southwest Museum cat. 202L98. Hough (1914 fig. 158b) shows a specimen from the prehistoric Pueblos, proving the unbroken line of descent of this ancient finger weave.

PLATE 3

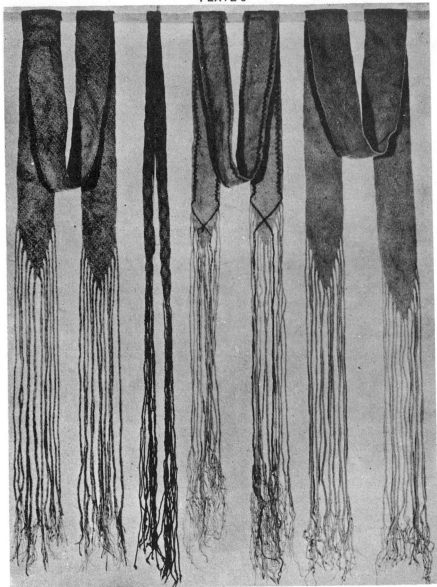

Basketmaker braided sashes, found in 1930 by Mr. Earl H. Morris in a cave in the Lukachukai Mountains, New Mexico. Colors natural white (dog hair) and brown (undetermined). Despite their age of some two thousand years, they are as fresh and strong as if newly made. The cave in which they were buried was perfectly dry, otherwise they would have decayed long ago.

Length of c, 9 feet, 2 inches. Courtesy Carnegie Institution of Washington and Laboratory of Anthropology, Santa Fe, New Mexico. Cat. (Laboratory) 846.

Coming down the centuries in the Southwest, we find the prehistoric Pueblos using braiding for sashes like those of the Basketmakers, as well as for tump-lines or carrying straps, and serviceable ropes; while in the cotton sash of their cultural heirs the Hopi(pl. 2c) we have the technic down to date. The Navaho are not known as braiders; yet this finger weave is so simple and widespread that they may well have practised it from an early time, for during the historic period they have braided ropes of horsehair and of leather, after the Mexican fashion.

Braiding is called the simplest of weaving methods because it needs no accessories but skilful fingers (most versatile of devices after all), and because it produces a fabric without the foundation required by the more complex methods. In our own times it is exemplified in the rag rugs which are getting old-fashioned enough to be popular again, and in various ornamental cords and ropes in use everywhere; but it was always a technic of limited value.

Plaiting in its more generalized meaning is a simple technic, yet its product is very near to that of the loom. Loom weaving, in effect, is plaiting done mechanically and in bulk instead of a stitch at a time. Its fabric is bonded in the same manner as the plaited fabric, by the overlap of the component strips (pl. 22a).

Modern furniture of wicker and cane is usually plaited; so too are many of our baskets—in particular the wire baskets used in offices, the willow clothes hampers in our homes, and the self-serve baskets in grocery stores. Oddly enough, the Hopi for centuries have made a counterpart of the latter two: a carrying basket of willow withes and a circular bowl-basket, called a ring basket, of yucca leaves plaited flat (pl. 2a). The last-named goes back to a remote prehistoric time without the slightest change in its structure or function, as many archeological finds have proved. Matting too was plaited by ancient peoples of the Southwest and by many others, using cedar bark, corn husks, yucca leaves, rushes—in fact, any material flat and flexible, for those are the requirements of plaiting.

---

earliest prehistoric Pueblo people in many Southwestern caves, hence Basketmaker preceded Pueblo. The latter, builder of the great villages like Aztec, Pueblo Bonito, Cliff Palace, and many others, around 1000 A. D., were then at the height of their career. But two well-defined culture stages preceded this "Great Period" before we get back to Basketmaker days—and those days were long, for they reveal in turn three stages: pre-agricultural, agricultural, pottery-making. Hence to place them at about the time of Christ is conservative enough.

For further evidence, the tree-ring method of dating Pueblo ruins (see Douglass, as listed in the bibliography) carries back to about 600 A. D. and is extending its time-reach constantly toward Basketmaker times.

For a good short account of these prehistoric culture periods see Roberts (Introduction).

LOOPING

The term looping[3] covers a variety of closely related methods of finger weaving, well exemplified in the knitted stockings so long considered an indispensable feature of civilized dress. Knitting and crochet are common

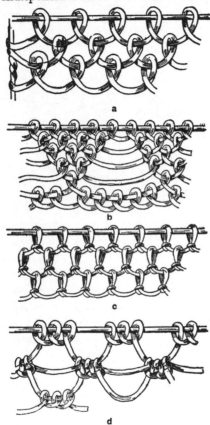

forms of looping, so called because they achieve a fabric bonded by a continuous series of interlocking loops, as shown in fig. 1. Like braided fabrics these have no foundation and have the same characteristic trend in one direction. They mark a technical advance, however, in requiring one very simple tool in their manufacture: the hook or knitting needle.

Looping is another ancient finger weave. Indeed, all the fundamental technics were invented thousands of years ago, modern man having merely elaborated and mechanized them to produce cheaply and in quantity the many textiles we have come to require in the complexity of our daily lives. Without extensive research one could not name the many aboriginal American peoples using this technic, but our immediate concern is with the Southwest, where Basketmakers and Pueblos

Fig. 1—Looping, various forms. a is the simplest type, figured by Guernsey from the Basketmakers (plate 46 e) and by Kidder and Guernsey from the prehistoric Pueblos (fig. 45 and plates 34a, 46c). After G. W. James, Indian and other basket making, figs. 60, 62-64 by courtesy of Mrs. James and Miss Edith Farnsworth.

alike were familiar with it. Here again the descent from ancient to recent times is unbroken, for the modern Pueblos knit their stockings, as do the Navaho; but more will be said of this in Chapter 7.

Having no steel for making needles, the ancient peoples used needles of

[3] Adopted at the suggestion of Miss Katherine Bartlett, Curator of Anthropology of the Museum of Northern Arizona, Flagstaff.

PLATE 4

Navaho basketry. **k** is a water bottle made tight with piñon gum inside and out, and provided with loop handles of horse hair. It is of the Ute type, coiled on a rod-and-bundle foundation. **j** is the typical Paiute "marriage basket" so common among the Navaho, made on a three-rod foundation. The other examples are of the old Navaho type, coiled on a two-rod-and-bundle foundation. Mason (II: 470) calls **j** a drum, the others meal baskets.

The designs suggest a progressive merging of the isolated figures characteristic of the Navaho type into the banded pattern of the Paiute. Height of **k**, 17 inches. Southwest Museum cat. **a** 31P1, **b** 31P2, **c** 31P3, **d** 29P1, **e** 30P1, **f** 31P4, **g** 31P6, **h** 31P5, **i** 31P7, **j** 29P2, **k** 501G14, **l** CFL22.

FIG. 4—Basketmaker bags, double-twined of apocynum or yucca fiber probably in the manner shown in fig. 7. a (after Goddard p. 47) is from Grand Gulch, Utah; b (Kidder and Guernsey plate 79f) from northeastern Arizona.

wood or of bone. For materials, various shredded vegetal fibers such as apocynum have been used, as well as cotton, wool, and hair both human and animal.[4]

COILING

We come now into that rudimentary field of weaving called basketry and encounter fabrics made upon a foundation. One category of basketry falls under our heading of looping, and an important, world-wide one it is: the coiled basket. Study of the detailed drawing in figure 2a reveals a structure of circular rods, the foundation, held in the form into which the maker has bent them by a series of looped stitches of stout grass or split twig, enclosing the rods. Each succeeding layer of foundation rods is bound to the preceding layer by these interlocking loops. Take away the foundation and a continuous fabric of stitching would yet remain —a looped fabric. Recognition of this fact is implied in the name Southwestern archeologists have applied to the technic of looping as exemplified in many fragments of textile found in ruins, calling it "coil without foundation." Coil with foundation seems merely an elaboration of the simpler form.[5] It yields a stiffer product, and in so doing marks an im-

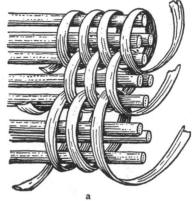

a

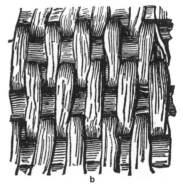

b

Fig. 2—Coiling, showing in **a** the method and in **b** the characteristic surface appearance of coiled basketry. The three-rod foundation shown in **a** is used in the ceremonial basket made by the Paiute for the Navaho, illustrated in plate 4J. After G. W. James, Indian and other basket making, figs. (a) 81, (b) 79 (from Mason figs. 50 (a) and 47 (b)).

portant advance along our chain leading to the Navaho loom: form becomes a factor.

---

[4] Knitting was known in prehistoric Peru in Early Nazca times, which go back to the initial centuries of the Christian era. (Means 1930: 23 and fig. 4).

[5] It is true that not all coiled baskets have a looped overstructure: in some the stitches clasp the foundation without interlocking among themselves, the effect being the same in either case. In this fact lies a possible objection to including the coiling method under looping.

Braiding and simple looping produce only flexible fabrics, formless; but the introduction of the stiff foundation coil makes possible an object that will retain the form to which the maker has modeled it, hence we have circular baskets, even rectangular ones, of a great variety of shapes. We must note, too, that an important esthetic factor has come into our field, that of graceful form, with its corollary consideration of proportion in the component parts, such as rim, neck, shoulder, body, and base.

All of our Southwestern peoples, ancient and modern, made coiled basketry; it gave the Basketmakers their name, for they were notably proficient in this technic. The Navaho of modern times, however, have largely surrendered this branch of their ancient heritage to neighboring tribes, the Paiute in particular. Some of their old-time coiled baskets are shown in plate 4.

TWINING

Plaiting and looping, as we have seen, produce fabrics without foundation, except for the coiled basket. Henceforth foundation is to be a factor in the weaving complex, and the fundamental technic next to be described is entirely dependent on the foundation for its successful application. Twining it is called, and figure 3 illustrates the methods. As the name implies, this form of weaving consists in wrapping or twining the outer strands around the inner ones, those comprising the foundation of the piece. The latter are entirely hidden if the twining is closely set, and the resultant fabric has the characteristic smooth surface texture with gentle undulations marking the hidden foundation ribs, which we associate with closely-woven loom textiles.

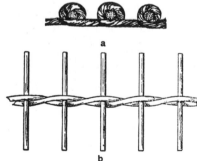

Fig. 3—Twining, two principal methods. a (seen in cross section) single (wrap weave); b double (plain) twine. The latter requires two weft strands, the former but one. After G. W. James, Indian and other basket making, figs. (a) 195, (b) 107 (a from Mason fig. 14, after Holmes 1884 fig. 71).

Twining has two principal divisions, known as single (called by Mason wrap weave) and double (plain twine); these are shown in *a* and *b* of figure 3. In the former a single strand of weft (the overlying material) is wrapped once around each string[6] of warp (the foundation

___

[6] More than one warp strip may be thus clasped; two are frequently used, but the method is the same whatever the number.

material), the fabric thus growing in layers of horizontal wrapping upon a vertical foundation. In double or plain twining two strands of weft are used concurrently. One passes below, the other above the foundation strip, then the two strands cross in the interval between the strips, reversing their relative positions before clasping the next strip of warp or foundation. This method differs from that of plaiting and of loom weaving only in the criss-cross of weft at every stitch, and with very fine and flexible materials it produces a fabric easily mistaken for one loom-woven.

Double twining is much the commoner form of the two in the prehistoric Southwest—for in historic times this technic has been little used except in basketry. The Basketmakers used it in making blankets of furred strips of rabbit-skin wrapped about a cord of yucca or apocynum, and bags and sandals of the latter materials, like those shown in figure 4 and plate. 107. These early people had no knowledge of the loom, hence were dependent for their fabrics on the simpler finger weaves already described. They made good use of the double twining process, however, producing sandals embodying many intricate patterns in stitches of varied width. In this feature the hand technics have a great advantage over the loom: they can vary at any point the stitch as well as the weft color being used, while the loom must plod along on the one stitch for which it has been rigged. Unthinkingly, one supposes that our modern machines produce endless variety in textiles; not so, they produce only monotony. The variety is in the machines, not the product, for each machine does just one thing, over and over, until its rigging is changed to a new pattern. Fortunately, though, we have many machines at work.

The prehistoric Pueblos acquired the loom at an early period of their development [7] and neglected twining of fabrics, although they practised the method to some extent in making sandals, occasional bags, and certain forms of basketry. The old double-twined blanket of the Basketmakers was frequently made, with feathers of the domestic turkey (a useful bird the Basketmakers did not have) used in place of rabbit-skin. Their modern descendants have carried this neglect of twining still farther, although rabbit-skin blankets are still made occasionally. The Navaho too may have been twiners in an earlier time, for they have traditions of having used vegetal fibers in garment making before the time of European sheep.[8] In later years, however, they have made the loom their sole reliance in the textile field.

---

[7] Apparently as early as their first culture stage, Pueblo I. See Guernsey: 9.
[8] "They had as yet no horses, domestic sheep, or goats. . . The women wore

Twining has little part in our modern life. Hard to adapt to mechanical processes, its main use in that regard is for making gauzes, especially surgical bandages, for it is best adapted to fabrics of very loose texture. But as a primitive process it ranks high, giving excellent results in patient and skilful hands, as the Basketmaker sandal and the Chilkat blanket attest.

OUTLINE SUMMARY OF THE FINGER TECHNICS

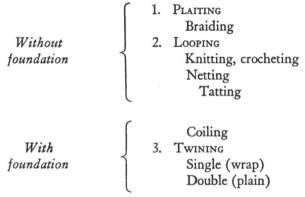

Without foundation

1. PLAITING
   Braiding
2. LOOPING
   Knitting, crocheting
   Netting
   Tatting

With foundation

  Coiling
3. TWINING
   Single (wrap)
   Double (plain)

THE INFLUENCE OF MATERIALS

Having reviewed the three fundamental technics of weaving and noted that all were extensively used by the two Southwestern peoples who in this particular were the cultural ancestors of those later comers, the Navaho, we turn from basic methods to certain adaptations and refinements in their use. This is no abandonment of our original quest, for there can be no loom weaving without a further advance in certain of the finger technics, an advance in which material plays an outstanding part. Plaiting and twining give us the methods on which loom weaving is based (looping may be dropped as a largely unproductive line), and they yield good results with a broad range of materials—most of them, however, either too stiff, coarse, or weak, for successful use in the loom. Hence the need of further developments before we reach the end of our chain.

Wool, in America, is the material on which the loom depends. The term includes cotton, for in the technical sense cotton is a wool, not a

a garment consisting of two webs of woven cedar bark, one hanging in front and one behind; all wore sandals of yucca fibre or cedar bark. . . Their blankets were made of cedar bark, of yucca fibre, or of skins sewn together." Excerpt from the legend of origins in Matthews 1897: 141.

bast, as Wissler (43) points out. Linen is the only bast to ride to high success upon the loom, and it was unknown to aboriginal America. Wool is a material which requires special treatment. Notably, it should be carded, and it must be spun or roved. Carding (pls. 10, 12) straightens the tangled short hairs, while spinning (pls. 13, 14) welds them into a smooth, continuous strand, as fine or coarse as the spinner may desire and of unlimited length. Carding is simply a process of combing. It is not indispensable, and in fact was dispensed with in Chilkat blanket weaving, the hair or wool being formed into a rove by rolling it on the thigh.[9]

Holmes (1896:21) comments as follows on the significance of spinning in the development of the textile crafts:

> The use of simple strands or parts in textile art precedes the use of spun threads, but the one use leads very naturally to the other. In employing rushes, stems, grasses, etc., the smaller strands were doubled to secure uniformity of size, and when a number of parts were used they were combined into one by twisting or plaiting. In time the advantage in strength and pliability of twisted strands came to be recognized, and this led to the general utilization of fibrous substances, and finally to the manufacture of suitable fibers by manipulating the bark of trees and plants. Spinning was probably not devised until the weaver's art had made considerable advance, but its invention opened a new and broad field and led to the development of a magnificent industry. Semi-rigid fabrics served for a wide range of uses, as already described, but soft and pliable cloths for personal use and ornament were made possible only by the introduction of spinning.

At this point our first special appliance for weaving comes into the picture: the spindle (the needle we have, but it has other uses). This vital adjunct to weaving in wool comprises a shaft and a round weight, commonly of stone, earthenware, or wood, slipped over the end of the shaft like a collar. The weighted end is generally placed on the ground, and from the other end the instrument is twirled—either in the fingers or by rolling it along the thigh (pl. 13) or the shin. The Navaho usually spin with the fingers. The whorl or weight, besides holding the wool in place

---

[9] The buffalo-hair bags of the Algonkian peoples underwent a similar preparation of material (buffalo hair being too coarse and short for successful spinning in any event); and it has been conjectured that the slit skirt of Iroquois women was meant to bare the thigh for this purpose.

PLATE 5

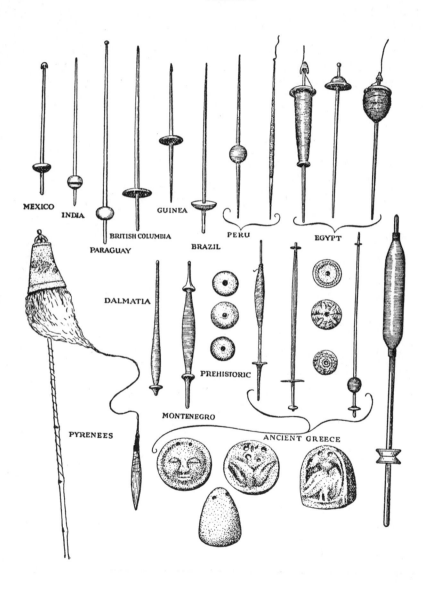

Spindles from many lands, with a distaff from the Pyrenees and loom weights from ancient Greece. The fundamental steps and accessories in loom development are similar if not identical in all times and places. After Hooper, plate 2.

on the shaft, acts as a flywheel, retaining the momentum of the twirl and giving an even movement to the revolving shaft. The free hand of

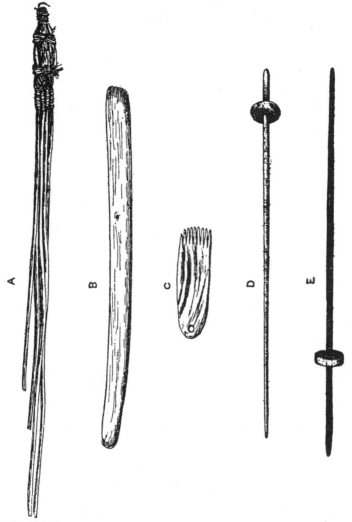

Fig. 5—Prehistoric Pueblo weaving implements, after Goddard p. 50. A, cotton beater; the Hopi used a similar device until recently, beating their cotton between two blankets until the fiber adhered to the wool and could be scraped into roves ready for spinning. B, batten. C, comb. D and E, spindles.

All are exact prototypes of modern Pueblo and Navaho implements, except that the Navaho, using no cotton, had no need of A. Block lent by the American Museum of Natural History.

the spinner manipulates the wool which is being wound upon the spindle and pulled and twisted into a continuous strand in the process. Spindles from various countries are shown in plate 5, while plates 13 and 14 show Navaho women spinning.

Another important accessory to wool weaving is the comb (fig. 5*c*, pl. 16). Its purpose is to straighten and press home the fine woolen strands after they have been enmeshed in the warp as shown in plate 16. On theoretical grounds the comb probably originated in the awl or bodkin of the basket maker—an implement with but one point. The comb is only an awl with multiple points. It is our second special appliance in weaving, and the influence of material—wool in this instance—is responsible for the existence of them both in the Southwest.

THE INFLUENCE OF METHOD

We come now to a final point of refinement in the finger technics before going on to the development of the loom: the question whether the foundation structure (warp) is to be left visible in an open or "basket" weave (pl. 27*b*) or hidden by pressing the overstructure (weft) so closely together that the other is obliterated (pl. 22*a*). In the latter case the result is known as tapestry weave. It was used by the Basketmakers in their bags and fine sandals, and it is invariable in Navaho blanket weaving; but the Pueblos in their cotton weaving have always preferred the open or basket weave (pl. 60).

The tapestry weave has had a great influence on the development of textile design, as will be explained. In the open weave the warp is visible throughout, hence the weaver must take it into account in creating her pattern. For that reason she cannot achieve a solid figure of any size, the nearest possible approach to it being a checkerboard outline produced by contrasting colors in warp and weft. This limitation of effect by structure is not without broad possibilities of its own, to be sure. In the basket type of weaving it was common practice to use different colors in the warp strings with a single color of weft. Thus, wherever unicolored weft met multicolored warp a visual contrast resulted, and with this the weaver fashioned her designs by manipulation of the strands of various hues into orderly arrangements.

In belt loom weaving as practised by the Navaho and certain Pueblos today, and by primitive peoples the world over, the many possibilities of the use of warp color in design are illustrated. Study of any specimen will reveal this significant limitation, however: warp color is

FIG. 6—The supporting stake. Attu Island woman weaving a twined basket of sea grass. After Mason, plate 144.

FIG. 7—The supporting frame. Plaited mat of cedar bark, showing one day's work by a Chippewa woman. After Mason, plate 122.

PLATE 6

The fixed-warp frame. Salish weaver at work, after Kissell, plate XVI, from a painting by Paul Kane in 1846.

invariable in the individual strip throughout its entire length. A pattern begun in white warp must continue in white to the very end. As a consequence, patterns in which warp color occurs—whether in basket weave or in its modified form, a tapestry weave with raised warp effects as exemplified in the belts and garters of the Navaho and Pueblos—tend toward a constant repetition of the unit figure along the straight lines of the warp. Structural considerations dominate the design, as plates 20 and 21 reveal.

Weft, on the other hand, can be manipulated freely, its color changed at will; and the tapestry weave, in concealing the warp, offers far greater freedom in design, with consequent stimulus to development of that important factor in the textile crafts. This stimulus must in turn have fostered progress toward the loom, manifesting itself in a desire to employ fine-textured fibers that lend themselves most readily to complexity of design. To employ such fibers an auxiliary device of some sort was obviously a necessity, and the pursuit of a suitable device led eventually to the loom. It must be borne in mind that in weaving—unlike pottery, for example—design is built in, not painted on. It is integral with structure, and method and material both have their influence upon it.

PLATE 7

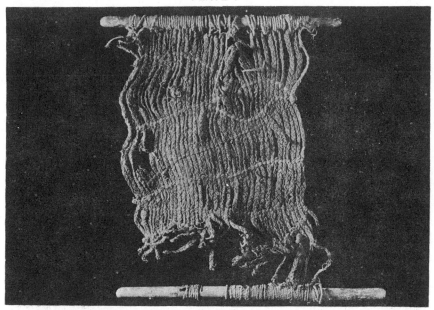

Prehistoric Southwestern twining frame, similar in many points to the true loom, but suitable only for hand twining. The lower figure shows in detail the method of attachment of the braided warp strings. Courtesy American Museum of Natural History, cat. 29.1/4581.

PLATE 8

A Navaho loom. For a description of its various parts see the drawing in fig. 12.
A. C. Vroman photo, Southwest Museum coll.

CHAPTER II

LOOM DEVELOPMENT IN AMERICA

ECHNICS and materials were the subject of the preceding chapter; accessories and appliances are the concern of this one. Loom weaving is the fruit of an alliance of material, method, and machine. We have sketched very briefly the development of the method and the influence of material; now for the machine, for it too had to develop. To assume that the loom, a relatively complex mechanical device, came into being as the result of a happy inspiration would flout the whole teachings of history. Discoveries may "just happen": inventions never do: they build up step by step as neatly as a block house, each the child of those that have come before and the parent of others to follow. There could have been no automobile without the wheelbarrow, no radio without Franklin's kite, and no loom without the supporting stake. Human needs in their fundamentals are constant, and their constancy has laid down lines of orderly progression for the great inventions to follow. Transportation, communication, clothing, are among those needs; but we are following now only the line determined by the last named.

There must be a word in explanation of the method of inquiry used in this chapter. It is not a historical method, although presented in the historical or sequential manner. We are dealing with developments that came about in prehistoric time, so must abandon the idea of having a chronological sequence to guide us, as we should have were we following the growth of the automobile, for example. The historian can say that the four-wheeled carriage, the gasoline engine, the rubber tire, were inventions of a certain definite time, place, and person, ranking each according to priority of appearance. In loom development we cannot do that, for want of knowledge; but we can do the next best thing. A skilled mechanic (to illustrate the statement) could step into a garage and without knowing anything of the development of automobiles (we shall assume his experience is with marine motors) could arrange a dozen of different makes and models into an approximately correct sequence of age on the basis of the growing complexity and perfection of their various mechanical features; and that we can do in loom development. The method has its limitations and weaknesses, to be sure; notably, it can prove nothing—as the historical method can—but it should convey some appreciation of the long course of experimental and practical development which culminated in mechanical weaving upon the loom as practised by only a few of the native peoples of America—among them the Navaho.

THE SUPPORTING STAKE

This chapter has for thesis the assumption that the evolution of the loom begins at the point of introduction of a device to facilitate manipulation of the material employed—for that is just what the loom does, mechanically and on a large scale. The germ of loom development therefore appears—on purely technological grounds, be it remembered—to lie within the stake upon which the soft baskets of the Northwest Coast area are woven, as illustrated in figure 6. It is significant in this connection that the basket woven on a stake is of material extremely fine and flexible, which has greater need of support than the coarser materials usually employed. Willow splints, for example, are rigid enough to retain the position in which they are placed, and in their use no support is needed.

The first step toward the loom, then, was probably dictated by the limitations of the available material. In all aboriginal crafts, for that matter, the material influences the technic quite as much as that affects the material. Stones which will not wear down are flaked; those which will not flake are shaped by abrasion. The plasticity of clay, the tendency of bone to split to a pointed end, the sturdy pliability of wood, have largely determined the form and function of objects wrought from these substances. Applying this principle to the textile crafts, it is natural to find that those materials which are easy to manipulate are handled without a supporting device; those which are too fine and flexible to maintain themselves in the process of manufacture are artificially controlled. The determination to make use of such fibers despite the difficulties inherent in their structure may well have been that spur of necessity which mothered the invention of the loom.

Closely akin to the supporting stake method of basket weaving is the manner of making twined bags of buffalo hair, with either a hair or a bast warp. This technic, of which little notice is found in the literature of American anthropology, is widespread among the Central Algonkian and Southern Siouan peoples, the Osage in particular having it highly developed. In this type of weaving the radial warp of the bag-to-be is suspended by a cord from overhead, bottom side up, and the weaver completes the fabric by twining the weft upon the warp foundation. The buffalo hair used is hand-spun, commonly by rolling it upon the thigh with the bare hand. This form of weaving employs no special devices except the means of suspension. It is an early form, and like most such was probably widespread in America. There is reason to believe that the Basketmakers of the Southwest employed it in making their twined bags of yucca and apocynum; and Kidder (1926: 623) thinks the extraordinarily complex sandal weaving of these early people was done in almost identical fashion, by suspension of the warp from a central point, as shown in figure 8.

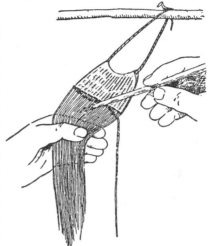

Fig. 8—Probable method of Basketmaker sandal weaving. After Kidder 1926, fig. 5.

THE FREE-WARP FRAME

From the supporting stake to the supporting frame, or from single-point to multiple-point suspension, is no great step. The two are used side by side in the Northwest Coast area, the region which affords the most abundant illustrations of the steps precedent to loom weaving. The stake offers only a single point of support: for that reason a mat or a blanket could not be woven upon it. Planting another stake alongside and stretching a cord or laying a pole transversely between the two, provides an adequate framework for mat weaving, as figure 7 makes clear. Strips of fiber are suspended from the transverse cord, and upon this warp rack every device known to foundation weaving—plaiting, twining, twilling, with their manifold variations—can be practised. This simple structure will do the work of a loom; but it is not by any means a loom, only a supporting frame upon which every step in the weaving process must be performed slowly and laboriously, handling each separate string of warp one by one.

Despite its theoretical possibilities, the weaving frame has its practical limitations. Its warp strings dangle loosely and tangle easily.[1] To work a

---

[1] The Chilkat blanket weaver's practice of making a little ball of the surplus

complicated pattern upon this shifting skein would be a slow and difficult process; to press home the individual strands of the weft, with no counter-resistance to the pressure, an exasperating and laborious task. The device is well suited to the function to which its highly practical users applied it: the weaving of coarse mats of rough bast, in the main. In this function it was widely distributed, probably throughout North America, wherever a suitable plant fiber grew in sufficient abundance to provide the requisite raw material.[2]

The weaving frame was adapted to the use of a fine fiber, wool, in a single known type of aboriginal American weaving, the Chilkat blanket of the upper Northwest Coast. Wool of the Rocky Mountain goat is used as weft, with a warp of cedar bark and wool together. This use of a coarse bast warp gives a certain rigidity to the structural foundation, in part overcoming the handicap of the free-hanging lower end. For the rest, the slow process of twining is employed, but it is done with such care and versatility in weft manipulation that the Chilkat blanket is justly renowned. No one would hesitate to call it a textile, in the ordinary sense of that word.

THE FIXED-WARP FRAME

The Northwest Coast affords another prototype of the loom, which in one respect is distinctly nearer to it than is the free-warp frame on which the Chilkat blanket is woven. The Salishan peoples of the region about the mouth of the Fraser and Columbia rivers used the wool of a domestic dog, bred for the purpose, on a rig which at first glance appears to be a true loom. It comprises two horizontal bars, an upper and a lower, fixed at an interval of perhaps three feet to two upright posts. The wool warp is wound around these two bars in a continuous strand. Thus a rigid warp is secured, and the apparatus would be a loom if it had heddles. Having none, it is merely a weaving frame of more specialized type than any yet considered; the weft is worked into the warp by hand, crossing one warp string at a time. Illustrations of this device (pl. 6) show that open or "basket" weaving

---

ends of her warp (which are to form the fringe of the blanket) by tying them up in a membrane bag, serves a purpose in keeping the strands untangled, besides keeping this protected portion clean. (Emmons: 339). The device thus is analogous to the weighted warp of the Old World, of which I can find no trace in America.

[2] Holmes (1884) figures pottery from the Southwest, the Mississippi Basin, and the Eastern Woodlands area, showing impressions of textiles which are matting for the greater part. Hoffman describes the process of mat making by the Menomini. Mason figures a weaving frame of the Chippewa (Ojibway). Wissler mentions the device among the Ojibway, and the great Algonkian family in general. Further search would doubtless yield much more evidence of distribution—but we have no record of its use in the Southwest; although both Basketmakers and Pueblos made mats, the method is not known.

was done upon it, and that the fabric grew from the top downward.[3] In the true loom progression is invariably upward, or away from the weaver, as will be seen.

It will be noted that the simplest devices for weaving—the supporting stake and the matting frame—have in common a free-hanging warp. They have likewise in common a strong association with twining, a rudimentary hand technic, as opposed to the in-and-out weaving which is characteristic of the loom. The transition from free-hanging warp to rigid warp, as just described, marks an important step in advance. There can be no true loom weaving without rigid warp, just as twining is impracticable, if not all but impossible (except by placing the twined strands at broad intervals, as was done in making the fur and feather blankets so common in the Southwest), on any but a loose warp; it is a technic requiring considerable manipulation of the warp strings, and taut strings reduce this freedom of movement very greatly. The weaver's craft is readily divisible into two broad phases of development. The first might be called the free-warp phase, beginning with the basketry stake and ending with the Chilkat weaving frame; the second, the fixed-warp phase, with the Salish frame above described as its first step, and the true loom its culmination.

The weaving of the Northwest Coast seems to mark very clearly the point of transition from bast to wool, and to exemplify a long stride toward the true loom. The Chilkat blanket—technically the cruder type, although it is much the finer product, as a rule—has a warp of wool and bast, a weft of wool. It is woven on the old primitive matting frame, and the method of its weaving is the ancient basketry technic of twining. The Salish type, on the other hand, employs the rigid warp and an all-wool material (with which the down of birds is sometimes intermingled). In both, the direction of weave is downward; and together they bridge a broad gap on the long road from the supporting stake to the loom.

Little by little, in this series of steps in a postulated development, weaving is emerging into full light to take its rightful place as one of the great fundamental industries. Its requisite special appliances have come into being: the rigid-warp frame, the spindle, and the comb, which make possible the use of fine fibers in tapestry weaving. The true loom lies not far ahead; yet one more step must be noted before it can take its place in the series, and of this step Peru offers the only example yet recorded, to my knowledge.

---

[3] See Kissell: 264; and Curtis: IX.

THE NEEDLE LOOM

On the authority of Joyce (200), the loom of early Tiahuanaco times in Peru was a fixed-warp affair like that of the Salish, but much smaller. A further point of resemblance lies in the fact that it was used in plain weaving, not in hand twining. Joyce calls this device a needle loom (fig. 9) because long slender needles worked the weft (of cotton or Andean camel wool) into the warp rack.[4] It was drawn and held taut by the weaver's own weight, being belted to her waist as shown in figure 9.

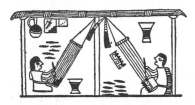

Fig. 9—Peruvian needle loom, from Mead p. 38, after Tello's Peru antigua. Means (1931: 74) figures the vase upon which this drawing appears, assigning it to Early Chimu times. It was found near ChanChan (Trujillo) and is now in the British Museum.

At first thought this type of weaving frame seems no great advance toward the true loom, for the needle is a common implement and a very ancient one. Yet the long Peruvian needle, capable under deft manipulation of lifting a number of alternate warp threads and thus forming a shed for the passage of the weft, has its significance.[5] Heretofore we have had no inkling of a means of handling more than one string

[4] A process somewhat similar is reported from the Osage, as quoted by Holmes (1896: 23-24) from Hunter: "The hair of the buffalo and other animals is sometimes manufactured into blankets; the hair is first twisted by hand, and wound into balls. The warp is then laid of a length to answer the size of the intended blanket, crossed by three small smooth rods alternately beneath the threads, and secured at each end to stronger rods supported on forks, at a short distance above the ground. Thus prepared, the woof is filled in, thread by thread, and pressed closely together, by means of a long flattened wooden needle. When the weaving is finished, the ends of the warp and woof are tied into knots, and the blanket is ready for use."

Fur blankets were commonly made in the Great Basin and the Southwest by staking out the strips of furred hide which formed the warp, and twining in the weft at broad intervals—a similar though more rudimentary technic. But Hunter's description fits Pima weaving more closely still. These people were true-loom weavers of long standing, using native cotton in a horizontal loom. See Russell: 148, Coues I:108, Bartlett II:225. And to make this now obsolete practice more intriguing still, we have Means' statement (1931:462) that the Peruvians sometimes staked out their looms horizontally. There may be a connection; we do not know, for our historic chain has many broad gaps the archeologist must fill.

The "long flattened wooden needle" referred to above may be ancestral, technologically, to the batten.

[5] Means says (1931: 465) the shed was formed with the left hand. Even so, the long needle might have picked out the alternate strings for the hand to grasp and hold forward while the weft was passed through.

of warp at a time. Weaving has been specialized, already in this series, to a high degree; but now it is about to become mechanized, and that is the ultimate step. "The loom is a machine," says Washington Matthews. He might have said yet more: that the loom is the only machine aboriginal America ever produced.[6] To make the loom a machine it wanted but one thing: a device for mass manipulation of the warp web; in other words, the heddle. The heddle marks the true loom.

ORIGIN OF THE TRUE LOOM

In the present state of our knowledge, one can only speculate upon the time and place of origin of the true loom in America. Peru would be a good guess, for there only, so far as known, has the needle loom come to light. There too the use of cotton, always associated with the true loom, was known in needle loom times. The heddle loom or true loom follows the needle loom closely, and it is quite possible that archeological research in Peru will settle the matter. If not Peru, then somewhere in Middle America; for we have every reason to believe that the loom came into the Southwest through the Pueblo culture, along with cotton; and cotton, as a cultivated plant, is associated with Middle America in the most generally accepted theory of the New World origins of agriculture. In speculating upon this point it is highly significant that nowhere in aboriginal America, so far as known, can the true loom be dissociated from cotton, nor cotton from corn.[7]

BATTEN AND SHUTTLE

The batten, a blade-like stick used in pressing down the weft strands to produce a tight fabric, follows the heddle more or less as a matter of course. Until a shed could be opened in the warp rack it could serve no purpose: the comb did the pressing home, over a small area, which the batten does over a larger area. The comb remains useful in straightening out twists and snarls in the weft, and in weaving those last few inches of fabric wherein space is so constricted that the batten has no room for movement. The latter has a function apart from that of tightening the fabric, however; it serves, when turned sidewise within the shed, to hold it open while the weft strands are passed through, as shown in

---

[6] With the possible exception of the two mechanical drills—bow and pump. I cannot learn whether they are aboriginal. Wissler (132-134) thinks they are not.

[7] The possibility of an exception to this statement must be noted: the Cherokee may have had a true loom, independently invented, used with a bast (apocynum?), not a wool, as will later appear.

plate 16. In this situation a shuttle would be of distinct service if weaving were being done in solid colors or plain stripes. New World fabrics show a great preference for figured patterns, however, and a completely special-ized shuttle was never evolved. The long needle was used as a sort of shuttle in Peru; but it is probable that the prehistoric Pueblos, like their modern descendants and the adept pupils of the latter, the Navaho, rolled their weft yarn into a little ball for greater ease of handling, or at best used a twig (an extemporaneous needle, as it were) for the purpose.

We may be grateful that the shuttle did not come into use. Its effect upon design is deadening, encouraging as it does a monotonous passing back and forth of the weft which gives at best but an unimaginative pat-tern of plain stripes. The shuttle tends toward rapid progress in weaving, but not, certainly, toward elaborate design. Witness for example the Chimayó (Spanish New Mexican) blanket and the modern Saltillo *serape,* both woven on the Old World horizontal loom with foot treadles for heddle manipulation, and a thrown shuttle for rapid intercalation of the weft. In them the mechanical factor in loom weaving comes too much to the fore; the art of weaving sinks to the level of a mere craft, over-mechanized: monotonous in method, and scarcely less so in result.

DIRECTION OF WEAVE

Two matters remain for comment before this brief review of loom development in America will have covered its allotted ground. The first has to do with the direction of weave, whether downward or upward. The basket woven upon a stake grows downward, as do the twined bag, the mat with free-hanging warp suspended between two upright stakes, and the Chilkat and Salish blankets. Were it not for the latter, woven upon a rigid warp, it could be stated axiomatically that free-hanging warp and downward weave go together, rigid warp and upward weave together. When the warp hangs free the fabric must necessarily grow from the bound end to the free end. When the warp is made rigid by fastening both ends, however, as in the Peruvian needle loom and the true loom wherever found, the direction of weave immediately changes, with the single exception of the Salish blanket.

The reason for this change of direction seems obvious. Gravity alone would ultimately dictate the method adopted. Mechanical weaving is a process of piling threads or strands of fiber one upon another within the clasp of a warp rack. It is naturally desirable that each new thread added to the fabric lie upon the firm foundation of others similarly laid, rather than hang suspended in air until another one can be inserted to maintain it. The batten is another reason for upward rather than downward weaving: it is natural to draw downward, or toward the body, rather than to push upward, away from the body; greater pressure can be brought to bear, with less exertion. The emergency brakes on our motor cars operate on this principle.

THE WAIST LOOM

The final point of technical character has reference to the method of suspension of the loom. The waist loom is the most common early form of the true loom and it is neither vertical nor horizontal, but diagonal. The weaver suspends it at a height which will present the warp strings at an angle convenient to her hands, when by attaching the lower or free end to a cord around her waist, she draws the loom taut.[8] This type of loom was used extensively in aboriginal America. It was common in Peru, for a number of complete looms have been found,[9] and the great majority of Peruvian fabrics, like those of the prehistoric Pueblos, are of such slight width that, inferentially, they were woven on the waist loom. Matthews' illustration of the Aztec weaver, from the *Codex Vaticanus,* proves the existence of this loom in a dominant culture of Middle America.

For the prehistoric Pueblos we have a vast number of fragmentary cotton textiles, evidently loom woven; none of them, on the authority of Hough (1919: 257), wider than 26 inches. There is evidence even more specific, however: Mr. Neil M. Judd found seven sticks in Kiva D at Pueblo Bonito, New Mexico, which beyond reasonable doubt are the end bars of waist looms. Only two could be saved, and these I examined through Mr. Judd's courtesy, in the National Museum (cat. 335284). They are about an inch and a half in diameter, and respectively 24 and 25 inches long. Each has a knob at either end, precisely as in Matthews' illustration of the Aztec weaver. These knobs, which are integral with the stick itself, probably served to keep the ropes by which the loom was suspended at either end from slipping off the stick.

A characteristic of fabrics woven on the waist loom is the long seam

---

[8] Matthews (1884) has illustrations of the waist loom as used by the Navaho (pl. XXXVI), the Zuñi (pl. XXXVII), and the Aztec (fig. 59). In each case the loom has an angular position, varying from the near-horizontal to the near-vertical. Logically, the weaver's own preference, rather than rule or custom, would determine the inclination. The needle loom shown in fig. 9 illustrates the method of suspension of the waist loom. See also pls. 19 and 20 for the Navaho belt loom, which was usually stretched on a frame as there shown.

[9] I have notes on two in the Brooklyn Museum: 27732 and 28846.

which indicates that two narrow strips have been sewn together (sometimes loom-joined) to form one wider piece. The cotton textile fragment from the Mesa Verde figured in Nordenskiöld's plate L shows such a seam very clearly, thanks to the excellence of the engraving. Thus we have fairly good evidence that the waist loom was in common use in the prehistoric Southwest.

THE VERTICAL LOOM

The wide distribution of the waist loom is well established. What of the vertical loom, the type that is suspended from above and lashed or weighted down at its base? Logically it might be considered the earlier type, by reason of the fact that the frames for weaving mats and hand-twined blankets are always vertically hung;[10] and a custom so long established would not be lightly broken. On the other hand, the adjustability of angle of the waist loom is a great point in its favor, particularly in such fine work as that done on the Peruvian needle loom. It seems probable that the latter is the immediate predecessor of the true loom, and that it set the fashion of diagonal suspension at the very outset. In that case vertical suspension might be a revival, or perhaps a regional survival, of an earlier custom.

There is some reason to conjecture that the vertical loom had its origin in the Southwest. Plate 7 shows an object from a cave in Cañon del Muerto, Arizona, which at first glance appears to be a miniature loom, such as the Navaho make today for the tourist trade. Its warp is strung between two sticks each about 12 inches long, the ends being bound to the sticks with a spiral winding of cord, just as the Navaho and the Hopi attach their warp strings to the horizontal supporting bars. Here the resemblance ends, for this specimen is not a loom but a twining frame. The evidence is incontrovertible, consisting in several rows of weft twined about the warp strings at intervals of about two inches. Yucca fiber is the material of this fabric, which is structurally identical with the fur blankets of the Great Basin and the Southwest. The piece is more of a net than a solid fabric, because of the wide spacing of the twined weft; in that respect it offers additional evidence that close-set twining cannot be done handily on a fixed warp, as previously pointed out. Whether this interesting specimen is attributable to the Basketmaker or the Pueblo culture horizon unfortunately is not known; hence it is impossible to determine

---

[10] Necessarily so: free-hanging warp cannot be made to take any but a vertical position.

whether it is a predecessor or a contemporary of the true loom. The significant fact remains that here is a device for twining, but with a rigid warp suitable for vertical suspension,[11] and like the vertical loom, so far as known, its occurrence is limited to the Southwest.

There is considerable evidence of the use of the vertical loom by the prehistoric Pueblos. Until quite recently this evidence consisted in loom holes and overhead supports found in ruins, usually in kivas, where, traditionally, the men did the weaving of the village. Judd found a number of loom holes at Betatakin, more often in living rooms than in kivas (24, 28, 31, 34; his fig. 18 shows a loom anchor as found in the floor). Kidder and Guernsey report loom holes, often with anchor loops still intact, from various cliff-dwellings in northeastern Arizona (60, 70, 73, and figs. 22 and 26), saying (60) that "there can be little doubt that these series of loop holders served as attachments for the lower bars of looms." [12] It is true that none of the series mentioned had a length of more than four feet, the holes being usually about one foot apart and arranged in a straight line. Four feet, however, is a sufficient width, particularly when it is remembered that a loom of even greater width could thus be secured by allowing the lower bar to project beyond its floor lashings.

It is difficult to reconcile loom lashings four feet in extent with textiles not exceeding 26 inches in width. Yet Hough's statement, as cited above, was incontrovertible at the time it was made, so far as I can learn; neither loom, nor poles, nor fabrics, which could be associated with a greater width had come to light in the Southwest.[13] In the summer of 1929 Mr. Earl H. Morris made a find in Cañon del Muerto, Arizona, which strengthens the case for the broad vertical loom. Wrapped about the mummified body of a man—a weaver, to judge by the many hanks of spun cotton yarn in the grave—was a large white cotton blanket, of plain "basket" weave; precisely such a blanket as a modern Hopi weaver might produce. It was recently on display at the American Museum of Natural History, where I was permitted to open the case and by working my ruler around the bundle a few inches at a time, to measure the width of the

---

[11] The waist loom can be vertically hung, as proved by the upright narrow loom on which the Hopi today weave their broad cotton sashes; and it is reasonable to conjecture that the broad vertical loom grew out of the fashion of suspending the waist loom upright.

[12] Little doubt indeed, as will be seen by consulting Mindeleff, wherein are described (132-133) and figured (figs. 27 and 31) loom attachments of identical form and position, in modern Hopi kivas.

[13] Dr. F. W. Hodge tells me, however, that in his excavations at Hawikuh New Mexico, he found (disintegrated), in graves, "what must have been loom poles, accompanied by battens."

blanket. It measured, perhaps a bit inexactly, 58 inches wide. The length could not be determined because of other wrappings.

Thus the existence of the broad vertical loom among the prehistoric Pueblos is all but proved. It would be a difficult task indeed to weave a fabric five feet wide on a waist loom;[14] and aside from that, we have the evidence of the loom holes and lashings of prehistoric time, identical with those of modern times.

Pottery accompanying the burial described above was of the "Mesa Verde" type.[15] Beyond a doubt, the old weaver was wrapped in his blanket and laid in his grave several centuries before European influence came into the Southwest. With the final statement that this cotton blanket was identical in every detail of construction with the woolen blankets of the Hopi and the Navaho of today, the aboriginal American art of weaving is brought down to the present time. "In the Southwest," as Lummis said, "we can catch our archeology alive."

LOOM DEVELOPMENT IN THE OLD WORLD

It is interesting to compare the development of the loom in the Old World with its progress in America. Hooper's admirable paper (see bibliography) makes this quite easy in summarized form. The great similarity of spindles has already been noted (pl. 5). In Europe, as in America, bast is the earliest material found in use: the Swiss lake dwellings have yielded numerous fragments of linen cloth, plain woven; but of the loom employed we are told

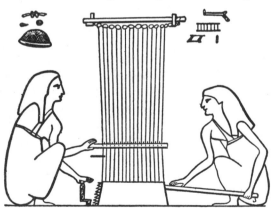

Fig. 10—Egyptian loom of about 2000 B. C. The bar across the warp rack is undoubtedly a heddle rod, proving this a true loom; one which a Navaho woman of today could operate. After Hooper, fig. 11.

14 There is at least a suspicion that the broad vertical loom was used in pre-Columbian Peru. O'Neale and Kroeber (29) mention a textile 47½ inches wide, and several more than 40 inches. That is rather an awkward width for waist loom weaving, but we cannot say it is impossibly wide. Archeology eventually will settle the point.

15 A type characteristic of the Great Period—Pueblo III—and dated by the tree-ring method roughly 1000 A. D.

little except that weights have been found, indicating a free-hanging, weighted warp. Egypt too used linen in early times and on a true loom, vertical, identical in all chief particulars with the vertical loom of the Southwest. Figure 10 shows a loom of this type, as conceived by an Egyptian artist of about 2000 B. C.

Perhaps most interesting of all is the loom on which Penelope wove the funeral pall of her father-in-law Laertes while awaiting the return of

Ulysses, as depicted on a Grecian vase of about 500 B. C. and reproduced in figure 11. It is very much like the proto-loom of the Chilkat blanket. The warp hangs free, weighted at the lower end, and the fabric grows downward from the top. Whether Penelope had the benefit of heddles is not clear; probably she used long slender needles, as in the Peruvian needle loom. At any rate she has achieved a complex pattern which is not suggestive of twining.

Fig. 11—Penelope's loom, in appearance more like the Chilkat than the Navaho type. The upper bar seems to be a roller, on which the completed web can be wound; above it is a rack for holding bobbins of colored weft thread. After Hooper, fig. 8.

Even this brief sketch will have shown that the principal weaving devices of the two hemispheres bear a remarkable similarity; but of their independent origin there can be little doubt. It is hardly likely that more than the bare outline of the development of the loom can ever be revealed in the Old World. In America, however, thanks to the aridity of such important archeological areas as the Peruvian highlands and the Southwest, there is good hope of recovering the whole story; apart from the fact that in America today many primitive weaving processes are in actual practice. Navaho weaving may be counted among the more advanced of these; so we see—as presaged in the preceding chapter—that its mechanical efficiency is by no means the measure of its significance.

LOOM DISTRIBUTION IN NORTH AMERICA

The distribution of the loom in aboriginal North America is another
point of interest. The existence of the waist loom among the Aztecs has
already been noted. Holmes (1884) figures 44 examples of textile impressions: from the Southwest, the Mississippi Basin, and the Eastern
Woodlands. Only five of them could have been loom woven; the rest
are hand twined, or are basketry fragments. Of the five, one is from Utah
(prehistoric Pueblo), one from Ohio, one from New York, two from
Tennessee. One of the latter is twilled, the only twill in the lot.[17] This
evidence, slender but extremely extensive, associates the true loom with
the higher cultures of the region now the United States; notably the prehistoric Pueblo and the Mound Builder. It indicates further that insofar
as Holmes' material is characteristic of conditions prevailing among the
makers of his pottery fragments, true loom weaving was in a very small
minority in comparison with the various hand technics revealed by the
pottery impressions.

Holmes mentions elsewhere (1896: 11) that "spindle whorls have in
rare cases been reported from southern localities." Finally, among the
scant bits of evidence of loom distribution in aboriginal North America,
we have an inkling that something very closely approaching the true loom
was in use by the Cherokee. Holmes (1896: 23-24) quotes Adair as follows:

> Formerly the Indians (Cherokee) made very handsome
> carpets. They have a wild hemp that grows about six feet
> high, in open, rich, level lands, and which usually ripens in
> July: it is plenty on our frontier settlements. When it is fit
> for use, they pull, steep, peel, and beat it; and the old women
> spin it off the distaffs, with wooden machines, having some
> clay on the middle of them,[18] to hasten the motion. When the
> coarse thread is prepared, they put it into a frame about six
> feet square, and instead of a shuttle, they thrust through the
> thread with a long cane, having a large string through the
> web, which they shift at every second course of the thread.

This shifting at every second course of the thread suggests that the
"large string through the web" was in fact a heddle of the most rudimentary and simple form. The "frame about six feet square" may have been a
broad vertical loom on a framework of posts, like the loom of the Southwest, or perhaps a horizontal rig. The whole description inclines one to

---

[17] For a definition of this term see Chapter 4.
[18] [The common type of spindle is easily recognized in this description.]

believe that here is a true loom of the simplest form possible; one which employs a bast (probably a species of apocynum) instead of a true wool. Was it an independent development or a borrowing from the loom presumably developed in Peru or Middle America? Another point for the archeologist's attention.

Viewing the textile development of aboriginal North America in general, insofar as our scanty knowledge permits, one gets the impression that everywhere experiments and developments were in process that were tending inevitably toward the loom; in most cases quite independently of one another. Some sort of device to facilitate weaving is found nearly everywhere. A variety of basts were in use, ranging from very coarse to very fine. Both hair and wool were frequently employed, and spinning had developed its own special technic and accessories. But of true loom weaving there is no definite evidence until cotton seemingly sweeps northward from "somewhere south." On the crest of that wave, to all appearances, rode the loom—and with it the economic destiny of the Navaho.

STEPS IN LOOM DEVELOPMENT IN AMERICA

			Device	Product		Material		Occurrence
Downward Weave	Free Warp	Wild Material	Supporting stake	Fine woven basketry		Sea grass, cedar root		Aleutian Islands, Northwest Coast
			Suspending cord	Twined bags, sandals (?)		Buffalo hair, apocynum, yucca		Great Plains, Basketmakers (?)
			Matting frame	Mats, bast fabrics		Barks, grasses		Mississippi Basin, Northwest Coast
			Weaving frame	Chilkat blanket		Wild-goat wool, cedar bark		Upper Northwest Coast
			Weaving frame (rigid-warp)	Salish blanket		Dog wool, fine fibers, down		Salish of Lower Northwest Coast
Upward Weave	Fixed Warp	Domestic Material	Needle loom	Narrow fabrics		Andean camel wool, cotton		Peru, Tiahuanaco period
			Heddle or true loom	Blankets, sashes, etc.		Cotton, domestic wools, apocynum (?)		Peru, Middle America, Mound Builders, Pima, Pueblos, Navaho, Cherokee (?)

The close correspondence of the bracketed groups will be noted, as they fall (horizontally) into two divisions: 1, Downward Weave, Free Warp, and Wild Material; 2, Upward Weave, Fixed Warp, and Domestic Material. The list is of course typical rather than inclusive; further research would lengthen it.

CHAPTER III

THE NAVAHO LOOM

HE loom of the Navaho is admirable not alone for the excellence of its textile product, but for its remarkable persistence as well. A native American device wedded to a material of European origin (the wool of the domestic sheep), it has been subjected to the influences of European civilization from the very moment of its adoption by the Navaho; for the whole craft of the Navaho weaver has been under constant pressure to change its methods, particularly since the establishment of the Navaho reservation and the advent of the reformer, private or Governmental, and of the Indian trader.

In consequence of this pressure, dyestuffs of native origin have disappeared; machine-spun yarns in the form of cotton warp and Germantown wool weft have secured a foothold; shearing and carding are done with devices of American manufacture; size and pattern of blankets are influenced by the preferences and prejudices of the buying public and by the fine artistic sense of the Indian trader who acts as middleman. The loom, however, has not yielded in the smallest particular. It is as completely aboriginal today as in the earliest time of which we have knowledge, and its product, as we have seen, is structurally identical with prehistoric Pueblo fabrics going back at least as far as the Pueblo III period. The Navaho loom of today (pl. 8) is the counterpart of the prehistoric Pueblo loom of perhaps the 10th century A. D. This statement holds as well for the accessory appliances of weaving—the spindle, batten, rudimentary shuttle, and comb. It is remarkable that this machine of a remote aboriginal and prehistoric time should have survived unchanged in the midst of the American people, whose mechanical ingenuity is unparalleled in history. The Navaho gladly accepts the automobile; but he will not change his loom in the least detail.[1]

Given the identity of the Navaho loom with that of the Hopi today [2]

---

[1] "There is no doubt that the ordinary Navaho loom is an aboriginal invention which has not been modified since pre-Columbian days." Matthews (1900: 641).

[2] See Hough (1919) for a description and illustration of the Hopi loom. Spier (1924) describes Zuñi weaving with comparative data from other tribes.

(pl. 9*a*), the structural identity of the products of these looms with pre-historic Pueblo fabrics, and the numerous bits of evidence unearthed by Southwestern archeologists concerning the loom of prehistoric times, we are forced to conclude that the Navaho have contributed precisely nothing to the development of their loom. That they have always been adept borrowers—whether of women, livestock, foodstuffs, or manners and customs—we have abundant evidence. Their debt to their Pueblo neighbors is particularly large:[3] many identities of custom, belief, and ritual exist in the cultures of the two peoples; and in view of the fact that the Pueblos are the heritors of an ancient and almost immutable culture, which archeology has revealed with exceptional clarity, there is good reason to consider them the originators, the Navaho the borrowers. Everything points to the conclusion that the loom was one of these borrowings.[4]

A corollary question is whether the Navaho were weavers before the introduction of domestic European sheep into their country. It is highly doubtful if they were. They are not known to have grown cotton, or to have woven it; and I know of no specimen of textile definitely attributable to them of which the material is not domestic wool.[5]

The remainder of this chapter will be devoted to a detailed description of the Navaho loom; but in order to give a complete account of loom construction, the preliminary processes of preparing the wool for the warp and weft must be considered. The first of these is shearing the sheep.

---

[3] Numerous references occur in the anthropological literature of the Navaho to beliefs and customs which are thought by the writers to be of Pueblo origin. See, for example, Franciscan Fathers 1912: 111, 115, 164; Hodge 1895; Hough 1902; Stevenson: 236; Reichard: 155 ff.

[4] James (16), accepting the hypothesis that the Navaho are of northerly origin because they are Athabascans, implies that weaving may have been practised by them before their migration southward. However, as pointed out in Chapter 2 herein, there is no true loom weaving in the Northwest Coast area: the Navaho blanket has little in common with the Chilkat and the Salish. Finally, there is not a shred of evidence, to my knowledge, that the Navaho ever did any sort of blanket weaving other than true loom weaving in wool.

[5] With one possible exception: Mr. B. I. Staples of Coolidge, New Mexico, has shown me a large fragment of loosely-spun, plain basket-woven blanket, without pattern, which he said is very old, with a history (not told to me) definitely attributing it to the Navaho. A wisp of the wool that Mr. Staples kindly let me take for identification was identified by Dr. W. H. Burt, Mammalogist of the California Institute of Technology, as probably that of the Rocky Mountain goat, as Mr. Staples had thought.

This bit of evidence is highly suggestive, but far from conclusive. The provenience of a "very old" specimen is always subject to doubt unless a record was made of its original acquisition. Blankets were widely bartered in all times, particularly between the Pueblos and the Navaho of an earlier day, and this specimen has no authenticated history. It may have been woven by a Pueblo; and I think it could be attributed even more plausibly, on the evidence of its very coarse, loose weave and its material, to the Salish.

PLATE 9

a

b

a, Henry Nappy, a Tewa from Hano pueblo, demonstrates Pueblo spinning and weaving. Courtesy of Mr. Fred K. Hinchman.

b, Navaho women shearing sheep. An old photograph, probably taken in the vicinity of Fort Defiance about 1890. Courtesy Signal Corps, U. S. Army.

PLATE 10

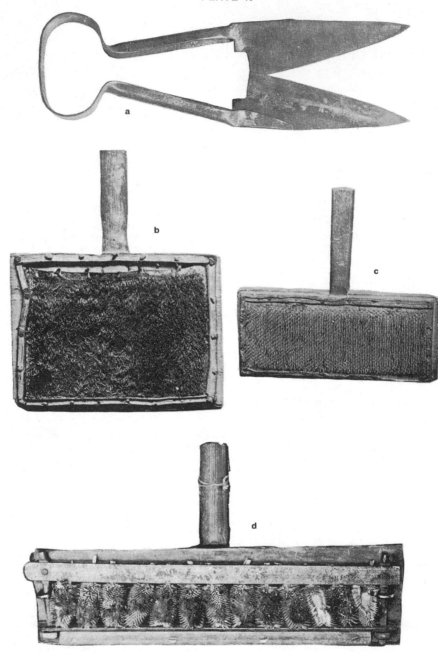

a, Old style steel shears, hand-wrought.
b, American wool card with fiber bristles.
c, Later American type with steel teeth.
d, Spanish type, burrs clamped in a frame; courtesy of Fred Harvey. a, b, and c, after Pepper 1923.

SHEARING

The goat-wool weavers of the Northwest Coast depended on collecting enough material for a blanket from bushes upon which the Rocky Mountain goat, in his passage, left bits of his fleece behind him. "First catch your hare" is as applicable in weaving as in cookery, and wild animals are not readily caught without killing or maiming them in the process. Domestic sheep are easily seized, and their wool is obtained by shearing or clipping, as shown in plate 9b. It has been stated, probably conjecturally, that the Navaho either pulled the wool from the animal or used flint knives for shearing, in very early times. Before the introduction of shears, metal knives or sharp-edged metals such as a sheet of tin were used, probably in imitation of the Spanish settlers, who had a special knife for the purpose. According to Major D. M. Riordan, Indian Agent at Fort Defiance in 1883 (Report of the Commissioner of Indian Affairs, hereinafter cited as RCIA, 1883: 122):

> The method of shearing among the Navajos is crude, wasteful, and barbarous in the extreme. They catch a sheep and throw him down, the shearer sitting on the animal in any manner to suit his convenience. He proceeds to hack rather than clip the wool from it with a case knife, a piece of tin, or any instrument which can be whetted on a piece of sandstone. The result is, the sheep is sheared in chunks, so to speak, and not half the wool is realized that should be.

Shears were the exception rather than the rule among the Navaho in the vicinity of Forth Defiance in 1884, for Welsh says (24-25), "The Indian by whose camp fire we were seated told Mr. Marshall that he was very anxious to get a pair of shears for sheep shearing." They are now in general use, but it is surprising, and indicative of the laggard development of Navaho weaving, to find them a rarity only fifty years ago. Modern steel shears (pl. 10a) now clip the fleece in a solid blanket from tail to head.

CLEANING

Writers generally agree that the Navaho did not wash their wool until the insistence of the traders, and Government regulations making sheep-dipping compulsory, brought them to it. After shearing, the wool was shaken to remove the sand clinging to it, then thrown over bushes and the entangled burrs and sticks pulled out (pl. 11a). Washing was coming into fashion about the time of Matthews' sojourn among the Navaho, ap-

parently; for Riordan, writing in 1883, states categorically that "the wool
is never washed." Matthews, however, says (1884: 376) that "the wool is
never washed until it is sheared." It is perhaps significant that Matthews
wrote from Fort Wingate, which was near the then newly completed
Atlantic and Pacific Railroad (now the Atchison, Topeka and Santa Fe)
and on a main artery of travel; Riordan from Fort Defiance, in the more
remote interior of the Navaho reservation. Any such innovation as washing would come into use soonest where American influence was greatest.
This was notably the case with aniline dyes.

James (109) describes the process of washing (pl. 11*b*) as follows:

> Bowls are prepared full of the clearest water obtainable,
> and if it is possible to be near a stream or spring advantage
> is taken of this close proximity. From the weaver's household
> stores several pieces of the root of the amole are taken. *Yucca
> glauca, Y. baccata, Y. angustifolia, Y. radiosa,* and *Y. elata*
> are all used for this purpose, though the second named seems
> to contain the largest and richest saponine. These roots are
> beaten between rocks until reduced to a mass of fibres, and
> are then splashed up and down in a bowl of water until the
> latter becomes covered with a rich and soft, foamy lather. In
> these suds the wool is soaked and more or less thoroughly
> washed, according to the habit of the weaver. If she be con-
> scientious and desirous of doing first-class work, she well
> knows the washing must be well done, or the dye will not
> "take" satisfactorily.
>
> In the case of white wool, which is to be used without
> dyeing, also of black, brown, and native gray, the careful
> weaver is extra particular to see that the wool is thoroughly
> washed. The fleeces are then spread out on whatever shrubs
> are nearest at hand to dry.

Pepper, writing as late as 1903, and having in mind the remote region
of Pueblo Bonito in Chaco Cañon, says (1903: 9-10):

> As a rule, there is no washing done. . . The scarcity of
> water in the Navaho country is responsible for this act of
> seeming negligence on the part of the blanket maker. But,
> in judging these worthy people we must remember that the
> wool of the Navaho sheep is not greasy as is that of the
> merinos and many other sheep and therefore does not re-
> quire the elaborate washing and scouring that must be under-

PLATE 11

a, Picking out the twigs and burrs.
b, Washing the wool. Both after Pepper 1923.

PLATE 12

Carding the wool. Courtesy of Mr. Philip Johnston.

gone ere the ordinary wool is workable. The Navajo herds-men are particularly careful about keeping their sheep from crossing with the merinos of the Mexicans, as they realize that the merino wool cannot be washed or bleached and that the use of the wool in its natural state causes unsightly streaks in their blankets.

In view of these conflicting opinions, it seems safest to summarize broadly with the statement that washing, unknown in early times, has gradually become the practice. The insistence of the buyer of blankets on the one hand, and the increasing greasiness of the wool as alien strains were introduced into the Navaho stock in the Government's effort to improve the breed, are no doubt largely responsible for the establishment of the practice of washing. Of late years some traders who were particularly interested in improving the quality of Navaho weaving have gone so far as to send the native wool to the woolen centers of the East, for a proper scouring by scientific methods, as told in Chapter 13.

CARDING

The purpose of carding (pl. 12) is to straighten the tangled individual fibers of the material employed, giving them a somewhat uniform longi-tudinal trend in the strand. It was pointed out in Chapter 2 that carding is not an indispensable preliminary to weaving. Rolling the material between the hands or along the thigh will accomplish the purpose. Basts were usually prepared for weaving in this manner, as was buffalo hair for use in making twined bags. Carding and spinning are both eliminated by this method, which seems better suited to basts than to true wools like cotton and domestic sheep wool.

James says (109) that the Navaho used teasels (thistles), which grow wild in parts of their country, for carding wool in early times. This is corroborated by Mr. H. Schweizer, whose long experience as head of the Indian Department of the Fred Harvey company has qualified him as an expert in the native crafts of the Southwest. Mr. Schweizer showed me at his headquarters in Albuquerque, New Mexico, the wool card re-produced, through his courtesy, in plate 10d. It is made by clamping a row of burrs to a wooden frame by means of two strips of iron held down by bolts. The device is of Mexican origin and the idea probably came originally from Europe, since our own pioneers knew it too. According to Mr. Schweizer, the Navaho adapted it to their use in very early times. Having neither the knowledge nor the facilities for working in metals, they tied the burrs to a wooden frame of their own fashioning with raw-hide thongs.

Today the tooth-comb card of American manufacture (pl. 10*b, c*) is in general use. Taking a card in each hand, the woman combs a handful of wool between them into a thick, fluffy rope, ready for the spinning, as shown in plates 13 and 14.

SPINNING

Shearing and carding have been revolutionized by the white man's appliances, but Navaho spinning remains as truly aboriginal as the loom itself: plates 13 and 14 leave no doubt on the point. Spinning has for its object the reduction of the loose fiber to a strand of requisite length and thickness, firmly compacted and surprisingly strong. This end is achieved by pulling and twisting in one operation, for spinning is essentially a process of twisting while pulling.

The Navaho spindle follows the general form described in Chapter 2, consisting of a wooden shaft with a wooden disk slipped over it and fixed at a point about midway between middle and butt of the shaft. Cottonwood and piñon were frequently the materials used in early times, but today a fragment of pine box, obtained at a trading post, is generally used.

James (110) has an excellent description of the spinning process, as follows:

> When everything is ready for the spinning—carded-wool on a blanket on the ground, distaff [6] in the right hand—the spinner squats down Turkish or tailor fashion, and picks up a little of the wool in her left hand, into which she sticks the tip of the spindle. With a few dextrous turns the wool is soon caught fast, and now the distaff rests upon the ground, and the wool is held so that it is on about a straight line with it. As soon as the strand is as long, and twisted as much, as the woman desires, she tilts the distaff so that it and the wool-strand are almost at acute angles, and, the spindle still kept twirling, the wool is wound up and down the upper portion of the stick. This is repeated until the stick will hold no more, when the stranded-wool is un-

---

[6] [James is avoiding the constant repetition of the word spindle and falling into error thereby. The Navaho woman uses no distaff—a device for holding wool to be spun. It was used in prehistoric Peru, say Means (1931: 458), and Crawford, who figures one (1915: 68).]

PLATE 13

Spinning the wool. The upper figure shows the first spinning after carding, the lower figure the second spinning. After Pepper 1923.

PLATE 14

Spinning, final operation, the yarn now fine and hard. Courtesy of Mr. Philip Johnston.

wound from the spindle, wrapped into balls and laid aside. As soon as all the wool is spun, or so much as the weaver thinks she may need, it is all respun, once or twice, or even more, according to the thickness and tightness of the yarn needed. The second twisting is generally enough for the making of the wool yarns, but the third twisting gives a tight, strong, bristly cord about as thick as the ordinary binding twine. For the extra fine blankets the yarn is both fine and extra tightly woven.

Enthusiastic apostles of modern methods have tried in years past to introduce the spinning wheel and the pedal loom among the Navaho (R. C. I. A. 1875: 71, 330), but the complicated and cumbersome devices had a cold reception. In spinning as in weaving, the Navaho woman prefers simplicity to speed. Perhaps she bears in mind that she is still in some degree a nomad, expected to transport her weaving gear when the family moves its flocks to new pastures. One can imagine a diminutive Navaho pony laden with a stout matron, a baby or two, a pedal loom and a spinning wheel!

RIGGING THE LOOM

The preliminary operations of shearing, cleaning, carding, and spinning completed, all is in readiness for setting up the loom.[7] Washington Matthews, living among the Navaho from 1880 to 1884, as surgeon to the Army post at Fort Wingate, New Mexico, observed the process of loom rigging so closely and described it so fully that I can do no better than quote his description (1884: 377-380):

Plate xxxviii and Fig. 42 [the latter reproduced herein as fig. 12] illustrate ordinary blanket-looms. Two posts, a a, are set firmly in the ground; to these are lashed two crosspieces or braces, b, c, the whole forming the frame of the loom. Sometimes two slender trees, growing at a convenient distance from one another, are made to answer for the posts. d is a horizontal pole, which I call the supplementary yarn-beam, attached to the upper brace, b, by means of a rope, e e, spirally applied. f is the upper beam of the loom. As it is analogous to the yarn-beam of our looms, I will call it by this

---

[7] These preliminary steps are more fully described in Hollister 96-98; and James 108-110. I have confined myself to the bare essentials, with emphasis upon the evolution in implements and methods, to which the above writers give little attention.

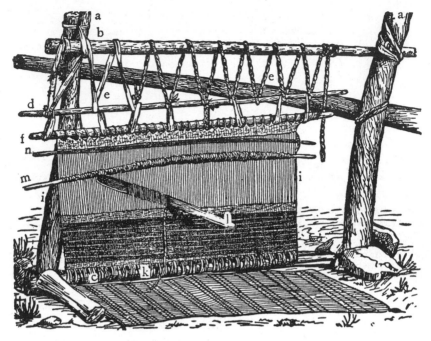

Fig. 12—Explanatory drawing of Navaho loom. Its various lettered parts are described in the text. After Matthews 1884 fig. 42, block lent by Denver Art Museum.

name, although once only have I seen the warp wound around it. It lies parallel to the pole d, about 2 or 3 inches below it, and is attached to the latter by a number of loops. A spiral cord wound around the yarn-beam holds the upper border cord which, in turn, secures the upper end of the warp i. i. [These attachments are shown in enlarged detail in pl. 17: 4] The lower beam of the loom is shown at k. I will call this the cloth-beam, although the finished web is never wound around it; it is tied firmly to the lower brace, c, of the frame, and to it is secured the lower border cord of the blanket. The original distance between the two beams is the length of the blanket. Lying between the threads of the warp is depicted a broad, thin, oaken stick, 1, which I will call the batten. A set of healds attached to a heald-rod, m, are shown above the batten. These healds are made of cord or yarn; they include alternate threads of the warp, and serve

PLATE 15

Stringing the warp. After Pepper 1923.

PLATE 16

Weaving. The batten turned horizontally holds open the shed while the weaver works the weft strand into place with the comb, preparatory to pounding it firmly down with the batten. A. C. Vroman photo from P. G. Gates coll. Southwest Museum. Note that one section of fabric is built higher than the rest; this practice explains the irregular diagonal lines, sometimes called "lazy lines," in large fabrics such as this "Moki pattern" rug.

PLATE 17

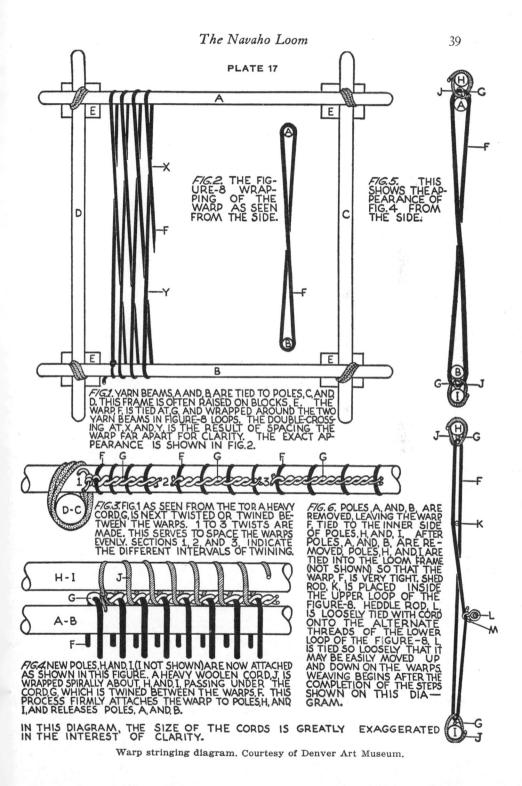

FIG.2. THE FIGURE-8 WRAPPING OF THE WARP AS SEEN FROM THE SIDE.

FIG.5. THIS SHOWS THE APPEARANCE OF FIG. 4 FROM THE SIDE.

FIG.1. YARN BEAMS, A, AND, B, ARE TIED TO POLES, C, AND, D. THIS FRAME IS OFTEN RAISED ON BLOCKS, E. THE WARP, F, IS TIED AT, G, AND WRAPPED AROUND THE TWO YARN BEAMS IN FIGURE-8 LOOPS. THE DOUBLE-CROSSING AT, X, AND, Y, IS THE RESULT OF SPACING THE WARP FAR APART FOR CLARITY. THE EXACT APPEARANCE IS SHOWN IN FIG.2.

FIG.3. FIG.1 AS SEEN FROM THE TOP. A HEAVY CORD, G, IS NEXT TWISTED OR TWINED BETWEEN THE WARPS. 1 TO 3 TWISTS ARE MADE. THIS SERVES TO SPACE THE WARPS EVENLY. SECTIONS 1, 2, AND 3, INDICATE THE DIFFERENT INTERVALS OF TWINING.

FIG.4. NEW POLES, H, AND, I, (I NOT SHOWN) ARE NOW ATTACHED AS SHOWN IN THIS FIGURE. A HEAVY WOOLEN CORD, J, IS WRAPPED SPIRALLY ABOUT, H, AND, I, PASSING UNDER THE CORD, G, WHICH IS TWINED BETWEEN THE WARPS, F. THIS PROCESS FIRMLY ATTACHES THE WARP TO POLES, H, AND, I, AND RELEASES POLES, A, AND, B.

FIG.6. POLES, A, AND, B, ARE REMOVED, LEAVING THE WARP, F, TIED TO THE INNER SIDE OF POLES, H, AND, I. AFTER POLES, A, AND, B, ARE REMOVED, POLES, H, AND, I, ARE TIED INTO THE LOOM FRAME (NOT SHOWN) SO THAT THE WARP, F, IS VERY TIGHT. SHED ROD, K, IS PLACED INSIDE THE UPPER LOOP OF THE FIGURE-8. HEDDLE ROD, L, IS LOOSELY TIED WITH CORD ONTO THE ALTERNATE THREADS OF THE LOWER LOOP OF THE FIGURE-8. L, IS TIED SO LOOSELY THAT IT MAY BE EASILY MOVED UP AND DOWN ON THE WARPS. WEAVING BEGINS AFTER THE COMPLETION OF THE STEPS SHOWN ON THIS DIAGRAM.

IN THIS DIAGRAM, THE SIZE OF THE CORDS IS GREATLY EXAGGERATED IN THE INTEREST OF CLARITY.

Warp stringing diagram. Courtesy of Denver Art Museum.

when drawn forward to open the lower shed. The upper shed is kept patent by a stout rod, n (having no healds attached), which I name the shed-rod. Their substitute for the reed of our looms is a wooden fork, which will be designated as the reed-fork.[8]

For convenience of description, I am obliged to use the word "shuttle," although, strictly speaking, the Navajo has no shuttle. If the figure to be woven is a long stripe, or one where the weft must be passed through 6 inches or more of the shed at one time, the yarn is wound on a slender twig or splinter, or shoved through on the end of such a piece of wood; but where the pattern is intricate, and the weft passes at each turn through only a few inches of the shed, the yarn is wound into small skeins or balls and shoved through with the finger.

The warp is thus constructed: A frame of four sticks is made, not unlike the frame of the loom, but lying on or near the ground, instead of standing erect [pl. 15]. The two sticks forming the sides of the frame are rough saplings or rails; the two forming the top and bottom are smooth rounded poles—often the poles which afterwards serve as the beams of the loom; these are placed parallel to one another, their distance apart depending on the length of the projected blanket.

On these poles the warp is laid in a continuous string. It is first firmly tied to one of the poles, which I will call No. 1 [see pl. 17]; then it is passed over the other pole, No. 2, brought back under No. 2 and over No. 1, forward again under No. 1 and over No. 2, and so on to the end. Thus the first, third, fifth &c., turns of the cord cross in the middle the second, fourth, sixth, &c., forming a series of elongated figures 8, as shown in [pl. 17: 1] and making, in the very beginning of the process, the two sheds, which are kept distinct throughout the whole work. When sufficient string has been laid the end is tied to pole No. 2, and a rod is placed in each shed to keep it open, the rods being afterwards tied together at the ends to prevent them from falling out.

This done, the weaver takes three strings (which are af-

---

[8] [Now generally called a comb, the term used herein.]

terwards twilled into one, as will appear) and ties them together at one end.[10] She now sits outside of one of the poles,
looking toward the center of the frame, and proceeds thus
[pl. 17: 3]: (1) She secures the triple cord to the pole immediately to the left of the warp; (2) then she takes one of the
threads (or strands as they now become) and passes it under
the first turn of the warp; (3) next she takes a second strand,
and twilling [twisting] it once or oftener with the other
strands, includes with it the second bend of the warp; (4)
this done, she takes the third strand and, twilling it as before, passes it under the third bend of the warp, and thus
she goes on until the entire warp in one place is secured
between the strands of the cord; (5) then she pulls the string
to its fullest extent, and in doing so separates the threads of
the warp from one another; (6) a similar three stranded cord
is applied to the other end of the warp, along the outside of
the other pole.

At this stage of the work these stout cords lie along the
outer surfaces of the poles, parallel with the axes of the latter,
but when the warp is taken off the poles and applied to the
beams of the loom by the spiral thread, as above described,
and as depicted in [fig. 12] and all is ready for weaving, the
cords appear on the inner sides of the beams [pl. 17: 6],
i. e., one at the lower side of the yarn-beam, and the other at
the upper side of the cloth-beam, and when the blanket is
finished they form the stout end margins of the web. In the
coarser grade of blankets the cords are removed and the ends
of the warp tied in pairs and made to form a fringe.

When the warp is transferred to the loom the rod which
was placed in the upper shed remains there, or another rod,
straighter and smoother, is substituted for it; but with the
lower shed, healds are applied to the anterior threads and the
rod is withdrawn.

The mode of applying the healds [or heddles, see pl.
17: 6] is simple: (1) the weaver sits facing the loom in the
position for weaving; (2) she lays at the right (her right)
side of the loom a ball of string which she knows contains

---

[10] [I have found two selvage cords, as shown in pl. 17: 3, 4, more common than
three. Usually they are of 3-ply weight.]

more than sufficient material to make the healds; (3) she takes the end of this string and passes it to the left through the shed, leaving the ball in its original position; (4) she ties a loop at the end of the string large enough to admit the heald-rod; (5) she holds horizontally in her left hand a straightish slender rod, which is to become the heald-rod—its right extremity touching the left edge of the warp—and passes the rod through the loop until the point of the stick is even with the third (second anterior from the left) thread of the warp; (6) she puts her finger through the space between the first and third threads and draws out a fold of the heald-string; (7) she twists this once around, so as to form a loop, and pushes the point of the heald-rod on to the right through this loop; (8) she puts her finger into the next space and forms another loop; (9) and so on she continues to advance her heald-rod and form her loops from left to right until each of the anterior (alternate) warp-threads of the lower shed is included in a loop of the heald; (10) when the last loop is made she ties the string firmly to the rod near its right end.

When the weaving is nearly done and it becomes necessary to remove the healds, the rod is drawn out of the loops, a slight pull is made at the thread, the loops fall in an instant, and the straightened string is drawn out of the shed.

WEAVING

Matthews (1884: 380-383) continues with a description of the weaving process, of which the essential passages are here quoted:

In making a blanket the operator sits on the ground with her legs folded under her. The warp hangs vertically before her, and (excepting in a case to be mentioned)[11] she weaves from below upwards. As she never rises from this squatting posture when at work, it is evident that when she has woven the web to a certain height further work must become inconvenient or impossible unless by some arrangement the finished web is drawn downwards. Her cloth-beam does not revolve as in our looms, so she brings her work within easy reach by the following method: The spiral rope [fig. 12*e*] is

---

[11] [The diamond twill weave, described in Chapter 4.]

PLATE 18

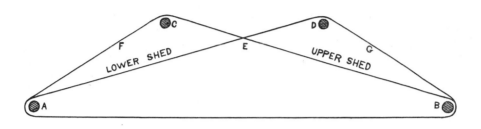

a

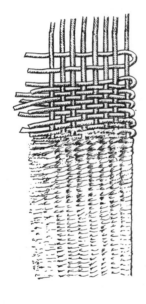

b

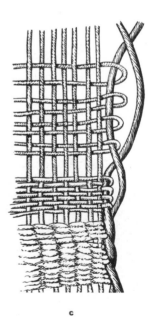

c

a, Warp diagram for belt loom. After Matthews 1884 fig. 56, from Pepper 1923.

b & **c,** Selvage details. **b** lacks the selvage cord, **c** has it. The former type is often found in Pueblo (particularly Zuñi) and Spanish weaving, seldom in Navaho work. Use of the cord strengthens the fabric. After Pepper 1923.

PLATE 19

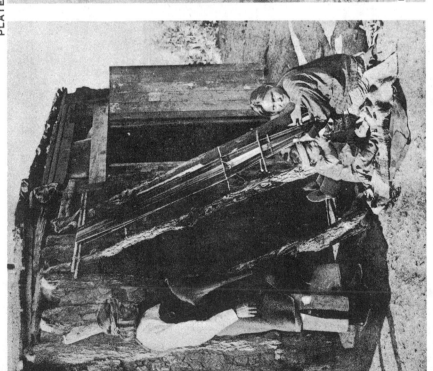

a, Belt loom weaving on a frame. Photo taken in the early 1880's near Fort Wingate, New Mexico. Wittick coll., Laboratory of Anthropology. b, Belt loom weaving without frame. Compare with the Peruvian weavers of fig. 9. After Matthews 1884 plate XXXVI.

loosened, the yarn-beam is lowered to the desired distance, a fold is made in the loosened web, and the upper edge of the fold is sewed down tightly to the cloth-beam. In all new blankets over two feet long the marks of this sewing are to be seen, and they often remain until the blanket is worn out. . . . . [pl. 51].

Except in belts, girths, and perhaps occasionally in very narrow blankets, the shuttle is never passed through the whole width of the warp at once, but only through a space which does not exceed the length of the batten; for it is by means of the batten, which is rarely more than three feet long, that the shed is opened [pl. 16].

Suppose the woman begins by weaving in the lower shed. She draws a portion of the healds towards her, and with them the anterior threads of the shed; by this motion she opens the shed about 1 inch, which is not sufficient for the easy passage of the woof. She inserts her batten edgewise into this opening and then turns it half around on its long axis, so that its broad surfaces lie horizontally; in this way the shed is opened to the extent of the width of the batten—about 3 inches; next the weft is passed through. In [pl. 16] the batten is shown lying edgewise (its broad surfaces vertical), as it appears when just inserted into the shed, and the weft, which has been passed through only a portion of the shed, is seen hanging out with its end on the ground. . . . When the weft is in, it is shoved down into its proper position by means of the reed-fork [pl. 16], and then the batten, restored to its first position (edgewise), is brought down with firm blows on the weft. It is by the vigorous use of the batten that the Navajo serapes are rendered water-proof.

When the lower shed has received its thread of weft the weaver opens the upper shed. This is done by releasing the healds and shoving the shed-rod down until it comes in contact with the healds; this opens the upper shed down to the web. Then the weft is inserted and the batten and reed-fork used as before. Thus she goes on with each shed alternately until the web is finished.

It is, of course, desirable, at least in handsome blankets of intricate pattern, to have both ends uniform even if the

figure be a little faulty in the center. To accomplish this some
of the best weavers depend on a careful estimate of the length
of each figure before they begin, and weave continuously in
one direction; but the majority weave a little portion of the
upper end before they finish the middle. Sometimes this is
done by weaving from above downwards; at other times it
is done by turning the loom upside down and working from
below upwards in the ordinary manner.

I have described how the ends of the blanket are bordered with a stout three-ply string applied to the folds of the
warp. The lateral edges of the blanket are similarly protected
by stout cords applied to the weft. The way in which these
are woven in, next demands our attention. Two stout worsted
cords, tied together, are firmly attached at each end of the
cloth-beam just outside of the warp; they are then carried
upwards and loosely tied to the yarn-beam or the supplementary yarn-beam. Every time the weft is turned at the edge
these two strings are twisted together and the weft is passed
through the twist; [12] thus one thread or strand of this border
is always on the outside. As it is constantly twisted in one
direction, it is evident that, after a while, a counter-twist must
form which would render the passage of the weft between
the cords difficult, if the cords could not be untwisted again.
Here the object of tying these cords loosely to one of the
upper beams, as before described, is displayed. From time to
time the cords are untied and the unwoven portion straightened as the work progresses. . . The coarse blankets do not
have them [pls. 46, 47, 77].

When the web is so nearly finished that the batten can
no longer be inserted in the warp, slender rods are placed
in the shed, while the weft is passed with increased difficulty
on the end of a delicate splinter and the reed-fork alone
presses the warp home. Later it becomes necessary to remove
even the rod and the shed; then the alternate threads are
separated by a slender stick worked in tediously between
them, and two threads of woof are inserted—one above and
the other below the stick. The very last thread is sometimes
put in with a darning needle. The weaving of the last three

---

[12][Shown in detail in pl. 18c.]

PLATE 20

Belt loom on a frame. This type has no ends and is sometimes called a tubular loom. Plate 19 shows an identical one in use. After Pepper 1923.

PLATE 21

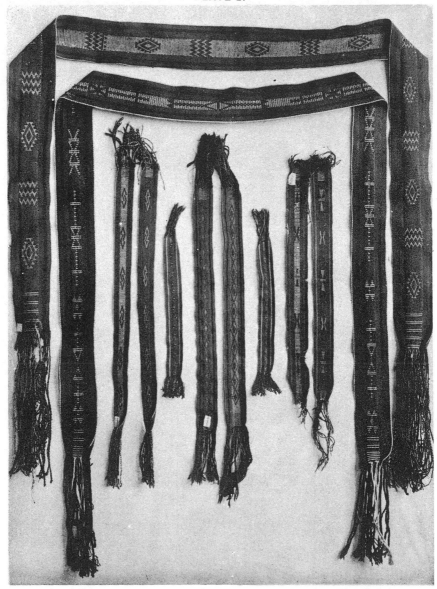

Belt loom fabrics: sashes and garters. Colors white figures on a red ground, with green stripes along each edge of the figured central band. In this type of fabric the warp hides the weft, except that the latter may occasionally peep through to form part of a figure. Southwest Museum, cat. (from left to right): B573 (length 5 feet 4 inches); B578; 491G212 (pair); ACV218; 200L3 (pair); ACV218; 491G210 (pair).

491G212 and 491G210 were collected among the Hopi but might be of Navaho make; 200L3, also from the Hopi, is an older specimen and was almost certainly made by them. It has indigo blue instead of green stripes. In most of these specimens the white yarn is trading store cotton, the rest native or Germantown wool.

inches requires more labor than any foot of the previous
work.

The description above quoted is based on a loom rigged for the
simplest of weaves—the plain. It holds good for all however, except in
heddle arrangement and manipulation. These are described for their
respective weaves in Chapter 4.

THE WAIST LOOM

The Navaho use each of the two types of loom known to be native
to the Southwest: the broad vertical loom, described above, and the
narrow belt loom of which the other is probably a development. Matthews
(1884: 389-391) describes the belt loom in these terms.

Their way of weaving long ribbon-like articles, such
as sashes or belts, garters and hair-bands, which we will
next consider, presents many interesting variations from the
method pursued in making blankets. To form a sash the
weaver proceeds as follows: She drives into the ground four
sticks and on them she winds her warp as a continuous
string (however, as the warp usually consists of threads of
three different colors it is not always one continuous string)
from below upwards in such a way as to secure two sheds,
as shown in the diagram Fig. 56 [pl. 18a herein].

Every turn of the warp passes over the sticks a and b;
but it is alternate turns that pass over c and d. When the
warp is laid she ties a string around the intersection of the
sheds at e, so as to keep the sheds separate while she is mounting the warp on the beams. She then places the upper beam
of the loom in the place of the stick b and the lower beam
in the place of the stick a. Sometimes the upper and lower
beams are secured to the two side rails forming a frame such
as the warp of a blanket is wound on [pl. 20], but more
commonly the loom is arranged in the manner shown in
Plate xxxvi [pl. 19b herein]; that is, the upper beam is secured to a rafter, post, or tree, while to the lower beam is
attached a loop of rope that passes under the thighs of the
weaver, and the warp is rendered tense by her weight. Next,
the upper shed is supplied with a shed-rod and the lower shed
with a set of healds. Then the stick at f [upper stick in pl.
19 a & b] is put in; this is simply a round stick, about which

one loop of each thread of the warp is thrown. (Although the warp may consist of only one thread I must now speak of each turn as a separate thread.) Its use is to keep the different threads in place and prevent them from crossing and straggling; for it must be remembered that the warp in this case is not secured at two points between three stranded cords as is the blanket warp.

When this is all ready the insertion of the weft begins. The reed-fork is rarely needed and the batten used is much shorter than that employed in making blankets. . . Fig. 57 [not reproduced herein] represents a section of a belt. It will be seen [see pls. 20, 21] that the center is ornamented with peculiar raised figures; these are made by inserting a slender stick into the warp, so as to hold up certain of the threads while the weft is passed twice or oftener underneath them. It is practically a variety of damask or two-ply weaving; the figures on the opposite side of the belt being different. There is a limited variety of these figures. I think I have seen about a dozen different kinds. The experienced weaver is so well acquainted with the "count" or arrangements of the raised threads appropriate to each pattern that she goes on inserting and withdrawing the slender stick referred to without a moment's hesitation, making the web at the rate of 10 or 12 inches an hour. When the web has grown to the point at which she cannot weave it further without bringing the unfilled warp nearer to her, she is not obliged to resort to the clumsy method used with blankets. She merely seizes the anterior layer of the warp and pulls it down towards her; for the warp is not attached to the beams, but is movable on them; in other words, while still on the loom the belt is endless. When all the warp has been filled except about one foot, the weaving is completed; for then the unfilled warp is cut in the center and becomes the terminal fringes of the now finished belt.

The only marked difference that I have observed between the mechanical appliances of the Navajo weaver and those of her Pueblo neighbor is to be seen in the belt loom. The Zuñi woman lays out her warp, not as a continuous thread around two beams, but as several disunited threads.

PLATE 22

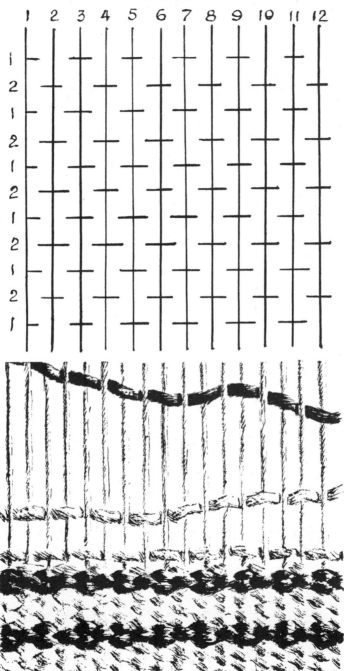

Plain weave, detail drawing and heddle arrangement. In this and following heddle diagrams the order of heddle shifting is shown at the left, color alternation (where important) at the right of the diagram, working from below upward as in actual weaving.

PLATE 23

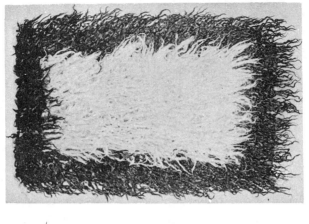

b

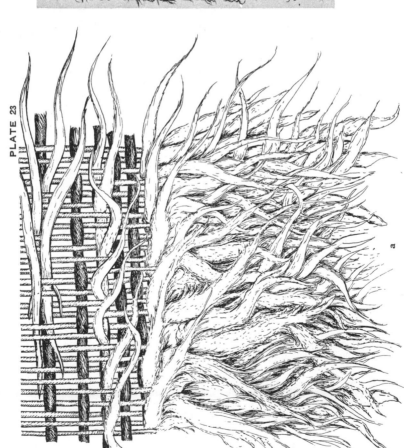

a

a, Tufting, detail drawing. After Pepper 1923.
b, Tufted saddle throw, white center, red border, size 27 x 44 ins. Author's coll. In this and following illustrations, the blanket is shown in its position in the loom: warp strings vertical, weft horizontal.

She attaches one end of these to a fixed object, usually a rafter in her dwelling, and the other to the belt she wears around her body. She has a set of wooden healds by which she actuates the alternate threads of the warp. Instead of using the slender stick of the Navajos to elevate the threads of the warp in forming her figures, she lifts these threads with her fingers. This is an easy matter with her style of loom; but it would be a very difficult task with that of the Navajos.[13]

_____

[13] [Matthews' plate XXXVII shows a Zuñi belt weaver.]

PLATE 24

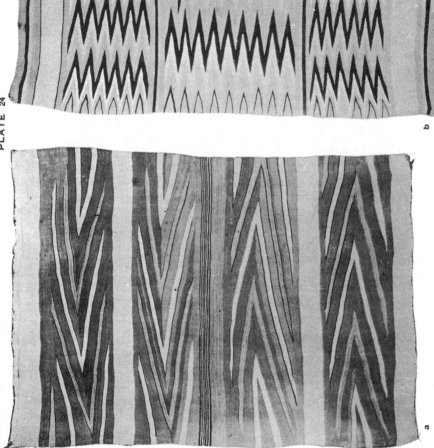

a

b

Pulled-warp blankets. a size 48 x 68 ins., colors yellow and white chevrons outlined in indigo blue and (machine-spun) green on a deep red ground; narrow center stripes brown and blue, ends white. b size 52 x 75 ins., colors black, white and orange chevrons on red ground. Earl H. Morris coll., both pieces dated about 1890. Dyes probably native and aniline mingled.

PLATE 25

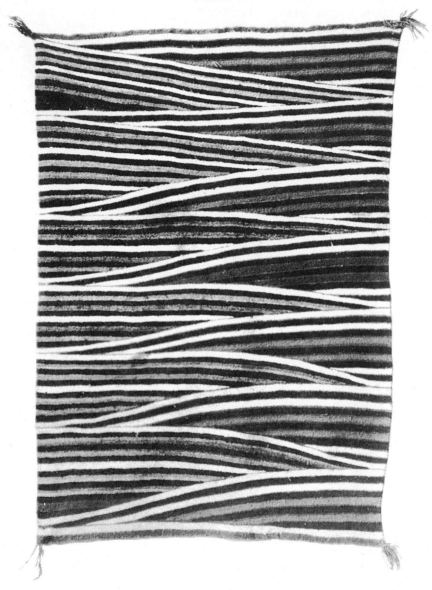

A pulled-warp blanket. Size 28 x 40 ins. (double saddle blanket dimensions although this has more the character of a child's shoulder blanket). Colors white, black, brown, red, and blue stripes. Mrs. C. Matthews coll., U. S. National Museum, number obliterated. Dates probably from before 1890, colors apparently native and aniline mingled.

CHAPTER IV

WEAVES OF THE NAVAHO

AVAHO weaving had attained considerable technical variety before the relentless pressure of American customs and the cheap products of Yankee manufacturing skill brought its development to a halt. Weavers of a generation ago were rejoicing in a new accomplishment, the two-faced weave. The diamond twill was a common part of their technical equipment, while the simple or diagonal twill was child's play, with the plain weave taken for granted as something every woman knew. Today the diamond twill is beyond the ability of most weavers, the diagonal twill considered somewhat of a feat. As for the two-faced weave, it nearly died a-borning; knowledge of its peculiar construction seems never to have become widespread among the Navaho themselves (probably because the weaving industry was in an enfeebled and apathtic state at the time of its appearance), and it is a complete mystery, almost a legend, to most weavers of today.[1] The ancient American craft of weaving as practised in the Southwest for a thousand years by the prehistoric Pueblos, the modern Pueblos, and the Navaho, seems destined to disappear; much of it is already gone, the rest is going. The plain weave stands almost alone today. A revival is in progress (Chapter 15) which may arouse certain of the moribund technics. But throughout the present century the technical trend of Navaho weaving has been steadily downward.

CLASSIFICATION OF WEAVES

A fundamental classification of weaves should include only those characterized by a distinctive loom rigging, or heddle arrangement. Under them as sub-classes come certain variants based on a manipulation of the heddles or of the weft, in the process of weaving. The fundamental classes of weave known (by me) to have been practised by the Navaho are nine:

---

[1] Of the thousands of Navaho blankets I have seen, not a dozen were two-faced. Most museums, even of those possessing excellent collections, have not a single specimen.

plain weave, diagonal twill, five diamond twills, two-faced, and double cloth. A doubt exists in the case of the last named, as will be seen in the section devoted to it herein. Each of these weaves has its own peculiar heddle rig as well as a definite order of heddle manipulation: no two of them are done upon the same rig. Each will be described in the order of historical development, so far as known, with the variants or sub-classes which have come under my observation. The list may not be complete; but certainly no technic of much importance can have been overlooked.

PLAIN WEAVE

The plain weave beyond reasonable doubt was the first ever adapted to the loom in any time or place. It is the simplest of all in loom arrangement and operation, requiring the minimum number of sheds, two. The single heddle controls one shed, the shed rod the other, to give the necessary interplay of warp and weft to bond the fabric. The description given in Chapter 3 of the setting up of a Navaho loom told in detail of the placing and function of the heddle and the shed rod. The heddle arrangement for plain weaving is shown in plate 22b. A simple over one, under one, or crisscross of weft over warp, is the formula for the plain weave, as plate 22a shows. The heddle clasps every alternate warp string and the shed rod clasps those jumped by the heddle—dividing the total warp evenly between them.[2]

While the plain weave is the simplest of all, it is also the most effective in such coarse weaving as that of the Navaho. Its small, even stitches and featureless surface lend themselves to smooth texture and elaborate pattern. The finest products of the Navaho loom are nearly always of plain weave; I do not recall a single instance of the use of bayeta, and only a few of Germantown, in any other weave than plain.

TUFTING

It is a common device in modern commercial weaving to make pile fabrics by allowing the weft (or even the warp, in some types) to project above the surface of the fabric in a series of little loops. These may be left as woven, as in Turkish toweling and terry cloth, or cut in the middle of

---

[2] In describing heddle rigging, terms are needed for distinguishing the strings of warp enclosed by the heddle or the shed rod from those not enclosed. I find the words clasp and jump simple and unmistakably clear, hence have used them exclusively. It should be understood that while the heddle actually encloses the warp string in a loop (as shown in pl. 16), the shed rod merely holds the string forward by being inserted behind it; but for simplicity, and because the result is identical in each case, I refer to each as "clasping" the warp string it controls.

each loop, as in velvet and mohair. The result is a pile, or mass of fiber standing vertically to the plane of the fabric. Oriental rugs and their machine-made imitations have this feature, the pile being an excess of weft material that renders the piece thick and soft.[3]

The Navaho formerly made (and do occasionally still) a species of pile fabric by looping long tufts of merino or Angora goat wool over certain strands of warp at regular intervals during the process of weaving, leaving the ends projecting beyond the surface of the piece in a series of tufts, as in plate 23. The effect is much like that of a sheep or goat pelt, and therein the inspiration of this type of blanket probably lies.

The attachment of the tuft shows variations of detail in different specimens. I have seen three: (1) Wisp of wool merely suspended at its middle from the warp string, both ends projecting to form tufts on the face of the blanket. (2) Wisp tied to the warp string with a single loop or half-granny knot near its end, either leaving both ends projecting as tufts, or clipping off the short or tied end even with the surface of the back of the blanket. (3) Wisp inwoven (like weft) for perhaps half its length, the other half projecting as a tuft. The last of these methods is shown in plate 23*a*. Each method seems to give security to the tuft if the blanket is soundly woven, for the hard-battened weft acts as a bond to the inserted wisps; but the knotted tuft should best withstand pulling.

Tufting is commonly done in diagonal twill as well as in plain weave. In either, the spacing of the tufts is variable. The specimen blanket shown in plate 23*b* has tufts at about every thirtieth row of weft and every fifth warp string. The weaver need follow no rule in this regard, provided she be generous enough with her material to assure a fair coverage of the surface with the shaggy wisps of wool.

Pulled Warp

Blankets are occasionally seen in which the pattern consists of vertical rows of interlocked zigzag stripes of various colors: specimens are shown in plates 24 and 25. They seem to be most characteristic of the end of the native dye period, around 1890. The peculiarity of these pieces lies in the fact that the warp bends along the lines of the pattern, giving rise

---

[3] The Navaho loom is almost a counterpart of that on which Oriental rugs are made, it is interesting to note: "The loom now generally used in the Orient is made by fastening two poles perpendicularly in the ground to a sufficient depth, leaving above ground as much of each pole as equals in length the desired rug. This framework supports two horizontal rollers, the warp threads being wound around the upper, while the ends are fastened to the lower; at this the weaving is begun, and on it the rug is rolled while in process of construction."—Holt: 11.

to the thought that they may be of a distinct weave. Having examined
a number of them (without, however, ever seeing one in process of
weaving), my conclusion is that the weaver, in order to save time and
avoid the constant manipulation of weft strands of different colors that
delays progress so greatly, builds one or more stripes higher than the body
of the fabric at that point, instead of working carefully across the entire
face of the blanket, one horizontal line at a time. Then, in battening down,
the batten strikes the fabric on a bias, since the zigzag lines of the pattern
lie diagonally to the perpendicular warp strings. This sidewise pounding,
with the subsequent pulling of the warp in another direction as a further
segment of the zigzag pattern was laid and similarly battened, would tend
to give the warp its wavering trend. The explanation is conjectural, but I
am certain that these blankets are woven on the plain loom rig and should
not be considered anything but a variant type of plain weaving.

WARP FLOATING

Another device employed by Navaho weavers that has its counterpart
in modern industrial textile manufacture is that of warp floating. The
damask weaves of our table linen are the most common examples. The
method is to leave certain warp strings unenclosed by one or more picks
of weft, or "floated" over the body of the fabric in an arrangement calculated to produce a harmonious pattern of repeated figures in the raised
warp. This pattern may be emphasized by a warp of different color from
its surrounding weft, although it is quite visible in warp and weft of one
color through the difference in surface texture produced by the floating.

The Navaho do warp floating with plain weave in their belts, garters,
hair cords, etc., on the belt loom described in Chapter 3, but I have never
seen the technic used in a blanket. The method is to raise certain warp
strings with a short stick—an extemporized, supplementary heddle, of a
sort—and pass the weft below them. The face of the piece shows a pattern
in raised warp, while the back has a corresponding effect in raised weft.
Warp strings of different colors are commonly used to heighten and vary
the effect. This is another ancient technic, as subsequent references will
prove. Plates 20 and 21 show examples of warp floating.

TWILLED WEAVES

Twilling is a constant diagonal progression of stitches produced by
the regular alternation of the point of intersection of warp and weft. The
plain weave, for example, uses but two sheds, permitting no alternation

PLATE 26

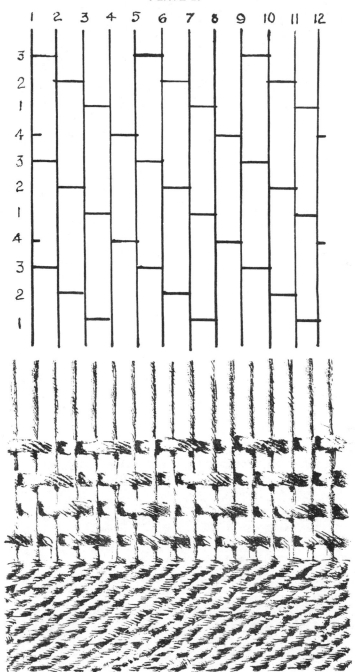

Diagonal twill, heddle diagram and detail drawing.

PLATE 27

a

b

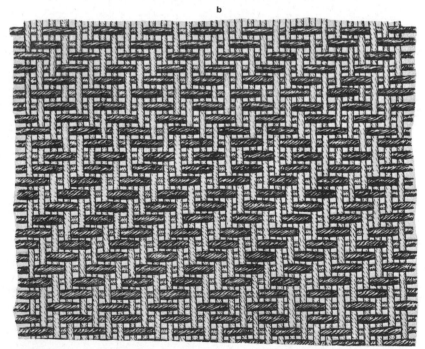

Reversed or herringbone twill, photograph and detail drawing. a is a single saddle blanket, size 30 x 24 ins., colors white, indigo blue and native green-gold on a red ground, probably aniline. Mrs. C. Matthews coll., U. S. National Museum, cat. 281481.

b is after Pepper 1923, a fabric in the open or "basket" weave.

of this point; the result is a fabric of vertical ribs with one string of warp (commonly) as the core of each. Twilling on the other hand (as done by the Navaho), employs four sheds, controlled by three heddles and the shed rod, the heddle arrangement being calculated to throw each stitch of weft one warp string to the right or left of the one preceding it. The result is a fabric of diagonal rather than vertical ribs.

DIAGONAL TWILL

In diagonal twilling, the simplest form of the technic, each heddle clasps two and jumps two,[4] but from one heddle to the next an overlap of one warp string occurs, as shown in the diagram, plate 26*a*. For example, Heddle 3 will clasp warp strings 1 and 2, Heddle 2 will clasp 2 and 3, Heddle 1 will clasp 3 and 4, and Heddle 4 (the shed rod) will clasp strings 4 and 5. Manipulation of the heddles in regular order, beginning at either 1 or 4 as the weaver pleases, produces a fabric of diagonal ribs through overlapping one warp string and advancing to right or left by one at each strand of weft. Each stitch climbs one strand higher than its predecessor, as in all weaving, but it also reaches out to right or left and encloses the adjacent warp string, and these two trends give the effect of a constant diagonal progression across the surface of the fabric.

Twilling is an ancient technic, extensively used in finger weaving for both basketry and textiles. The prehistoric Pueblos knew the diagonal twill in their loom weaving,[5] and the most prolific weavers among their descendants—the Hopi—use it extensively. I have never seen a twill from prehistoric Peru, however, in the hundreds of specimens and illustrations I have scrutinized.[6]

Reversed-Twill Patterns—It has been said that diagonal twilling may progress to either right or left, depending on either the diagonal trend chosen in rigging the loom or the order of heddle manipulation, whether regular (bottom to top) or reverse. *Ipso facto,* the order may be reversed

[4] This is the usual Navaho formula—2, 2, 2, 2; but other combinations are possible, provided always that at least each alternate heddle clasp more than one warp string, to provide for the necessary alternation of intersection of warp and weft.

[5] Judd (63) mentions "two specimens of twilled weave"; Kidder and Guernsey (115) describe two specimens of different formulas: one a 2—2 like the Navaho, the other a 2—1 (which the modern Hopi also use). Many other instances are of record.

[6] Peruvian weaving, for all its elaborate variety of finger technics auxiliary to the mechanical process of loom weaving, seems never to have reached the technical stage of even the simplest of twills. The prehistoric Pueblos of 1000 A. D. were in advance of the Peruvians in this particular—unless the latter simply did not care for twills.

at the will of the weaver, to produce banded "herringbone" effects in which the ribs trend in alternate directions, appearing to the eye as a constant series of chevrons or V's set sidewise. This expedient is not uncommon, the heddle order frequently being reversed to correspond with a change in weft color, in simple band or stripe patterns.

The diagonal twill is most often seen in a pattern of plain stripes or bands of various widths. Its broad stitches do not lend themselves so well to figured patterns, while their inevitable diagonal trend discourages the use of vertical lines in the design. Plates 43*a*, 60, show diagonal, and plates 42*a*, 43*b*, 65*a*, reverse-twill weaves in blankets.

DIAMOND TWILL

Navaho weavers of a generation ago were fond of making small blankets,[7] usually single or double saddle cloths, in which the pattern is a solid mosaic of diamonds-within-diamonds. Three colors are commonly employed, with each diamond of a different color from the ones enclosing it. Every rib of the surface thus shows a different color in regular alternation throughout, and each rib forms one side of a diamond figure.[8] The pattern is automatic, and is of that continuously flowing type known as diaper.

The diamond figure which comprises the entire pattern unit in this

---

[7] Twilled blankets are usually small, doubtless to enable the weaver to pass the weft strand from edge to edge of the loom without having to shift her seat, as she must do in weaving a blanket of greater width than her own reach. Large blankets of plain weave are built up in sections, sometimes with two sets of heddles side by side, each set covering half the width of the loom. Blankets thus made show diagonal lines at irregular intervals across their face, these lines being the point of junction of sections woven independently. They are visible in plates 106b, 111, 115.

These lines are considered an evidence of indolence in the weaver, and I have heard them called "lazy lines." Mrs. H. S. Colton of the Museum of Northern Arizona, Flagstaff, tells me that the Hopi male weavers will move constantly back and forth in front of their loom, rather than have "lazy lines" appear in the fabric.

Twills, with their complicated heddle rig, virtually require weaving across the entire width of the piece with each change of heddle. I have seen a few diagonal twills of perhaps five feet width; but never a diamond twill wider than about three feet, in Navaho weaving.

[8] Technical factors dictate the use of three colors if color alternation is to be constant—although the weaver may use any number of colors by taking the trouble to change weft color within the shed (as in pattern building in plain weave) instead of using a single weft strand throughout the length of the shed. Here is the reason: diamond twills require four different sheds; therefore the number of colors used must not be divisible by four, to prevent certain colors falling regularly into certain sheds. Two colors, or four, would not give the constant alternation required. With two, for example, red would fall regularly in sheds 1 and 3, white in sheds 2 and 4; and the result would be vertical lines of color violating the diagonal trend of the rib texture. I proved this by experiment.

PLATE 28

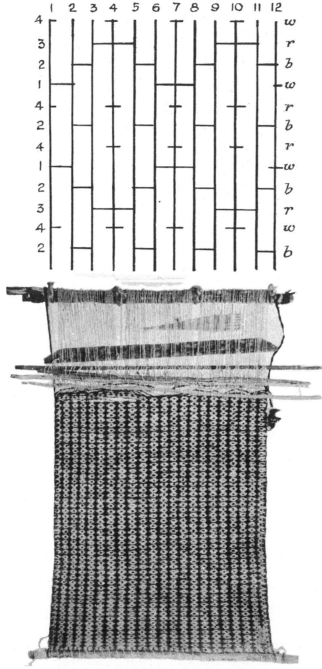

Two-unit diamond twill, photograph and heddle diagram, the former a loom from Crown Point Trading Company. Reeve coll. Southwest Museum cat. 491G303.

The diagram illustrates one complete heddle movement, to be repeated as shown **ad infinitum.** The heddle rig repeats from string seven onward.

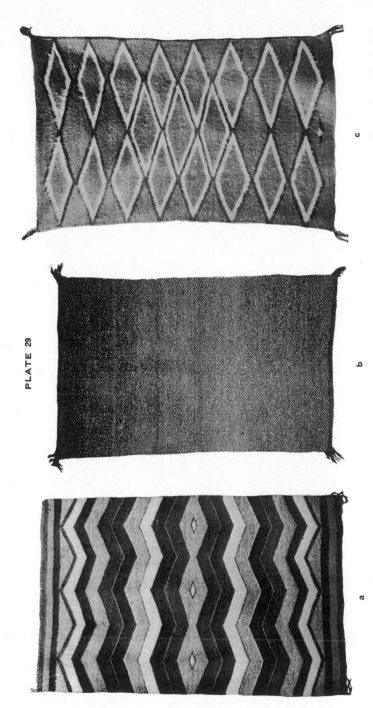

PLATE 29

a

b

c

Diamond twills in double saddle blankets. a is a variant of the diamond twill, made probably on a rig for large diamonds as illustrated in pl. 31; by reversing the heddle order only at the half-way point the weaver has produced a pattern of half-diamonds with a full-diamond center. Size 35 x 54 ins., colors red, white, black, yellow, grey.

b is the 7-unit diamond, size 32 x 52 ins., colors red, black, grey in regular alternation.

c is the 30-unit, size 34 x 53 ins. Instead of following the usual regular alternation of color, the weaver has repeated colors to give a pattern of black and white diamonds on a red ground.

The diamond twill has many such possibilities (see also pl. 89) in both color and heddle manipulation. a and b are recent pieces, c older but without known history. Author's coll.

type of weave is a product of that same basic arrangement of alternating stitches which makes its simpler associate, the diagonal twill: diagonal progression is the motive of each. But in the diagonal form the heddles are arranged to make this progression tend in one direction across the whole width of the web, while the diamond twill is the result of a heddle arrangement which sends the diagonal ribs outward in opposite directions from a common center. It is calculated to produce, in other words, a series of chevrons or V's in their natural position, point downward, and only the reversal of the heddle order is required to cap the V with another, point upward, to produce a diamond figure. Blankets are occasionally seen to have been woven without reversing this order, the pattern being a constant repetition of V-inside-V in vertical rows. Plate 29a shows this device used as part of the pattern at each end, the center of the blanket being a full diamond.

A comparison of plates 26a and 28 should make clear the similarity of the diagonal and the diamond twill heddle arrangements; closer scrutiny will reveal their essential difference. Plate 26a, the diagonal, shows the heddle clasps spaced at regular intervals in both horizontal and vertical orders. Every stitch is two warp strings in width, every one advances one string to the left of the predecessor just below it. But in plate 28, the diamond twill heddle rig, the order is broken. Attacking it at the point where its peculiar order is most understandable, we find that Heddle 4 at String 4 clasps one; Heddle 3, just below, is clasping three, our no. 4 and one to either side in addition. The next two heddles in order, nos. 2 and 1, continue this outward reach from the central string, no. 4, the whole pattern at this point consisting of a V, and this V is repeated in unbroken succession across the face of the diagram (which would be the face of the blanket in actual weaving): VVVV. Two V's side by side form one V inverted, so we have, automatically, a line of V's upside-down as well as a line in natural position. In weaving, the heddles are manipulated in regular order until a line of V's is completed, then both heddle order and color alternation are reversed and the V's cap themselves —and that is the diamond twill.

The heddle diagram chosen for exposition in the paragraph above (pl. 28) is the smallest and simplest diamond that can be made; I have called it the 2-unit diamond rig because it makes a pattern of only two diamonds, one inside the other. Plate 28 shows a photograph of this weave in the loom. The 2-unit figure is only one of a potentially infinite series. Larger figures, with a greater number of internested diamonds to each, may be made *ad infinitum* (except for the practical limitation of size), by merely increasing the distance between the nuclear stitches, of which String 4 in plate 28 was taken as an instance. Plate 31 *b, c,* and *d* shows heddle rigs for 5-unit (see also pl. 89) 7-unit, and 9-unit diamond figures. They are precisely like figure 28, the 2-unit, in fundamental arrangement, it will be noted, their only individuality being in the spacing of the nuclear stitches. In the 5-unit (pl. 31*b*), for example, notice that Heddle 2 at String 1 clasps one (a nuclear stitch), and this occurs again ten strings farther along, at String 11; but in the 2-unit (pl. 28), the simpler form, the nuclear stitch in Heddle 4 occurs at Strings 1, 4, 7, 10, etc.—an interval of only three strings. In plate 31*c* and *d* showing the 7-unit and 9-unit heddle rigs drawn in diagram, the interval is further lengthened; but I leave it to the reader to study it out for himself, for the exposition is becoming wearisome.

I have seen in Navaho weaving use made of the 2, 5, and 7-unit diamonds, the last two being most common; two blankets (one, dated 1893, is U. S. National Museum cat. 168239, another is plate 30) in a pattern with a unit figure of twenty-three boxed diamonds, counting from the center to the last complete figure in the outward progression; and one with no fewer than thirty such (pl. 29*c*). The 9-unit figure shown in the diagram (pl. 31*d*) is my own creation; I made it on paper, then wove it on my experimental loom to prove the statement that the diamond twill can be made in figures of any size from the 2-unit upward.[9] While speaking of experiments I should add that the Navaho too are experimenting, certain traders having apparently entered into a competition to produce weaves unknown to their rivals. I have seen on experimental looms weaves not here described, for I have never encountered them in practical use. The field is almost without limit, but the range of practicability is greatly restricted by the fact that one cannot evolve new weaves without getting into broad stitches. Any stitch of more than two warp strings width (although three may be used with restraint as in the diamond twill) is neither sightly nor practical. It makes for a loose, coarse fabric.

---

[9] I acknowledge, and very gratefully, the help derived from a set of miniature Navaho looms, made up for the Southwest Museum by an expert Navaho weaver at the instance of Messrs. Ambrose and Boardman of the Crown Point Trading Company, Thoreau, New Mexico, and presented to the Museum by its generous patron General Charles McC. Reeve as a part of the Reeve Collection in Ethnology. By copying the heddle rig used in them and tracing back the uppermost weft strands to determine the heddle order I obtained the technical data above heaped upon the patient reader—for little of it has hitherto been recorded, to my knowledge. Without an unfinished piece in the loom the task is formidable if not impossible, unless one sacrifices the specimen by tearing it down thread after thread.

The useful weaves were all discovered long ago, we may be sure, although many interesting manipulative variations of the diamond twill are possible.

The diamond twill is the most difficult of all the Navaho weaves, in my opinion (with the possible exception of the double cloth weave, the method of which is unknown to me). It requires a different arrangement of each of the four heddles, a complicated order of heddle manipulation, and a constant alternation of weft color in a predetermined order. The weaver must give close attention to her task in order to produce a perfect diamond pattern, for the possibilities of error are many.

I find no evidence that the diamond twill was used in mechanical weaving by the prehistoric Pueblos, although they used the diagonal twill, as was said. They knew the diamond twill as a finger method, certainly, as plates 2*b* and 35*c* prove. The first is a plaited mat, the second a cotton cloth fragment which appears to be loom-woven; close scrutiny shows, however, that the weft threads forming the diamond do not extend across the full width of the warp as they would if woven in the loom. The modern Hopi seem to have employed the diamond twill in relatively early times, and it may have originated with them, or reached the Navaho through them. O'Neale and Kroeber (plate 11*b*) figure a specimen from Peru that shows the diamond ribbing; but they call it a "twine-plaited wool fabric," hence it would not be a product of the loom. Their plate 39 likewise stands in evidence of the diamond twill in prehistoric Peru, but again in a finger technic: a brocade in wool on a cotton fabric, plain woven.[10] Inferentially, the diamond twill originated in a hand technic and was adapted to the loom by a weaver skilful enough to work out the complicated heddle arrangement.[11] When? Where? The archeologist must answer, when he is able.

THE TWO-FACED WEAVE

The Navaho loom produces, among other fabrics, one in which the two faces show quite different patterns, often in different colors (pl. 32).

---

[10] Brocade is secondary or overlaid weft, making a double weft at point of use. It is applied by hand in process of weaving and is independent of heddle rig. The Hopi use brocade as well as embroidery in decorating their white cotton fabrics. I have never seen it in Navaho weaving—perhaps because it is most effective with the open or basket weave, which the Navaho never employ.

[11] Unless it should prove another European trait introduced by Spaniard or American. The Scotch use it in their tweed weaving and I have seen it in Moroccan rugs. The earliest dated specimen of this weave I have been able to find for the Navaho is the saddle blanket shown in pl. 89 which was collected by Matthews, hence probably dates from the early eighties; but Schoolcraft (pl. 36) figures a pattern (in water color) which apparently is a diamond twill, this in 1860. The caption calls it Pueblo, the text reference (p. 436) Navaho.

This astonishing product was called the two-faced blanket by Matthews (1900), who was the first to describe it. Matthews attempted no technical description, his brief account in the *American Anthropologist* merely calling attention to the specimen figured therein, and giving some interesting historical information that will be quoted in following pages. Through the courtesy of Mr. B. I. Staples in lending me a loom completely rigged, with its blanket half woven, I have been able to record the heddle rig.[12] But to Mr. F. K. Hinchman of the Southwest Museum goes the honor of studying out the astonishingly simple method by which this weave achieves its mystifying effect, for he had solved the problem before I obtained the Staples' loom.

Matthews considered the two-faced weave a development of the twill. It requires the same number of sheds, four, necessitating three heddles and the shed rod;[13] but none of the several two-faced blankets that I have examined showed the characteristic surface appearance of twilling, having rather the vertical ribs of the plain weave, but with stitches of irregular width.

The heddle arrangement for two-faced weaving is shown in plate 32, and a specimen (the Staples loom), as seen from both front and back, in *c* and *d*. As the diagram in plate 32*a* shows, the heddle arrangement is in ratio of (1) 3 to 1; (2) 1 to 3; (3) 3 to 1; (4) 1 to 3. Sheds 1 and 3 have three warp strings to the front for one to the rear; therefore the strand of weft inserted in either of these sheds will jump three strings in four, passing behind them, to become visible from the rear for the width of three warp strings, and visible from the front for the width of only one warp string. In other words, these sheds throw three-fourths of the total weft color to the rear pattern, leaving only one-fourth visible in front.

Sheds 2 and 4 do the same thing inversely: their weft strands are visible in front over the width of three warp strings, and in the rear over one only. Thus it is obvious that if the weaver uses given colors with sheds

---

[12] Not a difficult task, despite Matthews' protest that he could not attempt a technical description without seeing the weaving in progress. The heddle arrangement of course can be noted only when the loom is not in use, by counting warp strings and recording the heddle that controls each one. The order of heddle manipulation in weaving is easily determined by tracing back several of the last weft strands woven, noting the warp strings that pass behind each pick of weft, and those that lie in front of it. The front strings are then followed upward to the heddle that clasps them, and the order of heddle manipulation, or shed opening, is thus determined.

[13] James' statement (112) that "as many as eight heddles are used" is taken from the Ethnologic Dictionary (244) and I am firmly convinced it is in error. At any rate four heddles suffice, as I have seen, to produce an excellent specimen of this weave, and pl. 32 proves this true, as do my own experiments.

PLATE 30

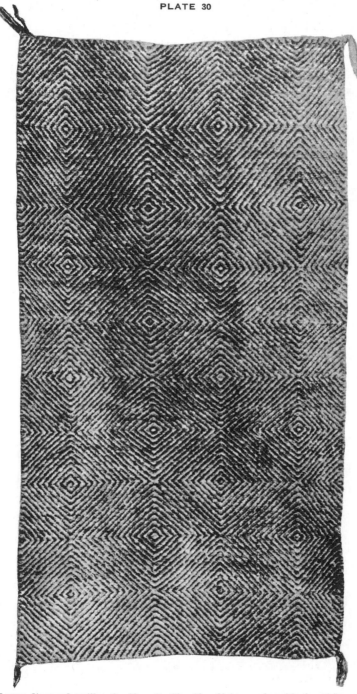

Large diamond twills: the 23-unit. Size 36 x 60 ins., colors black, white, gray, in regular alternation; Fred K. Hinchman coll. Southwest Museum cat. 202L85. Woven in 1931.

PLATE 31

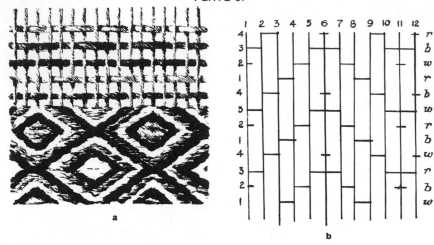

a

b

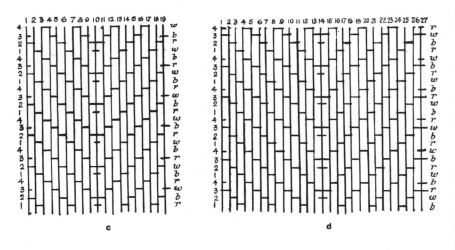

c

d

a and b, Five-unit diamond twill, detail drawing and diagram. Heddle rig repeats from string 11 onward; heddle order: five times on 1, 2, 3, 4, and W, B, R, as shown above, then five reversed, or 3, 2, 1, 4, and B, W, R.

c and d, Seven-and nine-unit diamond twills, heddle diagrams. c, seven-unit; heddle rig repeats from string 19 onward; heddle order: 1, 2, 3, 4, on R, B, W, as shown above, seven times over; then seven on 3, 2, 1, 4, and B, R, W, this making one row of diamonds.

d, Nine-unit; heddle rig repeats from string 27 onward. Run nine times in order shown above, then nine in reversed heddle and color order.

1 and 3 only, the back of the blanket will feature these colors predominantly; and likewise with sheds 2 and 4, on the blanket's face. By assigning certain colors to the rear sheds and others to the front sheds a totally different color effect is produced on front and back.

Where color change is possible, pattern is equally so. Instead of running a single strand of weft through the entire length of the shed, the weaver can change colors at any point and thus build up patterns, as in plain weave; and these patterns will be predominant on one side only, if the colors forming them are used only in the two sheds controlling that side. Thus the weaver can build up different patterns in different colors, on either side of her fabric.

One difficulty remains: that of the fourth stitch, which necessarily, in order to bond the fabric, shows through on the side to which its color does not appertain. This difficulty is overcome by using loosely-spun yarn and battening down the fabric in the usual tapestry weave. In this manner the wanted color, jumping three warp strings and surrounding the unwanted color in a preponderance of three to one, above and below, is made to overspread and efface the unwanted. The two-faced blanket is an optical illusion in this respect, for the back colors are actually present in front, but they are not visible if the weaver has done her work well. By spreading two weft strands apart and looking closely one sees them, tucked away at every fourth warp string, as shown in the detailed drawing, plate 32*b*.

It follows naturally that heddle manipulation is in the order 1, 2, 3, 4, over and over again, using first a back color, then a front color, and so on in regular alternation.

It would be difficult to work a figured pattern into the back of a two-faced blanket, merely because the weaver cannot see that part of her fabric, hence would have great difficulty in placing the weft colors in their proper arrangement for pattern building. She might conceivably carry the back pattern in her head and work from a mental picture of its exact layout, spacing, and progress toward completion; but to do so would be a mental feat fully equal to that of the chess expert playing several games at once. Two weavers, one building the back pattern only and the other weaving the front and manipulating heddles and batten, could produce an astonishing double pattern. One weaver alone, however, could scarcely handle the two patterns without rising from her seat and going around the loom to look at the back pattern at almost every shift of heddle—unless she used a large mirror back of the loom.

In practice, therefore, the two-faced blanket weaver contented herself with a simple pattern of stripes in the rear, building a figured pattern in front. Matthews' specimen, illustrated in his plate xxv [14] (and reproduced in James, fig. 138), is of this type; and so is every specimen I have ever seen.

History of the Two-Faced Weave

Matthews (1900) gives some interesting historical data concerning the two-faced weave, which is quoted below:

> While living in New Mexico during the years 1880-84, in daily contact with members of the Navaho tribe, I made a careful study of the Navaho art of weaving and wrote a treatise on the subject which appeared in the Third Annual Report of the Bureau of Ethnology. In that article I described all the important forms of Navaho blankets I had ever seen; but I had not seen a two-faced blanket, and, up to the date of writing, had not even heard of it; there is, therefore, no allusion to it in my treatise. I was absent from New Mexico, except during two short visits, for six years. Some time after I returned to it, in 1890, for another sojourn of four years, I saw for the first time, one of those two-faced blankets. Thus I may safely say that some time after I left New Mexico in 1884 the process of making this blanket was invented by a Navaho woman.
>
> During my second sojourn in New Mexico I tried to find a woman who wove this peculiar blanket in order that I might induce her by liberal pecuniary promises, as I had done on previous occasions with other weavers of special fabrics, to come to my residence and work under my observation; but I never succeeded. I was told that the blankets were made in a distant part of the Navaho country; my informants knew not where. If there were more than one maker, I never learned; but from what I know of the Navahoes I think it probable that the inventor has made no secret of the process and that now, at least, there are many weavers of the two-faced blanket.[15]

[14] The excellent photography of the illustration shows that this piece of weaving was inexpertly handled, unwanted color stitches showing through in a number of places, both front and rear. The specimen does not do full justice to the possibilities of two-faced weaving. The Staples loom, pl. 32, shows better workmanship.

[15] [The word "many" in my observation is too generous a term, for I found this type rare to non-existent in collections public and private throughout the United States.]

PLATE 32

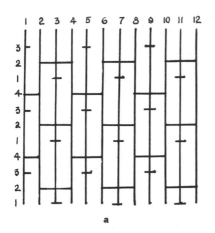

a

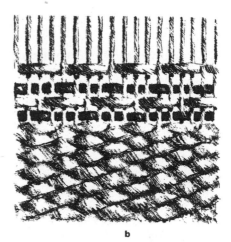

b

c

d

The two-faced weave, heddle diagram (a) and detail drawing (b). Heddle operation is in regular order, using "front pattern" weft colors with heddles 1 and 3, "back pattern" colors with heddles 2 and 4.

c and d, A two-faced loom, front and back views. Courtesy of Mr. B. I. Staples.

PLATE 33

Native American shirts. **a** from Pachacamac, Peru (prehistoric) after E. Hamy, **Galerie Americaine du Trocadero** (Paris, France) pl. XLVIII. **b** Navaho, J. L. Hubbell coll., after James fig. 40. **b** has a fashioned neck, (possibly done after weaving) otherwise all are woven in straight lines throughout. **c** Hopi, Fred K. Hinchman coll. Southwest Museum cat. 202L71.

The Peruvian specimen is of cotton embroidered in wool, the others of black wool.

d, Double cloth, a single saddle blanket, size 32 x 28 ins., described in the **text.** Courtesy of Fred Harvey.

Someone may question if this art did not exist during my first sojourn in the Navaho country previous to 1884, and if I might not have failed to observe it. This is by no means probable. Everyone in the Navaho country then believed that the distinguishing feature of the Indian blanket was that, no matter how richly figured, its two surfaces were always exactly alike in all respects. Mr. Thomas V. Keam, of Keam's Cañon, Arizona, is the Indian trader who has been longest established among the Navahoes, and is their most popular trader; he has dealt and dwelt with them, I think, for about thirty years, and he is an educated, intelligent, and observant man. Had such blankets been even occasionally seen among these Indians prior to 1884, some of them would have been brought to him to trade and he would not have failed to observe their unusual appearance. In 1896 I wrote requesting Mr. Keam to get for me a two-faced blanket from his part of the country and asking him what he knew of the origin of the new blanket. In his reply, dated January 27, 1897, he says:

"As you suppose, it is only about three years since I first saw this work, and to date there are only a few who understand this weaving. The diamond or diagonal twill is undoubtedly copied by them from the Moki (Hopi), but the double or reversible weaving I believe to be of their own (Navaho) invention, as I know of no other tribe that does such weaving."

Thus we see that it was not until about the year 1893 that the oldest trader in the Navaho land saw a two-faced blanket. (Matthews 1900: 639-640.)

My own investigations carry this weave back to about the year 1885, on evidence that seems entirely trustworthy. Mr. B. I. Staples has a very large two-faced rug (measuring 12 feet by 18 feet 2 inches) that he obtained from Mr. C. N. Cotton of Gallup, New Mexico. He was sure it dated back to about 1885. I asked Mr. Cotton for confirmation of the statement and he recalled the rug clearly, saying he was sure of the approximate date of its weaving as it was made about the time the Atlantic and Pacific Railroad (now the Atchison, Topeka and Santa Fe) reached Gallup. That was in 1882. This rug is shown in plate 90 at Ganado, Arizona, where it was made.

Mr. Staples has a fragment of another rug of similar size and style, very probably made by the same weaver, which through Navaho informants he had traced back to the early eighties.

I learned nothing in reading all available printed accounts of Navaho weaving, in talking with experts and in examining the catalogues and notes of museum collections of Navaho blankets, to arouse the slightest suspicion that the two-faced weave is older than the approximate date in the early eighties in which Mr. Staples and Mr. Cotton concur. All evidence procurable reveals this weave as a late development of very limited distribution.

The origin or inspiration of the weave is apparently unknown. One item of interest occurs in my notes, however: I learned at Field Museum in Chicago that the late Charles Owens of that institution was told by an old Navaho woman that she devised the two-faced weave from seeing a commercial fabric of that type at a trader's home. Some such explanation is at least plausible, particularly in view of the apparent complete absence of the technic in aboriginal American weaving. The machine-made, figured "Pendleton" blanket (pls. 11, 16, 80, 123) so common in modern Navaho dress, is a counterpart of the two-faced type and I strongly suspect it of being the father of the Navaho product.[16]

DOUBLE CLOTH

O'Neale and Kroeber (52) define double cloth in prehistoric Peruvian weaving as "a reversible fabric requiring two sets of warps arranged one above the other, each with its own weft. Commonly, the sets are of different colors. To make the pattern, certain reverse-side warps are raised to replace surface side warps which are lowered. Colors are exchanged and ties are formed between otherwise separate portions of the fabric. Since each set of warps, no matter what its position, is crossed only by its own weft of same color, strongly contrasted design areas are produced."

The authors quoted figure examples in their plates 24b and 44, showing, however, only one face of the fabric in each instance. Seemingly the reverse shows the same pattern and colors as the face, with an alternation of color arrangement to produce identical figures of different hue on front and back.

---

[16] The anonymous author of the Rudo Ensayo said (95) of the Pima, about 1762: "They also imitate ticking and any other thing they see, provided they are allowed to undo the warp of the model." A Hopi or Navaho weaver may have shown equal enterprise in the matter of the two-faced weave and of double cloth, next described herein.

The literature of Navaho weaving records nothing of this character and I should never have suspected the existence of a double-cloth weave in the Navaho weaver's technical equipment had a specimen not been laid before my eyes by no less an authority than Mr. H. Schweizer, head of the Indian Department of Fred Harvey at Albuquerque, New Mexico. Without knowing its history Mr. Schweizer considered the piece, a single saddle blanket measuring 32 inches in width by 28 in length, as of Navaho origin upon the evidence of its appearance and structure; it is reproduced in plate 33*d* through Mr. Schweizer's courtesy. With the reservation that it might conceivably be Pueblo, Hopi in particular, I agree with him; the specimen is almost certainly a product of the native Southwestern loom. It is woven in five colors: blue, orange, red, two shades of green, and yellow. With the exception of one of the greens and the yellow, which are of machine spun, probably Germantown yarn, the wool is native. The blue is certainly indigo, but it would be unwise to assert positively that the colors are of native dye.

The weave of this unique little blanket is a fine diagonal twill throughout, the pattern a broad band of red at top and bottom enclosing a checkerboard of squares in constantly alternating colors, each about two inches square. On the opposite side (there being no way of distinguishing face from back) the pattern is identical except that color alternation gives a different hue to each two squares lying back to back. The great peculiarity of the piece lies in the fact that any square figure on one side can be pulled apart from its opposing square, proving beyond question that the specimen is a true double cloth, bonded at every intersection of squares, both horizontal and vertical, by interweaving. Except that warp color does not figure in the pattern, the description of double cloth given by O'Neale and Kroeber, as quoted above, is generally applicable. The weaver must have used two sets of warp, weaving on them independently for the area of one square and interlocking them at every point of intersection, as Crawford (1916: 135) says the Peruvians did. He mentions too (140) that a few rare Navaho blankets have this weave, and that it is believed to have been known to the prehistoric Pueblos and the Choctaw. This I doubt.

It would be unwise even to offer a conjecture as to the heddle rig used in this weave. Mr. Schweizer had never seen a similar piece, nor to my knowledge have I. Unless a weaver could be found today capable of re-creating the weave, perhaps by studying this specimen, the technic may never be known. The existence of a weave almost identical in prehistoric

Peru is perhaps significant, but only a hardy imagination would dare consider it the technical progenitor of this isolated specimen from the Southwest, woven almost certainly within the memory of living men, as attested by the use of machine-spun and apparently Germantown yarn.

ANALOGIES OF PERUVIAN AND SOUTHWESTERN WEAVING

The previous topic suggests that a glance at other analogies between Peruvian and Southwestern weaving might fitttingly conclude this chapter. There are much stronger links than that possibly existent in the double cloth weave just mentioned. The poncho, or blanket with a slit in the center for slipping it over the head to form a sort of overcoat, is a Peruvian garment [17] found among the prehistoric Pueblos (Guernsey: 102) and the Navaho, occurring also in Mexico, and probably throughout the intervening area of Central America as well, at least from early historic times.

A more specialized garment of the same type is the shirt, a small poncho with its sides sewn together, leaving a gap for the arms at either shoulder. O'Neale and Kroeber figure specimens in their figure 10 and plates 8 and 33. This type of shirt was common to both Pueblo and Navaho in early modern times. The Ethnologic Dictionary has illustrations and a description and a further reference (458) stating that this style was copied by the Navaho from the Pueblos. James (fig. 140) illustrates a Navaho shirt of this type reproduced in pl. 33b. Sleeves were added to the garment, and the whole idea is precisely that of the Peruvian type, as plate 33 shows.

The belt affords another similarity between Peru and the Southwest. O'Neale and Kroeber (pl. 2) show a specimen of warp-float weave that might have been woven by either Navaho or Pueblo on their belt looms, which as we have seen are a direct and tangible link with Middle America. The Arizona State Museum at Tucson has a belt of identical type from a prehistoric Pueblo horizon, so in respect of this one type the chain of evidence is fairly complete. The braided belt of the Hopi (pl. 2c) and the Basketmakers (pl. 3) is quite different, however.

---

[17] But not prehistoric in Peru, says Means (1932: 71), who credits Montell with having shown "clearly that the poncho makes its first appearance in Peru about 1629." Mena agrees, for Mexico, saying (373) the native garment of pre-Cortesian days in the Aztec empire was a simple shoulder blanket (like that of the prehistoric Pueblos), the poncho being a post-Conquest hybrid. Yet we have the shirt in prehistoric Peru (pl. 33a) and a "poncho-like garment" in the prehistoric Southwest, while O'Neale and Kroeber call the subject of their plate 13 a poncho of Nazca times, hence prehistoric. On Peruvian dress see Montell, an exhaustive study of the subject.

It would be unwise in the present state of knowledge to insist too strongly on these analogies between Peru and the Southwest. The evidence is meager, the direct connection not established, nor as yet even tangibly envisioned. Yet the fact remains that Southwestern weaving has strong and obvious analogies with that of Peru and Middle America, and it may be anticipated with confidence that further archeological research will bridge the gaps and banish some at least of the doubts now existing. The tentative conclusion reached in Chapter 2 may be reiterated here in somewhat different form: that true loom weaving had its principal if not its sole origin in Middle America or Peru, with the Pueblo Southwest marking the northern (or perhaps more conservatively, the northwestern) limit of its distribution.

OUTLINE SUMMARY OF NAVAHO WEAVES
A. Plain
 Tufting
 Pulled Warp
 Warp Floating
B. Twilled
 Diagonal Twill
 Reversed or Herringbone Twill
 Diamond Twills
C. Two-Faced
D. Double Cloth (?)

PLATE 34

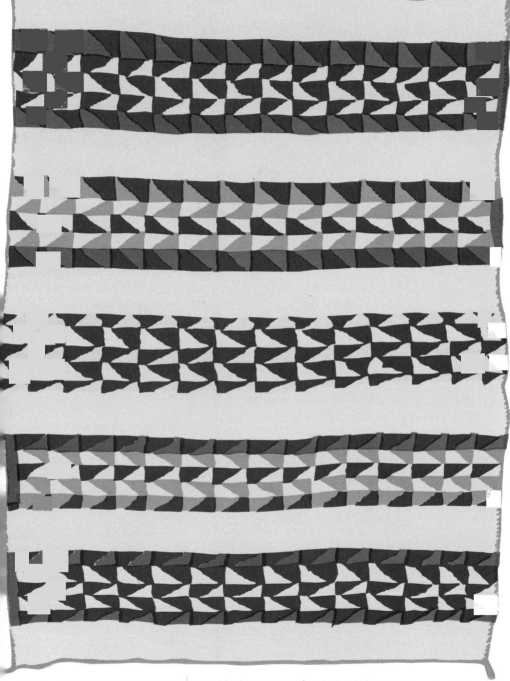

Native dyeing. The orange color probably is an example of the boiled canaigre root formula given in the following chapter, the yellow a rabbit brush dye, the black made after the formula given for that color. Of the red I am less confident; it may be native, or partly native, but may on the contrary be a faded aniline. Unfortunately only chemical analysis can give positive evidence in such matters. All colors but the black are pale and somewhat uneven in tone, a criterion of native dyes.

The blanket has a history back to about 1890 and probably is a few years older. Mrs. Walter Selden Ray coll., Southwest Museum cat. 171L5. Size 49 x 70 ins. Colorist: Mr. Clifford Park Baldwin.

PLATE 35

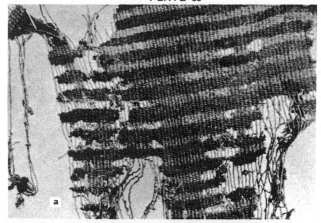

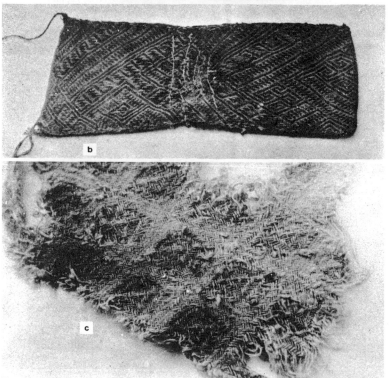

Prehistoric Pueblo textile fragments. **a,** striped natural buff and brown, is of Rocky Mountain goat and bison wool, as determined by Dr. W. H. Burt; P. G. Gates coll. Southwest Museum (see Hough 1914), cat. number lost, but apparently from the Tularosa or upper Gila region of Arizona or New Mexico. It may not be prehistoric Pueblo.

b, Cotton bag in black (blue?) and white, found in a cave near Montezuma's Castle where it now lies. In size 6 x 12½ ins., it was woven flat and sewn after being folded end to end. Such small fabrics probably were woven in a hand frame like that shown in pl. 7.

c is a diamond twill done by hand, not on the loom, found in a cave near Montezuma's Castle National Monument, Arizona, where it is now on display. Colors white, red, blue-black.

PLATE 36

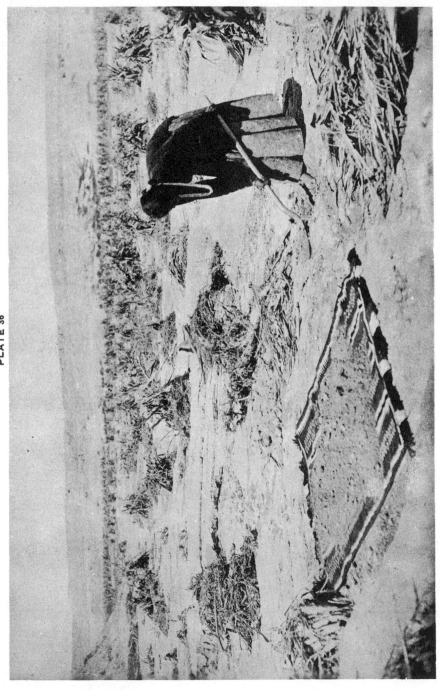

Cleaning a blanket by burial in wet sand for several days. A. C. Vroman photograph, P. G. Gates coll. Southwest Museum.

CHAPTER V

NATIVE DYES: DEVELOPMENT

NORDINATE love of color is popularly considered an outstanding trait of primitive people the world over. This belief, like a number of others similar, undergoes some modification on being examined closely. It is quite true that the American Indian, like the native of Africa or Polynesia, instinctively prized color for its own sake, however useless or outlandish the object embodying it. The error lies in confining this attribute to the under-civilized portion of earth's family, when in fact it is universal as a human trait. A man dying of thirst is quite certain to behave extravagantly when drink is obtained, whether he be savage or civilized, the previous scarcity of water making its present possession a major blessing. Similarly, primitive peoples revel in the possession of colored objects because they are color-starved. They see brilliant hues all about them in nature: the plumage of birds, the foliage and flowers of plants, the infinitude of chromatic range in the mineral kindgom; even the brilliant blue of the sky and the occasional wonder of the rainbow. Color surrounds them in prodigal abundance, yet how difficult to capture a bit of it for a permanent possession, how much more difficult still to make of it an adornment for their own drab persons or to embody it in some utilitarian object of their daily lives! Every such opportunity is seized upon eagerly, and the gewgaws brought by the civilized trader become prized possessions. For all that, the Indian woman with her beaded moccasins and painted deerskin dress is far less colorfully garbed than her white sister in conventional evening costume of tinted slippers, brilliant gown, and gaudy embroidered shawl. The pathetic wisps of red flannel with which the Indian warrior embellishes his accouterment are no more flamboyantly useless than the showy ribbons that civilized man wears about his neck.

Color apparently is a human need, without regard to social status or culture stage. Incalculable are the hours spent in times long past, in crude, unguided experimentation to capture and control this fugitive element in nature. And it is trite to say, although too often forgotten, that the colors we enjoy in such abundance today are the fruit of those early efforts (so strikingly exemplified, in our own time, in the native dyeing of the Navaho) to bring a natural phenomenon under artificial control. The truth of this statement becomes apparent when it is realized that the only truly artificial colors yet produced—aniline dyes—are less than a century old. Man learned to transfer and fix color some thousands of years back; but only in recent decades has he been able to create it.

The technic of dyeing with natural substances that is so well exemplified in the Navaho blanket represents an achievement which would have been a notable contribution to the progress of civilization had it come in the proper time and place. Astonishingly belated in time and somewhat isolated in environment, it appears today as an archaism of more interest than importance. Yet it is no less a triumph of human ingenuity and patience than those similar and much earlier experiments in the Old World that laid the foundation of our modern dye industries.

DID THE NAVAHO DEVELOP THEIR OWN DYEING?

It was shown in previous chapters that the Navaho deserves little if any credit for the development of his loom, although the last preceding chapter sets forth the fact that certain weaves practised upon it are apparently his own achievement. To what extent he pioneered in the development of the colors employed in his blankets is not easily determined. We have on the one hand the fact that the prehistoric Pueblos were fairly adept at using color in both paint and dye form, hence may have developed, wholly or partially, processes that the Navaho simply appropriated to his own use, as he appropriated the loom. As against that hypothesis is the fact that the Navaho was beyond question a pioneer in the use of wool in the Southwest, having learned to use it before it had made great strides among the Pueblos (Chapters 7 and 8); and wool, according to competent authorities on the chemistry of dyeing, has a wholly different reaction to dyes and mordants than has cotton, the principal textile fabric of the prehistoric Pueblos.[1] A successful cotton dye would serve poorly, if at all, for dyeing wool. Wool is an animal fiber, cotton a vegetable, and the two are quite different in composition. This fact is all-important in

---

[1] "There must always be some marked physical or chemical affinity existing between fibre and colouring matter, and this depends upon the physical and chemical properties of both. It is well known that the typical fibres, wool, silk and cotton, behave very differently towards the solution of any given colouring matter, and that the method of dyeing employed varies with each fibre." Article on Dyeing in Encyclopædia Britannica, 13th Edition, Volumes 7-8, p. 745.

that dyeing can be successtul only when it produces a fusion of components in material and colorant; in this fusion the mordant or "fixer" plays an important part.[2] Thus dyeing is not merely a physical impregnation or saturation of fiber with colorant; it is a chemical process. Impregnation alone will give color to the fiber, to be sure, but that color will be fugitive, not mixed. The laws of dyeing are immutable, and it does not follow that a vegetable paint—such, for example as the Pueblo peoples used successfully on wood and in basketry [3]—can be used as a textile dye. The Navaho themselves afford an illustration: they have green, black, and blue paints, quite different in composition from the wool dyes of equivalent colors.

The prehistoric Pueblos were dyers of cotton, as the Basketmakers before them were dyers of apocynum and yucca, so it must at least be said that the Navaho had before them a tradition of dyeing; and in the practices of the early Hopi, with whom they were in constant contact, they doubtless had actual examples as well. As was previously said, however, it is by no means certain that the technic and ingredients employed were applicable to the only textile material the Navaho are known definitely to have used—the wool of the domestic European sheep.[4] A brief summary of our scant knowledge of the attainments of the prehistoric peoples of the Southwest will place the reader in a position to judge for himself of the extent to which Navaho wool dyeing may be a heritage from the past.

BASKETMAKER DYEING

The Basketmakers (with whom, in our present state of knowledge,

[2] Means (1931: 467) says Valette in 1913 found silicates of chalk and aluminum, and oxide of iron, used as mordants in prehistoric Peruvian textiles, and cochineal and indigo as dyes. Both of the latter are native to America.

Alunogen, used by the Navaho as a mordant, is aluminum sulphate.

[3] The finest examples known to me of wood painting (and wood-working) recovered from the prehistoric Pueblo culture are the sunflowers and bird found by Kidder and Guernsey in Sunflower Cave, in northeastern Arizona. They are painted yellow, brown, pink, blue, and white—chemistry of coloring matter not specified. See Kidder and Guernsey: 94 and 145, and plates 33, 60, and 61, the latter in color.

On modern Pueblo paints and colorants, probably developed in the main by the prehistoric Pueblos, see Hough, 1902 and 1918.

[4] I find no evidence to support statements that the Navaho were loom weavers before the introduction of sheep by the Spanish. Those marvelous weavers, the Spider Man and Spider Woman of Navaho legend, are too poetic a concept to be taken as evidence upon a concrete, material point (See Ethnologic Dictionary: 222). Further, the Navaho creation legends embody references to Spanish settlers in the Rio Grande Valley, proving that some portions of the myth were brought into it after European settlements had begun: Navaho mythology is not entirely prehistoric.

See Matthews, 1893, for the creation legends, and Chapter 8 herein.

Southwestern culture begins) wove with great skill in apocynum and yucca, making baskets, sandals, and bags, for the greater part, that were decorated with designs in color (fig. 4, pl. 107). Goddard (46) says of the baskets that "they were decorated by the use of sewing material dyed black and red or brown." Nusbaum (106) found these same three colors in yucca and apocynum in Cave du Pont, Utah; and in the sandals, made usually of finely shredded yucca fiber, and the bags of apocynum, I have often noted them.[5] The natural yellow of yucca and brown of apocynum are consciously used for their color value in the design, as the Navaho use the natural browns, white, and blacks of their native wool, but the dyed colors thus far known seem limited to the three named above. I am not aware that the chemical composition of these colors has ever been determined.[6] Their quality is excellent, at any rate, for the black and the red in particular have in some instances survived the vicissitudes of some fifteen centuries underground with no visible diminution of their clarity. The brown, on the other hand, often appears to have turned drab and dingy, a fact that leads one to conjecture that the black and the red are of mineral origin, the brown vegetal.[7] Burial in absolutely dry ground (as in a cave, where the perfect specimens are almost invariably found) would have little effect on mineral colors, whereas vegetal colors tend to darken with age and close confinement.[8]

Hough (1914: 83) says of textile fragments from the upper Gila

---

[5] Notably brilliant in color and well preserved are the sandals in the Latter Day Saints Museum and the Museum of the University of Utah at Salt Lake City. Peabody Museum of Harvard, the American Museum of Natural History, and the Museum of the American Indian, Heye Foundation, have excellent collections, of broader scope, from the Basketmakers and the prehistoric Pueblos as well.

[6] Chemical analysis of colored fabrics is more of a problem than would be supposed. I submitted some wisps of wool to a textile chemist for an analysis of their coloring matter, and was told that unless several square inches of fabric could be supplied, no accurate analysis could be made; each wisp held so little of the colorant that after a single test nothing remained for further testing. A thorough analysis would involve the virtual sacrifice of a specimen.

[7] Black is not usually associated with mineral colorants, although a black mud was not uncommon in Southern California as a basketry dye. Hough (1902: 471) gives the Hopi and Navaho a black paint, consisting "of clay rich in oxides of manganese and iron with some organic matter. Dr. Matthews understood that the substance was found in the ground in this condition." The Vocabulary of the Navaho Language (134) mentions a "black ocher" used as a colorant—perhaps this same substance.

[8] Painted atlatl (dart-thrower) dart shafts found in Gypsum Cave, Nevada, by Mr. M. R. Harrington of the Southwest Museum, at depths far below the Basketmaker horizon, give even more striking evidence of the durability of mineral colors. Their deep red (hematite) and bright green (probably carbonate of copper) have come undimmed through perhaps thousands of years. See Harrington, frontispiece, for illustrations in color.

region in Arizona and New Mexico, as analyzed by Wirt Tassin of the U. S. National Museum:

> The materials are vegetal fiber in the main, with one or two specimens containing buffalo and mountain goat hair [see pl. 35*a*]. The colors were applied by the crude method of rubbing in ochers and earths practiced by many of the present Indian tribes; by dipping the yarn or cloth in a vegetal colored solution, technically known as a vat color; in some cases the fiber shows a mordanted color, the fixing substance not known, except in some specimens mordanted with iron tannate by burial in mud, an art applied to basket materials among many tribes. The colors represented are reds, browns, blue, and purple. . . The blue shades vary from dark to light, one specimen (Cat. No. 246045, U. S. National Museum, Bear Creek) tested reacting for indigo, probably of the *Indigofera anil* common in Mexico. The purple occurring on a loin cord bunch from a mummy in the Tularosa Cave resembles a color produced by rubbing the cords with the juice of prickly-pear fruit.

Prehistoric Pueblo Dyeing

The prehistoric Pueblos seem to have done most of their dyeing in cotton, a plant the Basketmakers did not possess. Strangely enough, we have fewer good examples of their textiles than of those of the earlier people. The most celebrated of them all is a cotton kilt from Grand Gulch, Utah, of which a part is in the American Museum of Natural History and the remainder of the piece as recovered in the Museum of the American Indian, Heye Foundation. The American Museum's portion is figured by Goddard (48), and this author says its colors are of "black, red and yellow dye." In addition to these hues, I have noted a drab brown, a blue, and an orange shade in prehistoric Pueblo cotton textile fragments. The well-known Mesa Verde specimen, figured in Nordenskiöld (pl. L) shows as natural white and dyed brown in color. The specimen from Montezuma's Castle, shown in plate 35*c*, is red, white, and blue-black in color; that in plate 35*b* is black (or blue-black) and white.

McGregor (1931: 3) says of prehistoric Pueblo dyes:

> Dyes or pigments used in coloring yarn or fabrics may be divided into two general classes: organic and inorganic. In prehistoric cotton fabrics the inorganic dyes are by far the

most common, and consist largely of three colors, red, produced from hematite or some other iron oxide; yellow, from a
yellow ochre; and blue or green, produced from copper sulphate. These inorganic dyes may be readily determined by a
superficial examination with a medium-powered microscope,
for the dye matetrial does not penetrate the fiber but clings to
it in the form of grains. Organic dyes seem to consist of black,
dark brown, and a light blue. These dyes are relatively permanent and cannot be washed out, as can the inorganic types.

I know of no instance of dyeing wool in prehistoric times in the Southwest—but there was little wool to be had in those times.[9] In fact, while
the dyeing of vegetal fibers, mainly for use in basketry, was widespread
in aboriginal North America, the dyeing of wool (north of Mexico) seems
to have been limited to the Northwest Coast until the introduction of
European sheep stimulated the Pueblos, and soon the Navaho, into activity. Hence it seems no more than their due to conclude that the Navaho
were pioneers, in their own time and place, in this highly specialized
phase of the great textile craft.[10] The possibility remains that the early
modern Pueblos, who were the first to receive sheep from the Spanish,
shared in the development of wool dyeing. But the Navaho so quickly
established a superiority in blanket making that I think the major credit
is rightly theirs, with due recognition of the fact that cotton dyeing had
already been proved practical. Modern Pueblo weaving in wool never
displayed the technical excellence, the range of color, or the freedom of
design found in Navaho work. The craft, during the historic period, has

---

[9] Hairs were used (domestic dog, human, wild animal), but of true animal
wool only that of wild sheep and goats was known, and it of course was scarce.

[10] At this point the hypothesis advanced by James, that the Navaho probably
came from the Northwest Coast and brought with them the technic of weaving
and inferentially of dyeing, presents itself. It is based largely on the facts that
the Navaho name for themselves, Dineh (The People) is very similar to the name
Dene, an Athapascan people of British Columbia, the Navaho likewise being classed
linguistically as Athapascans; and that the Navaho, like the Dene and others of
their area, are weavers.

As against the hypothesis there are the facts that the Athapascans are a
large family, not necessarily centering in the Dene region, and that the Navaho
might have come into the Southwest from any direction (my conclusion, set forth
in Chapter 9, is that they came from the east or northeast); that the Navaho
weaving apparatus bears little resemblance to anything in use on the Northwest
Coast, while it is identical with that of the prehistoric Pueblos, as demonstrated in
previous chapters; that there is no good evidence that they ever used either of the
wools of the Northwest Coast—domestic dog or wild goat; that Navaho design,
with its solid geometric character, is distinctly of the Southwest and foreign to
the grotesque naturalism of Northwest Coast art; finally, that the Apache, of
whom the Navaho are usually considered a late offshoot, have no weaving.

declined as steadily among the Pueblos as it has increased among the Navaho, until today it stands as a specialty, almost a monopoly, of the latter.

THE SPANISH INFLUENCE

No less difficult to appraise than the extent of the prehistoric ingredient in the technology of Navaho dyeing is the Spanish influence thereon. Some influence there must have been, even beyond that of which we have definite knowledge. The Spaniard brought in the sheep, sole provender of the Navaho loom from its earliest appearance in history. He brought indigo, most important of all the pre-aniline colorants, and that at a relatively early time—eighteenth century or before.[11] Those are facts, incontrovertible; and from them we are amply authorized to draw certain conclusions scarcely to be gainsaid. Wool undergoes several processes from sheep's back to loom, as we saw in Chapter 3. Where would the Pueblo craftsmen, skilled cotton weavers though they were, learn these unfamiliar operations of shearing (or cutting without shears) and carding, except from the Spaniards? Where would they learn the only successful formula for dyeing wool with indigo within the scope of their abilities (the urine recipe), except from the alien who gave them that colorant? [12] Hence, by a deduction eminently plausible, we augment the known Spanish influence; for to assume that the Indian took the sheep without taking at least the elemental methods of handling it, that he accepted lump indigo from Mexico without a word of query as to its use, would be unwarrantably naive.

Navaho mordants (except urine with indigo) almost certainly are independent of Spanish influence. Alum, it is true, was one of the standard mordants of the Old World, back to the Greeks or earlier; Pliny the Naturalist describes its use (35th Book, 15th Chapter) in dyeing and in medicine, says the Encyclopaedia Britannica (article Alum). Alunogen or native alum does not precisely roll about underfoot in the Southwest; its occurrence is widespread, but always in limited quantities and generally in highly inconspicuous spots. Its peculiar virtues nevertheless seem to have been discovered by the native unaided, for Benavides wrote in 1630 of the mountains of the "province of Navajo" (44):

---

[11] One of the Massacre Cave fragments (pl. 60) has the characteristic deep blue color of indigo. They date from 1805. The undated but very old specimen shown in pl. 63a has a strip of rich blue; so has one of the White House burial fragments shown in pl. 62a.

[12] The case for prehistoric indigo is not proved, although a vegetal blue for use on cotton apparently existed. In modern times both blue beans and blue corn have yielded the color—and both beans and corn are prehistoric.

And as all these town-dwelling and Christian nations are inclined to dyeing, to have wherewith to dye (*pintar,* lit. paint) their clothing they need alum, which exists only in those ranges.

If written a century later, we might dismiss this passage on the probability of the Spanish having taught the Pueblos to use alum in dyeing. But only thirty-two years have passed since the founding of New Mexico in 1598: too little time for a few hundreds of Spaniards (few if any of them experienced dyers, all too busy in their new home to occupy themselves thus) to have fixed a complex alien craft in the tribal economy of a score of scattered Pueblo villages. Nor can we justifiably flout the accuracy of this particular passage in Benavides. It is of no consequence to him or his missionary work—a mere passing detail noted with the off-hand simplicity of perfect truth.

Wood ashes, the companion mordant to alunogen in Navaho technology, are quite certainly native to America in this use. They figure widely in tanning, and both Basketmakers and Pueblos used dressed animal skins.[13] Their only recorded use in Navaho dyeing, in fact, is in a recipe designed primarily for tanning hides and adapted to the new purpose with only indifferent success, as will be seen.

The other dyeing practices of the Navaho, as recorded in detail in the following chapter, have every appearance of being native. Some doubt may arise in the reader's mind as he reads the formula for black, of the purely casual discovery of its complicated interaction of mineral and organic ingredients; but we have only suspicion to guide us here. There can be little doubt that the plants used in Navaho dyeing were found adaptable to such use by experimentation on the spot, and presumably (in many instances certainly) by the Indian uninfluenced. Our best conclusion on this topic of Spanish influence would be to the effect that Spanish wool, Spanish indigo, Spanish weaving in general, gave a new impetus and new trade secrets to a craft already familiar to the native Pueblos; and that the Navaho, coming along with minds open and inventive, took over all they could from the joint sponsors of the weaver's craft and in course of time made some contribution of their own. But where to draw the lines between these three unwitting partners in the enterprise is far beyond our present knowledge. I have a suspicion that the Spanish craftsmen were not by any means silent partners,[14] a suspicion based in part on the fact that

---

[13] This is merely evidence, not proof of the use of ashes in prehistoric time.
[14] James had reached this conclusion too, to judge by his statement (29) that

Don Eologio Gallegos, octogenarian Spanish-American weaver of Abiquiu, New Mexico, gave me last summer (1932) his entire mental stock of dye formulas. His yellow from rabbit brush and reddish-brown from mountain mahogany (*palo duro*) were almost identically the Navaho recipes given in the following chapter; his use of indigo for blue and green was the same; and he told of a brown wool dye made of yellow ocher, the same substance the Navaho use in making their black. Here again is influence, either of the Spaniard upon the Indian or vice versa; but the reader's guess is as good as mine.

COLOR RANGE OF NATIVE DYES

Various writers on Navaho weaving have recorded bits of information on processes of dyeing: first Washington Matthews in the early eighties of the past century, then George H. Pepper soon after 1900, and the Franciscan Fathers at St. Michaels, Arizona, whose excellent Navaho Ethnologic Dictionary was published in 1910. The difficulties of the task have increased steadily, for already in Matthews' time commercial yarns and aniline dyes were invading the field, and the native art was in its decline. Today few weavers indeed know the old processes, although a revival is in progress, which is discussed in Chapter 15.

The native dyes recorded for the Navaho with sufficient evidence to justify their acceptance [15] are of the following colors: black, four kinds of red, three kinds of yellow (one of which is more of an orange or red-yellow), two kinds of green, and indigo blue. The latter is not strictly native, for the Navaho produced no indigo. The natural wool colors employed undyed were brown, black, white, and gray. Thus the Navaho technology of dyeing embraced a broad range, including the three colors regarded by artists as primary: red, yellow, and blue. By combination any hue was theoretically attainable. Practically, such combination had its handicaps, for the dyes employed were of widely different chemical character requiring, as the user well knew, different mordants; and it is likely that certain combinations were denied a successful issue by the laws of chemistry. Purple, for example, is never encountered, to my knowledge,

"when the Navahos began to dye wool for themselves they were dependent upon the less [sic.] experienced Mexicans and Pueblo Indians for their knowledge of dyes and mordants."

[15] James (37) speaks of a "pale violet doubtless obtained from berry juice;" and Hollister (108) refers to a yellow color as "doubtless a decoction of peach leaves and bark." I have heard of piñon nut brown and lichen yellow or green. But all of these remain undescribed and unverified by the testimony of other persons. Incidentally, one learns to beware the word "doubtless," for in the two quotations above it masks an out-and-out conjecture.

in native colors; yet when aniline dyes came into use purple had such a vogue that traders in self-defense stopped selling it.[16] It has been said that certain colors were traditionally *tabu,* but to my mind the riotous use of aniline, which runs the entire chromatic range in Navaho blankets, tends to discredit the statement.

There is general agreement among contemporary observers as to the colors found in Navaho blankets of native dye, as the following citations show:

"The colors are red, blue, black and yellow; black and red being the most common." (Letterman: 291.)

Matthews (1884: 376) mentions "yellow, reddish, and black;" indigo blue, and "the three natural wool colors of white, rusty black, and gray."

"Black, red, russet, blue and yellow" are mentioned by C. E. Van-dever, government agent for the Navaho in 1890 (R. C. I. A. 1890: 161).

"The leading colors used are red, brilliant orange yellow, a blue: and by combination a green, and finally black, white and gray." (Shufeldt: 392.)

According to the Vocabulary of the Navaho Language (81) there are words in the Navaho language for red, black, yellow, navy blue or indigo, green, with the variant hues of red-brown, brown-yellow (orange?) and Indian-red. Some description of the composition and method of use of the dyes producing these colors is available in the works of various writers, which I shall quote freely under the heading of each color. First, however, the Ethnologic Dictionary's statement covering the general process and apparatus of dyeing is pertinent (229):

> For making native dyes the Navaho dyer needs the vegetable and mineral ingredients required for the specific dyes; a pot in which to make the decoction of barks, flowers, twigs or roots, for which their own native pots are preferred, probably because the acid of the mordants will not act chemically upon earthen vessels as it will upon tin or iron; a skillet, or frying pan, to prepare certain of the ingredients, and a few thin, slender sticks to immerse the wool with, or take it out of the dye, and to spread it out to dry.
>
> Each dye consists of at least two ingredients, a coloring matter and a mordant, usually some acid substance to fix the color fast.

---

[16] I am told by Mrs. H. S. Colton, herself a painter, that purple is difficult to achieve by color mixing, even with the best of pigments.

PLATE 37

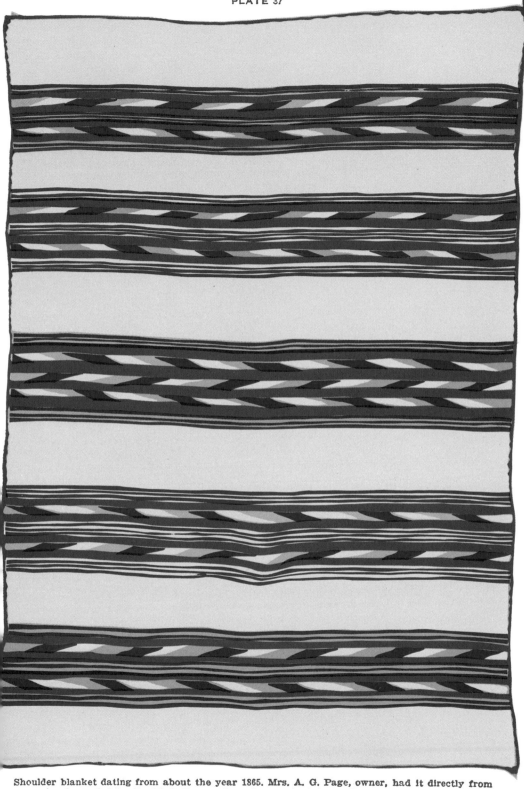

Shoulder blanket dating from about the year 1865. Mrs. A. G. Page, owner, had it directly from an uncle who traded for it with Indians, tribe unknown, in Arizona. It may be Hopi, but is much like the Navaho native shoulder blanket of pre-aniline times. The orange is almost certainly a native color, probably the black and the red as well; here at any rate is a red used on native wool and antedating by at least a decade the advent of trading-store dyes. Size 41 x 61 ins., cat. Southwest Museum 200L1. Colorist: Mr. Clifford Park Baldwin.

It may be added that dyeing was usually done after spinning, and that the wool of the old-stock Navaho sheep was sufficiently free from grease to take the dye without washing, although the later introduction of foreign strains, notably the Merino (see Chapter 13), made washing a prerequisite to successful dyeing.

PLATE 38

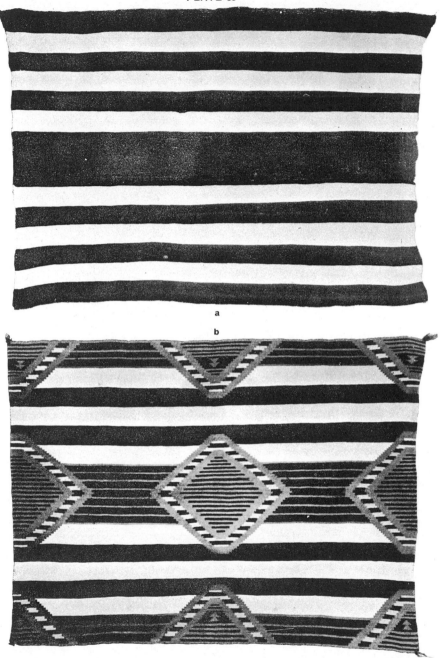

Typical chief blankets. **a** size 74 x 52 ins., colors black and white (compare with pl. 63).

b size 72 x 54, colors large stripes black and white, narrow stripes black and indigo blue, bars forming figures alternate indigo blue and native-dye yellow on bayeta red ground.

Both specimens in Mrs. Philip Stewart coll. Laboratory of Anthropology cat. **(a)** no. 11; **(b)** no. 1.

PLATE 39

The sources of native Navaho colorants, a flowering head of rabbit brush, **Bigelovia graveolens**, b leafy branch with catkins of alder, probably **Alnus tenuifolia**. c is sumac, **Rhus trilobata**, and d a sprig of mountain mahogany, **Cercocarpus parvifolius**.

The group e is five separate and whole plants of the ground lichen **Parmelia molliuscule**, called by the Navaho **ni'had'lad**. f shows the characteristic paired needles and small cone of piñon, **Pinus edulis**; g a flower stalk of the Western thistle, **Cardus occidentalis** Nutt. The Navaho are said to have used the spiky seed pod of this or a similar plant for wool carding, as teasels were often used by European weavers.

h figures two of the tuberous roots of the canaigre or wild rhubarb plant, **Rumex hymenosepalus**. i a sprig of juniper, **Juniperus monosperma**, with its scaly leaves and small bluish berries. Here we leave the plant kingdom for the mineral: J is a lump of ocher, k one of alunogen or native alum.

CHAPTER VI

NATIVE DYES: METHODS AND FORMULAS

 HIS chapter is based on investigations both in the library and in the field. It gives, under the heading of the various colors produced by native processes, both the data hitherto recorded and those I obtained at first hand in the summer of 1932. My principal informant was a Navaho woman of some fifty years, living on the Navaho reservation south of Farmington, New Mexico. She had not been to school, and apparently had not been sought out for questioning before. Her replies to my queries err on the side of understatement if at all, for she was a shy witness and talked only because her son Auran Bassett, an excellent interpreter, served as intermediary. I had been advised by Mr. O. J. Carson, Indian trader and good friend to the Navaho, to seek Mr. Bassett's mother as a woman experienced in weaving and trustworthy in statement. *N'dan des pah* is the name she told me hers,[1] and I give her testimony under that name, at appropriate points. No better evidence of its reliability could be found than its general agreement with published accounts;—for I was careful not to prompt or suggest replies. I had with me samples of the plants reported by other investigators as used in Navaho dyeing[2] which I exhibited for her verification at the close of the interview, so I am certain that every ingredient named is the very one she had in mind. This point has troubled every previous investigator, as will be seen. Plates 39 and 40 show both detailed and general views of these plants.

BLACK

For their finest blankets (pl. 38) the Navaho commonly used dyed wool because it yielded a deeper, more truly black color than the somewhat rusty natural hue of the undyed black wool. Matthews (1884:

---

[1] A conventional name, I suspect; Navahos have personal names but are not known by them. She was reluctant to pronounce a name, even to her own son— and he instead of telling me his mother's name, dutifully asked her to name herself.

[2] Identified at the Boyce Thompson Southwestern Arboretum, Superior, Arizona—a living library of native flora—whose courteous help I acknowledge with gratitude.

376) describes this dye and its preparation very fully, and later writers have generally accepted his account as adequate. It follows:

> The black dye mentioned above is made of the twigs and leaves of the aromatic sumac (*Rhus aromatica*); a native yellow ocher, and the gum of the piñon (*Pinus edulis*). The process of preparing it is as follows: They put into a pot of water some of the leaves of the sumac, and as many of the branchlets as can be crowded in without much breaking or crushing, and the water is allowed to boil for five or six hours until a strong decoction is made. While the water is boiling they attend to other parts of the process. The ocher is reduced to a fine powder between two stones and then slowly roasted over the fire in an earthen or metal vessel until it assumes a light-brown color; it is then taken from the fire and combined with about an equal quantity in size of piñon gum; again the mixture is put on the fire and constantly stirred. At first the gum melts and the whole mass assumes a mushy consistency; but as the roasting progresses it gradually becomes drier and darker until it is at last reduced to a fine black powder. This is removed from the fire, and when it has cooled somewhat it is thrown into the decoction of sumac, with which it instantly forms a rich, blue-black fluid. This dye is essentially an ink, the tannic acid of the sumac combining with the sesquioxide of iron in the roasted ocher, the whole enriched by the carbon of the calcined gum.

Here Matthews leaves off; but Pepper gives us the final details of the process (1903: 9): "The boiling continues for fully half an hour. The wool is then introduced, allowed to boil, and the dyeing is complete."

N'dan des pah: "Yellow ocher is powdered on a stone and cooked dry—half a large frying-pan—and stirred till it turns purple or dark red. Then add a large can (2½ size) of piñon gum and stir till all black and no more smoke.

"Boil branches (leaves, berries, and all) of sumac, folded up to go in the pot, all you can get in, while cooking ocher and gum. Take out branches, put ocher and gum in pot. Put in wool—black wool, white not good—and boil about a half hour. Takes about an hour in all."

Q.—"Any other uses?"
A.—"Yes, dye for basketry."
Q.—"Where is ocher found?"

A.—"Dug up around Pueblo Alto (Chaco Cañon)."

Pepper says this same black dye was used also on leather and buckskin (in notes on a collection of native Navaho dyestuffs in Peabody Museum, Cambridge. Catalogue number of collection 89875). He remarks elsewhere (1902: 36) that black was the only native color still in use when he first came in contact with the Navaho in 1896.

It will be noted that this black dye is an entirely different substance from the black paint attributed by Hough to both Navaho and Hopi, as quoted in footnote 7, Chapter 5.

RED

The authorities disagree somewhat on the subject of the red dyes of the Navaho, leaving one wondering if something has not escaped their attention in this particular. Matthews (1884: 377) leads off with:

> The reddish dye is made of the bark of *Alnus incana*
> var. *virescens* (Watson) and the bark of the root of *Cercocarpus parvifolius;*[3] the mordant fine juniper ashes. On
> buckskin this makes a brilliant tan-color; but applied to wool
> it produces a much paler tint.

Pepper (1903: 5-7) describes in great detail a process that is surely the one alluded to by Matthews as above, for the ingredients are the same. He concludes, however:

> The color resulting from this process is a dull red. It
> gives a very satisfactory color when applied to buckskin, but
> it cannot be used to dye wool. It has been tried but the resulting color is too light a red to be of use for blanket work.

Such was Pepper's experience; but there is no reason to doubt that Matthews' dyer did succeed in applying this same dye to wool. Living some twenty years before the time of Pepper's activities, she probably was more experienced in the selection and compounding of the ingredients than was Pepper's helper. A pale, thin red is sometimes seen in old Navaho blankets, as in plates 34 and 37.

A possible explanation of Pepper's failure lies in the description of this same dye given in the Ethnologic Dictionary (232) which includes a mordant not mentioned in Pepper's account:

> To make this dye the woman first burns some twigs of
> the juniper tree, *Juniperus occidentalis.* . . [4] The roots of . .

---

[3] [For full botanical descriptions of the various plants used in Navaho dyeing I recommend Wooton and Standley.]

[4] [Navaho words omitted as not essential to the description in the present connection. The reader especially interested will find them in the work cited.]

Cercocarpus parvifolius, a kind of mountain mahogany, are crushed and boiled. To this is added the juniper ashes and the powdered bark of the black alder, *Alnus incana* var. *virescens...* [4] together with a plant called *ni'hadlad,* a moss, which acts as a mordant.[5] After this mixture has boiled until it is thought to be right it is strained and the wool or yarn is soaked in it over night. The result is a fine red color.

The dull reddish dye is made of the powdered bark of the mountain mahogany, which makes a fine tan color on buckskin, but produces a rather pale shade of wool.

What are we to conclude? Three first-hand students of Navaho dyeing agree on a dye that is particularly adapted to buckskin. One, Pepper, says it is not adaptable to wool. The other two, Matthews and the Franciscans Fathers of St. Michaels, find that on wool it gives a pale red. The last-named of the three authorities adds a mordant of "moss" to the compound and records "a fine red color" as a result. Given the soundness and painstaking care that distinguish the field observations of these three students, it is incumbent on us to accept the buckskin dye as applicable to wool, although with a considerable loss of color value; and to recognize another shade of red resulting from the use of a mordant of lichen with the same basic ingredients.

Pepper in his collection of native dyes in Peabody Museum, Cambridge, includes a sample of reddish-brown wool (cat. 89875-3) with the note that it is dyed with the bark of alder: possibly akin to the "dull reddish dye" of the Ethnologic Dictionary, as quoted above. Elsewhere in these same notes he says that red was obtained from the rootbark of the aromatic sumac used in the black dye described previously, by boiling and using the liquor. No specimen of this red was found in the collection.

Thomas V. Keam, Indian trader of Keam's Cañon, Arizona, from 1882 to 1904, wrote to Washington Matthews of a third red which I suspect is primarily Hopi; both because Keam's Cañon is in Hopi territory and the Navaho did not commonly cultivate sunflowers, while the Pueblos did: "Their [Navaho] red was of a dull dark color and obtained by boiling the husk of sun flower seed; which was also the means of obtaining the

---

[5] [Ni'hadlad is a ground lichen, identified by Miss Joyce Hedrick and Dr. Melvin R. Gilmore of the University of Michigan as Parmelia molliuscule Ach. I have sought it in many localities but found it only near Coolidge, New Mexico, where Mrs. B. I. Staples pointed it out and had a Navaho girl identify it for me by the native name.

yellow from *Khil'soey* (rabbit brush). In preparing them they put alum in the water." (Letter dated April 16, 1904; copy in Southwest Museum Library.)

N'dan des pah: "No red until we got trader's dyes." She gave me the formula for the buckskin red above quoted, however, saying it was effective with "moccasins and baskets" but not with wool. Incidentally, I asked her if she herself made baskets, and she said yes: "Little baskets, with yucca (foundation) and split sumac branches; not like Ute baskets." She later made one for me, a two-rod-and-bundle basket like those of plate 4*a-i*. It has been questioned by some if the Navaho made baskets, hence this evidence. Three types, the Ute, the Paiute, and the Navaho, are shown in plate 4.

Don Eologio Gallegos had no formula for a native red in Spanish-American weaving, saying, "*Colorado colorado no había.*"

Reviewing the evidence as presented, one gets the impression that red was produced somewhat experimentally, and not always successfully, by different processes, in sharp contrast to the clear-cut, widespread formula and method for producing black. A study of old blankets leads to the same conclusion. One finds little but bayeta (machine-made) red yarn in pre-aniline blankets, and I am convinced that many reds which pass for natives are early anilines or mixed aniline and native, nicely toned by time.

INDIAN RED

The Vocabulary of the Navaho Language is our sole authority for this shade of red; even the Ethnologic Dictionary, published two years previously by the same authorities, does not mention it. The Vocabulary (112) defines the expression as a "mixture of red and a tinge of blue for dyeing wool." The category of red dye used is not specified; the blue would be of indigo—unless this is a modern color tone, produced with aniline dyes. I cannot identify this shade of red with anything in my experience, although deep aniline reds are common enough in modern rugs.

YELLOW

Three processes are of record for achieving a yellow color, each yielding a different shade. Yellow in Navaho dyeing ranges in color from a pale bright lemon through a light orange to a distinct red-orange, on the one hand; and on the other it leans distinctly toward the green—although the full deep blue-green of old Navaho blankets was produced by a different process, as will be seen.

Matthews (1884: 377) describes the most common yellow dye as follows:

> There are, the Indians tell me, three different processes for dyeing yellow; two of these I have witnessed. The first process is thus conducted: The flowering tops of *Bigelovia graveolens* are boiled for about six hours until a decoction of deep yellow color is produced. When the dyer thinks the decoction strong enough, she heats over the fire in a pan or earthen vessel some native alunogen (an impure native alum), until it is reduced to a somewhat pasty consistency; this she adds gradually to the decoction and then puts the wool in the dye to boil. From time to time a portion of the wool is taken out and inspected until (in about half an hour from the time it is first immersed) it is seen to have assumed the proper color. The work is then done. The tint produced is nearly that of lemon yellow.

Pepper's version is much the same (1903: 9-10):

> The native yellow dye, in common use when the traders entered the Navaho country, was made from the flowering tops of the Rabbit weed or bush (*Bigelovia graveolens*). This plant is a member of the aster family and grows on the open prairies. It has a slender stalk which is crowned by a mass of yellow blossoms. It grows in clumps, as a rule, and there are three or four varieties in the Southwest. The flower-clusters are gathered and placed in a large pot containing water. This is allowed to boil from four to six hours. During the boiling the squaw places native alum, alunogen, in a frying pan and heats it until it is reduced to a pasty consistency. When the boiling has extracted the juices from the weed, the alum, which is to act as a mordant, is added. The liquid is now ready for the reception of the wool.
>
> In dyeing the wool with the yellow decoction, it is placed in the pot of boiling liquid and allowed to boil for fifteen or twenty minutes, after which it is tested every few minutes until it has assumed the color desired. The tints obtained from this dye range from a canary yellow to an old gold, and even an olive green may be produced.

That the same process and ingredients should yield both a bright yellow and an "olive green" may seem strange. I was told, however, by Mr.

PLATE 40

Complementary to plate 39, this shows the various plants thereon identified as they appear in growth. The hat in each gives a scale of size. Some it will be seen are trees, others low shrubs.

a juniper; b alder; c sumac; d piñon; e rabbit brush; f canaigre; g mountain mahogany.

Alder is found along streams in the Transition Zone; the others are common to the Upper Sonoran.

PLATE 41

a, Single saddle blanket, size 28 x 32 ins., colors: end figures red, yellow, white; middle stripes red, blue, grey, white. Catalogue says: "all native dyes but one—red." Mrs. C. Matthews coll., U. S. National Museum cat. 281482; probably woven before 1890.

b, Home-made loom at Tierra Azul near Abiquiu, New Mexico, of Don Eologio Gallegos. Made of hand-hewn pine, it has stood nearly a century. Photographed in 1932. To those who suspect Navaho weaving of being a modification of the Spanish, a comparison of this loom with those shown in pls. 8 and 17 is suggested.

B. I. Staples of Coolidge, New Mexico, who has done much in his district to revive the use of old native dyes, that the explanation is simple enough: if the dyer is careful to include only the mature blossoms of the shrub, a clear yellow will result; but if immature flowers, leaves, or green bark are used, a green tint proportionate to the quantity of green portions of the plant used will appear.[6] In my own observation this green shade is not uncommon, and is easily distinguishable from the blue-green dye made of indigo by the strong tone of yellow pervading it. Often yellow and green are so evenly balanced that one hesitates to designate the color by either word alone.

N'dan des pah: "Take bunches of yellow flowers, put in cloth made like a sack. Boil and boil. Heat some alunogen in fire till warm and put it in. Water foams, then settles down and is yellow. Put in white wool and boil quite a while (after removing flowers). When wool real yellow it is done. That bucket [ten quart size] of flowers will dye half a sheep's fleece."

Q.—"Can flowers be used dry, any time of the year?"

A.—"Yes; in old days, gathered in season and hid in holes under rocks with dirt on top; sumac bark and leaves kept that way too."

Q—"Was this method used for green dye too?"

A.—"I don't know of it; I heard of green and tried to make it (with indigo) but could not."

The Ethnologic Dictionary (230-231) also describes this process in full agreement with the accounts quoted above. It refers to the plant as goldenrod, giving also, however, its botanical name *Bigelovia*. Thus this yellow dye, like black, is amply documented in every detail.

Orange-Yellow

Another dye rests on the authority of both Matthews and the Ethnologic Dictionary. Matthews' description follows as a continuation of the last quotation from him, above:

> In the second process they use the large fleshy root of a plant which, as I have never yet seen it in fruit or flower, I am unable to determine. The flesh root is crushed to a soft paste on the *metate,* and for a mordant, the alunogen is added while the grinding is going on. The cold paste is then rubbed between the hands into the wool. If the wool does

---

[6] Similarly, if the flowers are withered and dry when used, the tint will be more of a dull gold color than if made of fresh blooms. In short, the dye is an extract of color and its hue is that of the ingredient. This, generally speaking, is true of all vegetal dyes made of a single plant.

not seem to take the color readily a little water is dashed on
the mixture of wool and paste, and the whole is very slightly
warmed. The entire process does not occupy over an hour and
the result is a color much like that now known as "old gold."

The account of this process in the Ethnologic Dictionary (231) seems
to have been based on Matthews' description, as given above.

A third process for making yellow is given in the Ethnologic Dictionary in which Matthews' "large fleshy root" is identified as:

A plant, or rather a weed, belonging to the *Pogonaceae*
or buckwheat family, of the species Rumex, commonly called
dock or sorrel. Dr. W. Matthews calls it *Rumex hymenose-
palum* and Dr. Geo. H. Pepper says it is commonly known
as canaigre. It has a long, fleshy tap root, not unlike a slender
parsnip, throws out a dense bunch of almost lanceolate leaves,
from the midst of which rises a slender stem, sometimes two
or three, with a long spike of blossoms and seed. The plant is
a perennial and besides multiplies fast by seed. It is difficult to
eradicate, which can be done only by digging out the root.[7]

The dye in which this plant is used is described in the same quotation very briefly as a "decoction of the plant, with native alum or salt
rock," and the Dictionary continues in another paragraph on the same
page: "Dr. Pepper describes a third process of making yellow dye, in
which the bruised roots. . . are boiled and [native alum] added during
the boiling. The wool or yarn to be dyed is boiled in this solution."

Pepper's own description is available, as quoted below (1903: 4):

She (Pepper's Navaho woman informant) said that the
roots of a certain plant are gathered and crushed. They are
then placed in a pot and allowed to boil. This plant is called
Chad-inney[8] or *Jhild-oey*. While this is boiling, alunogen is
added. The wool is dyed by being boiled in the solution. My
informant said that she did not know of the practice of using

----

[7] [This plant is also known as wild rhubarb because of the resemblance of
the thick, juicy flower-stalk to the petiole of rhubarb. I have seen it in a half-
dozen States, from California to Colorado. Dr. Wm. T. Hornaday, in his book "Camp
Fires on Desert and Lava," pages 77-78, notes this interesting fact concerning its
roots: they "contain more tannin than anything this side of oak bark—but unfortunately cannot be grown in sufficient quantities to constitute an important
factor in the leather industry."

A factory for commercial exploitation of this plant was opened in Deming,
New Mexico, some years ago, but the venture failed.]

[8] [The Ethnologic Dictionary spells the word "chat'ini, or jat'ini;" a neat
commentary on the difficulty of reducing Indian speech to writing.]

b

a

Native dye blankets, double saddle size. a is of diagonal twill weave, size 28 x 46 ins., colors: narrow stripes red and indigo blue, 2 broad center panels gray, 2 broad end panels yellow, certainly native. b in plain weave is 35 x 49 ins. in size, colors red, indigo blue and native yellow-green stripes on gray. The reds probably are anilines, by their bright, hard colors.

Both in Mrs. C. Matthews coll., U. S. National Museum, cat. (a) 281477, (b) 281476. Both probably antedate 1890, as most of the Matthews collections were made during Dr. Matthews' tours of duty in the Navaho country: 1880-84 and 1890-94.

PLATE 43

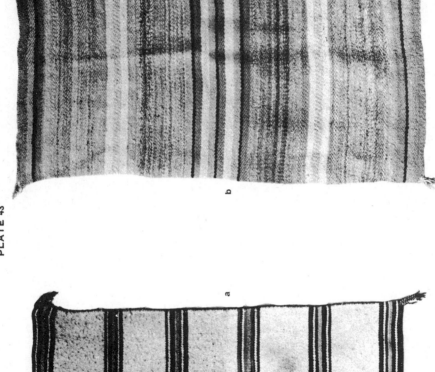

Native dye blankets. a size 30 x 42 ins., diagonal twill weave, colors narrow stripes of indigo blue, Germantown red, native yellow-green, on white panels. Washington Matthews coll., U. S. National Museum cat. 129957.

b in reversed twill weave is 35 x 53 ins., colors indigo blue, a maroon red which is almost certainly aniline, and native orange and green-gold. Mrs. C. Matthews coll., U. S. National Museum cat. 281474. Both pieces would date not far roots in the way mentioned by Dr. Matthews" (in cold paste form, presumably).

N'dan des pah: "To make that color [pointing to son's orange-brown suede coat], get about a shovelful of canaigre roots and pound fine with rocks. Put in a bucket of water to boil; no alum needed. Boil a long time, take out the roots, put in the wool and let it set a day."

Q.—"Can you make dye with these roots without boiling, using them cold?"

A.—"I never heard of it."

Is this the dye that yields the brilliant orange color seen in old blankets? Pepper does not specify its shade of color, although he does say (1903: 2-3):

> Orange colored figures are also seen. This color is doubt-less the one resulting from the dye mentioned by Dr. Matthews as being made from the roots of a native sorrel, *Rumex hymenosepalum,* but the writer was unable to verify this statement nor was it known by those interviewed in obtaining the notes that form the substance of this paper.

Again a regrettable confusion prevails, although it seems apparent that Rumex used in cold paste form with alum gives the deep, dull yellow described by Matthews as "old gold," while the same root, boiled either with or without alum, gives the brighter, redder tone of orange. The second formula seems to be the better known of the two, as its shade of color is by far the more common, in my observation. Plate 37 gives the color tone nicely.

This very confusion, noted in the case of both red and yellow dyes, is perhaps significant. Does it not indicate that native dyeing was in an unstandardized, experimental state until the very moment of its extinction by commercial aniline dyes—hence that the Navaho were, as has been said previously, pioneers in the development of native colors for use on wool? We know that European sheep came into the Southwest less than four centuries ago; that the two-faced blanket weave is of very recent origin and the diamond twill is found only in textiles of the last half-century; that Navaho design (see Chapter 14) has undergone a steady and rapid evolution; and now we have this strong suggestion of constant experimentation with natural colorants: all signs pointing to the conclusion that Navaho weaving is a late and largely independent development, thwarted while yet in full career by the constantly increasing pressure of an alien culture.

GREEN

The yellow-green resulting when green portions of the plant *Bigelovia graveolens* are used along with the flowers was described under the heading Yellow.

A combination green, our authorities agree, was made by adding indigo blue to this same yellow dye. Another process, given me by Don Eologio Gallegos but not recorded among the Navaho, uses indigo only. The solution is prepared as for dyeing blue (described in next topic), but the wool is immersed for only a short time—until it has taken a good green color—and is then removed and left to dry. I suspect the Navaho used this method too, for its simplicity would popularize it. The strong hint of blue in colorants made by either process using indigo affords easy identification. This green, however, in my observation, is perhaps the rarest of the old colors—a great deal rarer than the highly-prized bayeta red. Ordinarily a large bayeta blanket will have only small touches of green, used in a few lesser figures of the pattern. I have never seen green used as a background color, and seldom in figures of much prominence in the pattern. Why this sparing use of a dye that was eminently satisfactory is not known to me.[9] Indigo blue, to which it is so closely akin, occurs in large masses in old patterns, as for example in the woman's dress.

PRE-ANILINE COMMERCIAL DYES

Aniline dyes appeared among the Navaho soon after 1880, as told in greater detail in Chapter 12. Commercial dyes had been in use among the Spanish colonists of New Mexico from earliest times, and various conjectures have been made on the extent of their infiltration into the Navaho dyer's craft. Brazil wood, logwood, fustic, cochineal, indigo, were standard dyestuffs among the Spanish of the New World, as in Europe generally, in pre-aniline days. Not all of them, however, were in common use in the remote northern province of New Mexico, on whose borders dwelt the Navaho. One caravan a year trekked northward from Chihuahua to Santa Fe before the Santa Fe Trail opened an easier avenue to the marts of civilization. Space was at a premium in this lone annual file of lumbering ox-carts on its journey of five hundred miles across rugged and dangerous terrain, and articles of the commonest utility bore the value of luxuries on arrival at their distant point of consignment. The New Mexicans consequently were accustomed to fill their own needs, relying

---

[9] Possibly a rooted aversion to the color; yet green is quite common in Germantown and aniline-dyed blankets.

but little on outside sources for anything they could possibly provide for themselves.[10]

Don Eologio Gallegos, patriarch in whom memory and direct hearsay together span easily a century of time, has told me of Brazil wood in billets two feet long, arriving in the remote Spanish villages of the upper Rio Grande on mule-back, directly from Chihuahua City. Indigo, too, came in great lumps by the same mode of transport. Cochineal was less bulky, cheaper to carry but much more expensive to buy. Don Eologio used Brazil wood and indigo commonly, throughout his long career at the loom. But he was a country-man, living far from the busy capital that was Santa Fe, and he knew nothing even of cochineal. Brazil wood and indigo, and for the rest of his colors, native plants and minerals of the province—those were the materials with which this old weaver embellished the serapes toilsomely woven on the home-made loom shown in plate 41*b*.

In fine, the expensive dyestuffs of pre-aniline days were none too common among the Spanish colonists who were the Navahos' only point of contact with the source of supply. We may assume, then, that they did not reach the latter in quantities sufficient to establish them (in a tribe numerous and widely scattered) in common use. No doubt there was some use of these dyestuffs, cochineal in particular,[11] on the fringes of Spanish territory and by Navaho women in Spanish households. Yet I find no definite evidence to this effect, and I am convinced that only one such dyestuff really established itself in the Navaho practice; that one is the subject of the following topic. I have mentioned that Don Eologio Gallegos knew nothing of cochineal; neither did my Navaho informant,

---

[10] Gregg, Davis, Bancroft, Prince, and other chroniclers of the period, give good pictures of these times. Especially recommended are the brief files of the New Mexico Historical Review (begun in 1926) for excellent papers on various phases of life in Spain's ultima Thule, New Mexico.

[11] I have seen several blankets, pre-aniline by their history and every point of appearance, with native-spun weft dyed in a color that had all the aspects of cochineal. But I recall no strong suspicion of other commercial dyestuffs (barring indigo, of course), except in that peculiar category of weaving known as "slave blankets": woven by Navaho women captive to the New Mexicans, or vice versa, with mingled Spanish and Navaho characteristics in color, pattern, size (see pls. 44 and 45).

This term is popular in Santa Fe, particularly among dealers who neglect no opportunity to add color and romance to the history of their wares. Of its authenticity one finds it difficult to judge, for slavery was common throughout the Spanish and well into the American period. Agent Riordan at Fort Defiance in 1883, for example, tells (RCIA 1883: 121) of freeing twenty slaves from their Navaho masters. The Ethnologic Dictionary, as late as 1909, can say only that "slavery has disappeared to a great extent." On the Spanish side slavery was quite as common: references to it are frequent in the literature of the period, and J. K. Graves, Special Indian Agent for New Mexico, reported in 1866 that "no less than 400 Indians are thus held in Santa Fe alone" (RCIA 1866: 137).

N'dan des pah; neither did a Navaho woman of more than eighty years
to whom Mr. B. I. Staples gave some of the powder—although she was
familiar with all the old native dye processes. Finally, none of our authorities on Navaho dyeing mentions any pre-aniline commercial dye but indigo.

BLUE

According to the Ethnologic Dictionary (232) "in former years the
Navaho had a native blue made of a kind of blue clay which was pulver-
ized and boiled with sumac leaves to obtain a mordant. Later this was
entirely superseded by indigo obtained from the Mexicans." Matthews
(1884: 376)) bears the same testimony: "There is good evidence that they
formerly had a blue dye; but indigo, originally introduced, I think, by
the Mexicans, has superseded this." Pepper, seeking to throw more light
on the point, "could find no one who knew how it [the original blue]
was made" (1902: 37). So the strictly native blue remains more or less a
tradition only. Indigo at any rate displaced it quite completely, and more
than a century ago. The Ethnologic Dictionary says (245-246) that the
woman's dress was dyed with native black and indigo blue even before
bayeta came into use, and the Massacre Cave fragment of plate 60 (dated
1805) is dyed with indigo.

Apparently boiling did not figure in the process of dyeing with
indigo. I can find nothing to indicate that either Matthews or Pepper
took the trouble to record the process, although Pepper says (1903: 2):
"This blue was prepared with great care, the time required to produce the
proper tint being over a month. Indigo was the basic principle and urine
was used as a mordant." The Ethnologic Dictionary (232) agrees: "Urine,
preserved in large Zuñi pots, was used as a mordant into which the indigo
was poured and the wool dipped. This was then allowed to stand from
five to ten days after which it was removed from the vessel and after dry-
ing was ready for use." Letterman (291) says that blue was obtained "by
dissolving indigo in fermented urine," but gives no further details.

From Mr. R. T. F. Simpson of Farmington, New Mexico, a trader
among the Navaho from the year 1895, I learned further details out of his
own experience and observation. He recalled selling indigo in his trading
store until about 1905, when the demand, which had been failing for
some time, ceased to justify its continuance as a trade item. He bought
the dyestuff in lumps from an Eastern supply house, selling it at two to
three dollars a pound. A bit would be broken from the lump and sold
by weight to the customer.

PLATE 44

A "Slave blanket." The Spanish influence is hardly apparent in this monotone illustration; the reader must imagine stripes of indigo blue and brown-black (natural wool), with light blue diamonds, their centers black or occasionally red, on white. The size, 53 x 81 ins., is more Spanish than Navaho, while the bound edge is a Navaho trait. Laboratory of Anthropology, cat. Indian Arts Fund. no. 189.

PLATE 45

A "slave blanket". As in the preceding illustration, lack of color robs this specimen of much of its peculiar character. Its red center figures and stripes of red,
orange, purple, gray-pink suggest the Chimayo (native Spanish-New Mexican)
rather than the Navaho; so too the proportions and size, 53 x 82 ins., but the
bound edge is Navaho. Laboratory of Anthropology, cat. Indian Arts Fund no. 21.

Navaho families in which weaving was done kept a pot outside the *hogán* for storing urine, as mentioned by the Ethnologic Dictionary. Letterman's reference to "fermented urine" strengthens the impression one gets from the other accounts, that ageing the solvent fluid was a part of the process, beneficial probably because of the evaporation of the water and consequent strengthening of the acid content. I was told at Crafts del Navajo that the pot of urine was sometimes buried in the ground for a period of several weeks. At any rate, it is clear that the process was one of dissolution of the indigo in urine and immersion of the wool in the solution for a considerable length of time.

N'dan des pah: "Blue made from something like this but darker [fishing around in a bag for a piece of blue carpenter's chalk.] We got it from Santa Fe or from the Pueblos, long time ago, in lumps. Must use Indian pot for this, bucket no good [the chemical reaction of metal to indigo is said to spoil the dye]. Use big pot to hold lots of wool, get it from Pueblos—Jemez or Laguna mostly. Keep pot outside *hogán* for children to urinate in mornings. Put in blue chunk size of fist, wrapped in a cloth; leave it till urine gets green and nothing left in cloth, about half day. Put in spun wool, leave it three days. That's all."

Indigo, as indicated above, was one of the last of the old dyes to fall out of use. I have a Navaho blanket known to have been woven near Farmington, New Mexico, soon after 1900, in which aniline red, green, and orange are used with indigo blue. Connoisseurs agree that aniline blues with their harsh, slightly purplish tint are unworthy successors to the deep rich blue of indigo.

RECOGNIZING NATIVE DYES: A NOTE FOR COLLECTORS

Lest blanket-loving readers wish me ill for neglecting a point that is to them perhaps the most important of all in the matter of native dyes, something must be said of the characteristics by which native dyed colors may be recognized as such. As in the case of bayeta,[12] I know of no sure criterion. In a blanket that has been kept as new, whatever its age, the problem is found in simplest form; but most blankets have not had this good fortune. Aniline has been in use long enough that many blankets dyed with it have faded and toned down to soft and pleasing shades. Particularly is this true of red: the sultry, hard crimson hue most characteristic of aniline red sometimes fades to a delicate rosy tint after a few washings in soapy water or a few years of exposure to sunlight. Orange is an-

---

[12] Chapter 10 is devoted to bayeta.

other shade in which native and aniline colors are much alike; and black, of course, is hardly to be identified with certainty.

But there are several old dyes that can be recognized with fair assurance. Indigo is easiest of all. It has a bright richness and depth of color that the cheap trading-post aniline does not even remotely approach. Indigo blue is quite literally recognizable at a glance, even from a distance. Another inimitable native color is the bright lemon yellow of the rabbit-brush dye (*Bigelovia graveolens*); it has a pale, delicate (almost always due in part to fading) brightness that the deeper and more lifeless hue of aniline yellow cannot equal. Further, yellow is a color seldom used in aniline-dyed blankets, in my observation. The green of this same native dye is equally characteristic, having the same delicacy of tint in which green and yellow blend most pleasingly. The green made of indigo or indigo and native yellow combined is ordinarily recognizable, although not perhaps so easily as the yellow, by the strong suggestion of those qualities of richness and solid depth that make indigo so attractive. The aniline greens have a metallic, hard quality suggesting the apt term "poisonous green." Finally, aniline colors are generally uniform in density throughout their extent in the blanket, while native colors (again excepting black and indigo) tend toward a variability of shade which gives a faint effect of horizontal streaking, particularly noticeable where the color occurs in large masses.

Generally speaking the native colors, indigo and black excepted, have a pleasingly light, sunny tone, a liveliness that makes the color almost indecisive at times, whereas the anilines are heavy and lifeless in their effect; they are more striking but decidedly less attractive to the eye sensitive to color values. One thinks of the anilines as colors, of the native hues as shades of color; to borrow a simile from music, the former are full tones, the latter half-tones. These diverse qualities are hard to put into words, it is admitted. The person who would learn to distinguish them should spend hours in a museum where Navaho blankets are displayed, or with his own collection, studying and comparing the blankets intensively from the sole standpoint of their color effects and values. Some help may be given by plates 34, 37, 48, and 59, in which are good reproductions of native colors. The subtleties and difficulties of this subject are foremost among the factors that make blanket collecting so exasperating—and so well worth while. Anybody can identify a postage stamp.

Aside from color alone, there are criteria which help solve the prob-

PLATE 46

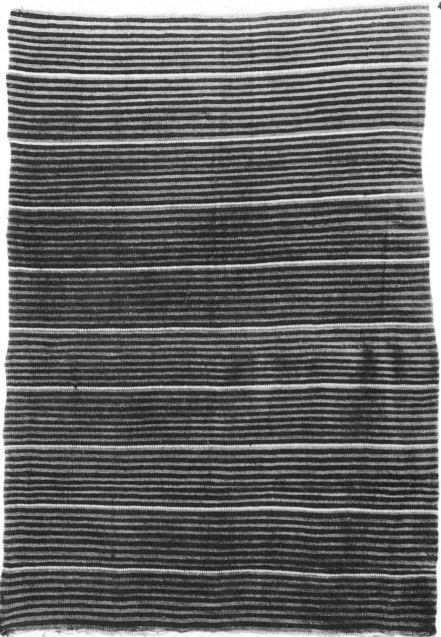

Indigo-dyed blanket. This and the following illustration (plate 47) are figured by Matthews 1884, figs. 54 and 55. Thus they antedate 1884, and despite their strong Hopi character we must bow to the fact that Matthews (who evidently collected them) considers them Navaho. They may of course have reached that tribe through trade; on the other hand Matthews makes it clear that the Navaho made many such **serapes**.

Size 53 x 72 ins., colors: narrow stripes of indigo blue, native black, white. U. S. National Museum, Washington Matthews coll., cat. 281469.

PLATE 47

Indigo-dyed blanket. This like its companion piece of plate 46 is a large, coarse **serape** or shoulder blanket, size 55 x 77 ins., colors: gray panels, stripes of white, indigo blue, and a mixture of green and red weft strands which gives a mottled effect to certain stripes. The green is quite certainly native, the red possibly so. Note the warp fringe in this, and the unbound edge in both specimens. Washington Matthews coll. U. S. National Museum cat. 281478.

lem of determining whether the dyestuff in question came from a plant of the desert Southwest or from an envelope in the trader's store. If the blanket has a pattern completely enclosed by a border, or "boxed," it is almost certain to be aniline-colored, for the practice of boxing patterns came in about the time that aniline dye and trader influence in pattern became paramount in the craft, and it increased in favor very rapidly, as told in Chapter 14. Similarly, if the figures of the pattern are large and bold, tending in vertical lines, lengthwise of the blanket, rather than in horizontal lines, crosswise, the probabilities strongly favor aniline. If the warp is of cotton [18] the color is likely to be aniline—for cotton warp always comes from the trading post, being nothing but the common white twine with which grocers tie their packages. Germantown wool is never native dyed, although the early machine-spun yarns have vegetal dyes.

These are unscientific and uncertain methods; what of chemical analysis? Several chemists (among them Dr. R. E. Rose, Director of the Dyestuffs Department, Sales Division, Technical Laboratory, of E. I. du Pont de Nemours and Company) have assured me that no simple, practicable test for aniline versus vegetal is known. An expert can make a test if furnished only "a few fibers" of material, but there is no magic fluid the amateur could use in furtive drops to set his mind at rest. All I can offer the reader are the following apparently simple tests for certain commercial dyes, taken from J. J. Hummel, *The Dyeing of Textile Fabrics* (Cassell and Co., London, 1885):

Cochineal (the usual colorant of bayeta): Nitric acid turns it yellow; hydrochloric has no action.

Madder (possibly used in bayeta, but not common): Turns bright yellow under nitric acid.

Vat Indigo: Sulphuric concentrated dissolves color. Chloroform also extracts blue color. Strong nitric makes a bright yellow spot (best test).

---

[18] Cotton warp is another trader contribution to the craft, beginning however as early as about 1880; from then until about 1910 it grew in popularity with the weavers; but traders of late years have discouraged its use, for it is far weaker than wool. Germantown wool blankets usually have a cotton warp, although many have both Germantown warp and weft. To recognize cotton warp, burn a fragment of exposed end with a match: if it burns down with a steady glow, like a match that has been allowed to consume itself, it is cotton. Wool fizzles slightly and ceases burning the moment the flame is withdrawn. Also, cotton burns with a woody smell; burnt wool smells acrid and unpleasant, like burnt hair (which of course it is). Cotton warp untwists more cleanly, with less of fuzzy edge, than wool; and with some practice one can recognize it by the hard, smooth appearance of the strand, without touching it.

CHAPTER VII

TYPES AND USES OF NAVAHO TEXTILES

HE product of the Navaho loom is commonly referred to today as a "Navaho rug." Purists have objected to the phrase, holding that it is unjust as well as misleading to consider Navaho weaving a rugmaking industry. In so far as they speak historically, the objectors are right: Navaho looms were not devised for rug making. From the standpoint of the existing situation, however, the objection is overruled, for the weavers of today are engaged in making rugs and little else. To be painstakingly correct in phrase, one should speak of an old-time specimen, one that has seen use among the Navaho, or was woven before the era of the trading post, as a blanket. The remainder of the output, with a few exceptions such as the saddle blanket and the pillow-top, may quite properly be alluded to as rugs. The Navaho woman of today is weaving for the market, producing a great variety of sizes from the pillow-top eighteen inches square to the veritable carpet, large enough to cover the floor of a living room.[1] Her product—stiff, tight, heavy—is best suited to use underfoot, where it will render incredibly long and satisfactory service. The weaving of rugs is of course a modern development with an alien stimulus. In the days when weaving was done to fill a domestic need the Navaho loom produced little but garments. Rugs were not in demand among the natives of the Southwest.

An enumeration of the various uses of Navaho textiles with a brief

---

[1] The largest piece of Navaho weaving known to me is the two-faced (pl. 90) rug owned by Mr. B. I. Staples, which was mentioned in Chapter 4 as being 12 feet by 18 feet 2 inches in size. A Germantown yarn rug formerly in the possession of the late J. F. Collins of Santa Fe, now owned by Mrs. C. F. Baisley, Palm Springs, California, measures 14 by 14 feet, the largest Germantown I know. Southwest Museum has a specimen of native wool, shown in pl. 91b, measuring 11½ by 16 feet.

These large rugs are woven on the typical Navaho loom, expanded for the purpose, of course. Their making requires many months and is such an ambitious and costly undertaking that weavers will not attempt them except as special orders, payable in part in advance of completion. It is said that the late Lorenzo Hubbell, old-time Indian trader of Ganado, Arizona, had a number of these large rugs made for wealthy American customers. In this connection it may be said that the Navaho always weave in a single piece, never joining separate strips as do the Chimayo (native Spanish-American) weavers.

description of the more or less standard type which each use called into being will serve to emphasize both the widely diversified character of Navaho weaving and its economic and social importance to the tribe. The remainder of the chapter will be devoted to this enumeration. It will be seen that the principal types are either outright imitations or modifications of garments used by the prehistoric and the early modern Pueblos,[2] or introduced from Mexico by Spanish colonists.

THE WOMAN'S DRESS (*bil*) [3]

Historical evidence bearing on the early products of the Navaho loom is meager indeed, but there is no doubt that the woman's dress is among the oldest of all. It imitates the garment the early Spanish explorers found in general use among Pueblo women before the middle of the 16th century: a straight, sleeveless dress hung over the left shoulder, leaving the right shoulder bare.[4] It was belted at the waist with the sash woven on the belt loom, and it extended below the knees of the wearer. The Pueblos wove this garment in a single piece, its height (in the loom) being the length of the dress, and its loom width sufficient to permit doubling and sewing the two sides together to make a straight, formless gown (pl. 50*b*). Thus it was of slightly greater breadth than length—a common feature of Pueblo textiles, but more rare in Navaho weaving.

The Navaho woman's dress (pls. 49, 50*a*) was woven in two pieces of identical size and pattern. These were sewn together after weaving, the sides being joined except for a gap of several inches at both top and bottom. The bottom gap formed a slit in either side of the skirt, designed to give freedom in movement to the wearer, while that at the top provided neck and arm room, the garment being sleeveless. The upper edges were joined for a few inches on each side to form straps over the shoulders, the middle portion remaining open to allow passage for the woman's head. The style of the dress was thus roughly that of the Pueblo woman's (except for the one bare shoulder in the latter), of which it was almost certainly an adaptation.

Early Spanish descriptions of Pueblo women's dress, as in the quotation from Castañeda given in note 4 below, clearly imply a one-piece garment like that of modern times, leaving the two-piece Navaho dress without historic explanation. Possibly some native Navaho dress, most likely

---

[2] For native garments of the Hopi see Museum Notes 3: 1.

[3] Navaho names of garments are taken from the Ethnologic Dictionary: 245ff.

[4] "The women wear blankets, which they tie or knot over the left shoulder, leaving the right arm out." Castañeda writing of 1540-42 in Winship: 517.

of deerskin, set this two-piece fashion for the loom to follow. Such dresses are a widespread type: two skins sewn together down the long sides. Apache women, first cousins of the Navaho, have long worn them.

Each of the two small blankets comprising this garment was woven in plain weave, with the selvage cords of ends and sides projecting to form short tassels at all four corners. The size varied somewhat, a stout matron obviously requiring more coverage than a slender girl, but a width of about thirty inches and a length of about forty are typical dimensions. In color and pattern a rigid conservatism prevailed. The Ethnologic Dictionary (245-246) says the dress was originally woven in black and blue; the black a native dye, the blue a Mexican indigo. "The top and bottom of the blanket alternated in four lines of blue and three of black, with the body of the blanket, or its center, a plain jet black. The whole was bordered and tasseled in blue. With the introduction of bayeta (Spanish flannel), red was substituted for the blue in the body of the blanket, though the blue border and tassels were retained. The solid black center, too, was retained, and gradually various designs of red and blue were woven with the black at each side of the center belt."

I have never seen a specimen of the early black and blue dress (the traditional modern Pueblo colors, incidentally), but many of these later red, black, and blue dresses are in existence today, having been prized for their bayeta content. More often than not they are only half complete (like pl. 49), the two pieces having been cut apart and sold separately as small blankets.

This standard woman's garment was worn from the early days of Navaho weaving down to the twentieth century. It is barely possible that a very few old women cling to it still; I saw one wearing a native dress in the year 1913.[5] Cheap cotton cloth changed this long-established style, apparently rather suddenly in some parts of the Navaho country. I was told by Mr. R. T. F. Simpson, retired Indian trader of Farmington, New Mexico, that about 1895 the tribe was "going calico" as he expressed it, very rapidly, and he had so many native dresses in pawn in his trading store that he sold them for as little as five dollars each. He kept one, however, for which he says he has refused more than one hundred dollars. In more recent years the demand for the garment has been so strong that traders have sometimes had old weavers make dresses solely for sale to collectors. Otherwise the woman's dress is one of the most characteristically and completely native products of the Navaho loom, the more so for the

---

[5] Mr. J. L. Ambrose of Thoreau, New Mexico, has told me of an old woman who keeps a native dress to serve as her shroud.

fact that unlike many Navaho textiles, it was used only by the tribe that made it.

THE MAN'S SHIRT (*æ dotl'izhi,* blue shirt; *æ ndädeshchi,* red-striped shirt)

In former days the Navaho apparently imitated the Pueblos, who in turn were probably imitators of some ancient weaving peoples of Middle America, in making a shirt for men on their native loom. The body was woven flat and rectangular, like a small poncho,[6] with a slit in the center through which the head was passed. Tacking down the sides and adding sleeves, woven flat and later doubled, made a complete garment on a pattern entirely rectangular. Plate 33 exemplifies the wide diffusion in both time and space of this type of garment by illustrating shirts from prehistoric Peru, from the modern Pueblos, and from the Navaho.[7] The resemblance to a modern athlete's sweater will be noticed. The Navaho shirt was generally of blue or black color, sometimes striped with red; and an illustration on page 248 of the Ethnologic Dictionary suggests that it was sometimes fringed at the bottom, apparently by allowing the warp strings to project beyond the end of the web, as in certain blankets.

SHOULDER BLANKETS

It has been said that the Pueblos weave many textiles of greater breadth than length. The white cotton shawl woven by the Hopi man for his bride-to-be is of such proportions; so too is the common woman's dress of black wool, woven in one piece and doubled to form a sleeveless gown. The Navaho on the other hand have adhered more closely to the general proportions of the ancient waist loom fabrics in their weaving, making the length definitely greater than the breadth. Two standard types, however, follow the Pueblo tradition: they are the shoulder blankets, men's and women's. Both are ancient styles, and in them one seems to see a survival of that Pueblo influence which molded the destinies of Navaho weaving in the time of its beginnings.[8] The woman's is always smaller

---

[6] Such small ponchos, unsewn, are in use in Latin America today.

[7] I doubt if the shirt has ever been found among the prehistoric Pueblos. These people knew how to make a full-fashioned woven garment, however, for the Arizona State Museum in Tucson has a sleeveless, low-necked sweater or blouse, made of cotton yarn by a process of netting, which was found with the mummified body of a child in a cave in the Tonto Basin, Arizona. The pottery found in the ruin was of a late prehistoric type, establishing the relative age of the piece beyond question.

[8] A friend who has spent most of his life in the Navaho country, and who wishes to remain nameless because of his tribal standing, once happened on a Navaho burial in a cave filled with prehistoric Pueblo and Basketmaker remains. A cist or roofed pit had been formed, after the old Navaho fashion, and it held the

PLATE 49

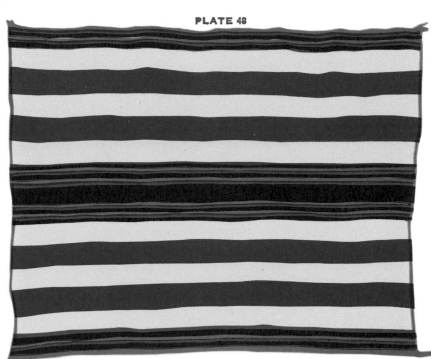

Man's shoulder blanket (chief blanket) of the 1850's. Native black and indigo blue, bayeta red. Size 68 x 54 ins. Museum of the American Indian cat. 8-8038.

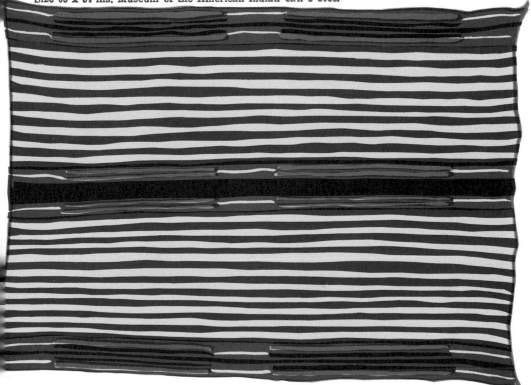

Woman's shoulder blanket, size 58 x 42 ins., colors and materials as above. Found wrapped about a baby girl (Sioux) found on the battlefield of Wounded Knee in South Dakota, December 29, 1890 beside her dead mother. Owner Dr. Spencer R. Atkinson.

than the man's which is commonly called the chief's blanket. Both follow certain general rules of proportion, color, and pattern, however, and seem to have their inspiration in a common source.

THE WOMAN'S SHOULDER BLANKET (*bīl babá dotl'ízhi:* blue borders; *bīl łagaí:* white shawl)

The Ethnologic Dictionary says (246) that the woman's shoulder blanket was of two patterns. One was called by the Navaho "blue borders," owing its name to "the two borders of blue which flanked the center of black." The color and pattern were much like those of the early type of woman's dress, while the general resemblance of the garment to the Hopi woman's embroidered shawl of white cotton will be noted. Thus the two principal garments of the Navaho woman, dress and shoulder blanket, are strongly reminiscent of the Pueblo.

The other pattern, that of a type known as the "white shawl, was so called from the alternating white and red color which was woven horizontally in narrow strips throughout. The border and tassels were blue. It was the only woman's garment in which white was used, and was therefore appropriately designated." In later years the same general pattern apparently was modified to include three broad bands of color, usually blue or black, in which figures of contrasting color might be framed. These bands extended horizontally across the blanket at ends and center, the intervening space being filled with narrow horizontal stripes in black or blue and white or gray. Dimensions of about 45 inches length by about 60 inches width are characteristic of the type. It is always of greater breadth than length, and always bears a pattern in which horizontal stripes predominate. Plates 48*b*, 50*a*, and 106 show typical patterns. This garment was sometimes made in a small size, evidently for children's use.

----

mummified body of a Navaho man. The body was clad in one of the woven shirts just described, it is interesting to note.

Various articles, including buffalo robes and native woolen blankets, were buried with it, and my friend could not resist the temptation to retrieve one of the latter for his collection. He then closed the grave. I have notes on a personal examination of the blanket which is illustrated in pl. 63a. It is 66 inches wide and 48 inches long, woven of coarse wool in a loose basket weave, with a pattern of broad horizontal stripes in the natural hues of brown and white. A thin band of indigo blue traverses the center, the only artificial color in the piece. In proportion, size, and pattern this blanket is a typical shoulder blanket, with Pueblo and Navaho characteristics in about equal measure. Its age cannot be determined, but the mummification of the body it accompanied should justify a guess of perhaps a century. Such bits of evidence as this have convinced me that Navaho weaving followed Pueblo styles closely in its early years, gradually asserting its independence and assuming the individuality it later demonstrated. The point is discussed further in Chapter 13.

THE MAN'S SHOULDER BLANKET OR CHIEF'S BLANKET (*hǎnolchǎde*)

This highly standardized and well-known form of Navaho blanket was once so widely bartered and so popular that it might be seen over the shoulders of influential Indians from the northern Great Plains to the Mexican border. Many of the finest specimens in existence today were obtained from tribes far removed from the Navaho. Never in the strict sense a badge of chieftainship, this garment did have a certain connotation of power and affluence wherever seen.

Fine material and careful workmanship went into the chief's blanket of olden time. The broad white stripes must be truly white, the black stripes paralleling them a deep glossy black. As in the woman's blanket, the horizontal stripe pattern of two strongly contrasting colors was varied by the three bands of a third color at ends and center. These were usually of indigo blue, set with plain bars of bayeta red (in earlier specimens) or with geometric figures, usually a serrated diamond, likewise in red. It was traditional to introduce these red figures in stated positions: one complete figure or group of bars in the very center of the blanket; one-half of an identical figure or group in the center of each end band and similarly at each end of the central band; and one-fourth of one figure or group at each corner of the blanket. Thus when the blanket was folded to bring the corners together, the four quarter-figures matched to form one whole. The two ends and the two sides could each be brought together to match their half-figures. This layout therefore required a precision in size and spacing which was a supreme test of the weaver's eye. The size of this blanket is ordinarily about 50 inches in length by about 70 in width, being slightly larger than the woman's garment, in the same general proportions. Plates, 38, 48*a*, 64, 74, 75, 91*a*, 98 show typical patterns.

The Ethnologic Dictionary mentions three variants of this general pattern type, indicating that the details of the layout and coloring had their significance (246-247): one was "horizontally striped, a blanket woven in alternating stripes of black and white, with an occasional narrow strip of red added in the center, and the end belts of black [pl. 38*a*]. Red tassels decorated each corner. A similar blanket, and one much in demand by the Utes, was known as . . . the blanket with the black (streak) belt in the center. While the body of the blanket was laced with strips of white and black, the center was mounted with a wide black belt, with additional red and blue stripes woven in between [pl. 48*a*]. Similar belts were woven in equidistant intervals between the center belt and the ends, though they were narrower than the center belt. The corners were decorated with black

PLATE 49

A woman's dress, (half only). Colors: black center, bayeta red stripes and end panels, with figures in indigo blue. Size 31 x 48 ins.

It is recorded that Mr. S. E. Day Jr. found this piece in Massacre Cave, Cañon del Muerto, inferentially dating it from 1805, for no Navaho dares venture into the cave since the massacre commemorated in its name. Courtesy of Laboratory of Anthropology.

PLATE 50

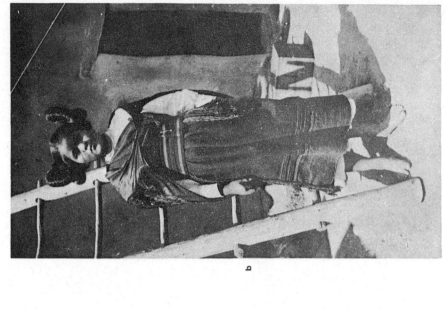

b

a

The woman's dress, Navaho and Pueblo.
a Angelina, a Navaho girl. Compare her shoulder blanket with plate 48b. Photo from Wittick coll., Laboratory of Anthropology; taken probably around 1890.

tassels, making a very attractive blanket." Finally, "the Mexican rug or pelt, was a pattern borrowed from the Mexicans. The center was woven in a belt of blue flanked by narrow stripes of black, the remainder of the blanket alternating in belts of white, black and blue, interspersed at optional intervals. This design was a very plain one and made for the Mexican trade."

The Ethnologic Dictionary would restrict the term chief's blanket to a specific design of diamond figures, although usage sanctions the broader interpretation and recognizes the generic type of man's shoulder blanket characterized by a pattern of broad horizontal stripes, however the details of the design and coloring may be worked out. Furthermore, the diamond-figured pattern is of later date than the all-striped, as the dated illustrations herein prove.

THE SERAPE or ZARAPE [9]

The various types of woven garment hitherto considered bear a strong flavor of the aboriginal Southwest. The serape, however, is definitely associated with Mexico. Mena (375) derives the word from the Nahua language through a series of phonetic modifications. He characterizes the serape as a garment of mixed Spanish and native Mexican origin, a composite of the Spanish *manta* or quilted cloak and the native Mexican *tilmatli,* a cotton cape about 40 inches square, which must have borne a close resemblance to the cotton capes of the Pueblos seen by the early Spanish explorers of the Southwest. The word serape today connotes a blanket of garish colors, three or four feet wide and six or seven long, which Mexicans of high and low degree carry, folded the long way, over the shoulder. It is woven on the European horizontal loom, sometimes in two strips which are sewn together side by side, often with an aperture in the center for slipping the garment over the head, making of it a poncho. The serape is an overcoat, a raincoat, a cushion for sitting or kneeling, a blanket for sleeping. The Chimayo blanket of today is a serape in origin and form.

The Pueblos came to weave serapes of wool in one piece, usually without the poncho slit, on their upright loom; in the latter years of their

___

[9] The coarse serape type goes by the general native term of diyugi: soft fluffy blanket. For the fine serape and the poncho I find no specific name—but this type never fixed itself in the tribal economy, being woven rather for trade. I suspect Letterman had it in mind when he wrote (291): "Occasionally a blanket is seen which is quite handsome, and costs at the same time the extravagant price of forty or fifty dollars; these, however, are very scarce, and are generally made for a special purpose."

weaving this type was one of their most characteristic products. The Navaho did likewise: whether in imitation of the Pueblos or of the Mexican settlers is not certain, but probably for trade with those neighbors.

Matthews (1884: 387-388) speaks of "coarse blankets made more for use than ornament. Figure 55 is made of loosely-twilled yarn and is very warm but not water-proof. Such blankets made excellent bedding for troops in the field. Fig. 54 is a water-proof serape of well-twilled native wool."

These two typical specimens (pls. 46, 47) have fringed ends and a pattern of horizontal stripes and bands. They have a decidedly Pueblo or Mexican look. Matthews says elsewhere (ibid. 382) that the "coarse blankets" do not have the selvage cords on their side edges,[10] and this feature, too, is characteristic of Pueblo as well as Mexican serapes. All in all, there is good reason to believe that the serape has little of the native Southwest except the loom on which it is woven; although the Pueblos adopted it wholeheartedly, as did the Navaho in later times.[11] Gradually this foreign type, longer than broad, displaced the native type, broader than long, of which the men's and women's shoulder blankets are survivals.

THE PONCHO

A variant of the serape which is more typically Navaho in pattern and excellence of workmanship (if not in style) is found in the *poncho* blanket, a rare type, of which I have seen only a dozen in all.[12] It is woven after the sound Navaho tradition of battening down hard and tight, with the characteristic selvage cords all around, and a figured pattern instead of the banal horizontal stripes of the usual serape proper. A slit is left open in the center for putting the garment over the head.[13] The size is about that of the Pueblo and Mexican serape, perhaps a foot shorter. Every specimen

---

[10] The use of the selvage cord, a characteristic feature of Southwestern weaving in ancient and modern times, is described in Chapter 3, shown in pl. 18.

[11] When the Navaho tribe was returned to its home-land in 1868, after its sojourn at Fort Sumner where Kit Carson had taken it bodily to break the spirit of the people once for all, it was in desperate straits for clothing. Blankets were woven as hastily as possible, and I think the coarse, loose-woven serape had a revival of popularity at that time, this fact helping to explain the presence of many serapes when Matthews went among the Navaho in 1880, only twelve years later.

[12] Three of them are in the Charles F. Lummis Collection in the Southwest Museum.

[13] Not to be confused with a small slit which the Ethnologic Dictionary (247) explains as follows: ". . . any blanket might be woven so as to leave a slit about four fingers wide in the center of the blanket, which was afterwards laced with blue yarn. It is generally stated that this weave had to be occasionally resorted to in order to avoid overdoing weaving."

I have seen this small slit only thrice; in a bayeta blanket of modified serape

PLATE 51

A bayeta **serape.** Colors native white and indigo blue on a two-ply bayeta red ground, size 54 x 72 ins., thread count 14 warp, 30 weft. Plainly visible are the four horizontal folds showing where the blanket was sewn down to the lower loom bar in weaving; they never entirely disappear in these fine, hard-battened old specimens.

Bought at Taos about 1880 by W. A. Givens; his daughter Mrs. Jim Clay sold it to the Laboratory of Anthropology in 1932. Cat. T 209.

PLATE 52

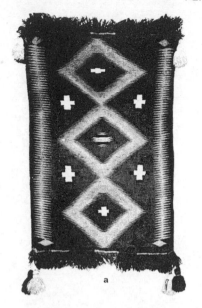

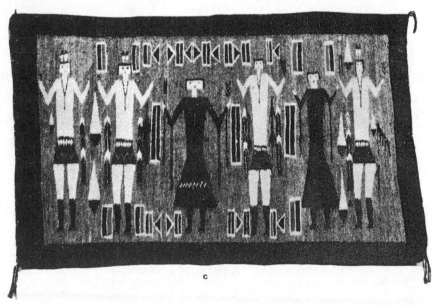

a and b, Saddle throws of Germantown yarn. Both have a cotton warp. a is white, purple, green, black, on red; size 17 x 27 ins. Tassels of both 3-and 4-ply yarn. b is white, green, yellow purple, light red, on dark red ground; size 19 x 29 ins. a woven about 1905, b undated. Author's coll.

c, A Yei blanket, recent (seen sidewise, warp strings horizontal). Size about 40 x 60 ins., colors red, black, yellow, green, blue, on gray. Courtesy of Mr. Philip Johnston.

of Navaho poncho serape I have seen was a bayeta piece of exceptionally fine weave and intricate pattern. Obviously this type was made rarely, for persons of wealth and standing; probably for trading to Mexican settlers, through whom so many of the fine old Navaho blankets have been preserved. One of the Lummis poncho serapes is shown in plate 59; another of the type in plate 67a.

The serape, modified though it has been in many details, must be considered the universal type garment of the Navaho, the type that more than all others is behind the broad phrase of "Indian blanket." The wealthy tribesman might flaunt his chief's blanket or bayeta poncho, but the humbler men and women of the nation contented themselves with a coarser blanket of similar size and general proportions, as shown in plates 46, 47, 69, 77, 78. In this useful garment, worn over the shoulders and frequently belted at the waist, the wearer could muffle his head against the cold or shield his face from the sun or the driving sand of desert windstorms. Burdens of every description, from firewood to babies, were carried in its folds. Like the Arab's *burnous* it was a garment by day, a blanket by night, an inseparable companion in all seasons. Today, the machine-made blankets and shawls known as "Pendletons" have replaced it; but its form and proportion survive still in the longish-rectangular rugs, five by eight feet or thereabouts in size, which are among the characteristic products of the modern Navaho loom.

THE SADDLE BLANKET (*akidahi'nili*)

So rapidly is the horse vanishing from the American scene that it is perhaps advisable to explain that a pad or saddle cloth is always used to protect the animal's back from chafing under the saddle. The Navaho early adopted the Mexican settler's high-cantled, hornless saddle, made of wood covered with leather and studded with large brass nails. Two decades ago this type of saddle was still in common use. For a saddle pad the Navaho turned to his womenfolk, they to their looms, and a short, squarish blanket was produced that served the purpose excellently.[14] The

type in the Arizona State Museum at Tucson (cat. 8418), in that shown in pl. 101a and in one of similar style in the F. K. Hinchman Collection, Southwest Museum (cat. 202L118). In each the opening is about 1½ inch long and is not laced with blue, but with the colored yarn of its surrounding fabric.

[14] So well, in fact, that Navaho saddle blankets were in general use through the latter days of the cowboy's glory, all over the West. A merchant on the Mexican border once told me he bought quantities of Navaho saddle blankets every year for sale to the vaqueros of his region. The dyed-in-the-wool Westerner of today prefers a thick Navaho blanket under his saddle to the scientifically-constructed pads favored in more effete circles where horseback riding is known as "equitation."

double saddle blanket is the more common type today, although the single was probably the earlier type. Without evidence on the point, it is my impression that the increasing use of heavy American saddles, coupled with the market demand for a substantial pad, has brought the double saddle blanket into favor. The single blanket is generally about thirty inches square, being used under the saddle without folding. The double blanket is woven to about twice the size of the other, on the same width, and is doubled end to end for use.

Twilled weaves were popular for saddle blankets as they resulted in a thicker, softer fabric than the plain weave. The diamond twill is seldom seen except in saddle blankets. Typical specimens of this article, both single and double, are shown in plates 29, 33*d*, 41*a*, 42, 43.

The saddle blanket was no article of merely commonplace utility to the Navaho horsemen. It was no less a feature of his accouterment than the silver-mounted bridle or the brass-studded saddle. The blanket under the saddle might pass unnoticed while in use, but when the rider unsaddled to spend a few hours in friendly visiting it was spread out to lounge upon, and there it underwent critical inspection. Bayeta, always a costly material and a difficult one to prepare for weaving, was frequently used in saddle blankets, as was Germantown wool yarn in later times.[15] In color, pattern, workmanship, and material, the saddle blanket was often one of the finest products of the Navaho loom. The fact seems surprising in view of the rought usage to which these utilitarian articles were subjected; yet the Navaho were merely typical of equestrian people the world over, in holding that nothing is too good for the horseman and his mount.

It was not uncommon to weave double saddle blankets in two quite distinct patterns or colors, or both. Having completed the lower half of the web, the weaver would weave the upper half quite differently. When folded and in use the blanket showed only one of its two patterns; it was a two-in-one affair, like the reversible coats women sometimes wear today.

THE SADDLE THROW (*A yăh năl sósie*: "used as a pad to sit on")

The importance of the horse to Navaho life has called into being another distinctive small blanket, the saddle throw. It is thrown across the saddle for the double purpose of comfort to the rider and embellishment to his equipage. In size some twenty by thirty inches, this blanket is easily mistaken for a single saddle blanket—but it is too narrow for such

---

[15] A word of caution is needed here: child's serapes often are called saddle blankets because of the similarity in size.

service. Saddle throws usually are handsome little fabrics, most of those I have seen being made of Germantown yarn [16] with tasseled ends, like those shown in plate 52*a* and *b*. Tufted saddle throws are known too (pl. 23*b*), being especially popular with women riders.

THE SADDLE GIRTH (*ăchŏshtl'ŏl*)

The Navaho often made their own saddle girths or cinches by string-ing the warp between two iron rings and weaving a strip of fabric five or six inches wide and perhaps thirty inches long, upon this foundation. These articles bore characteristic patterns and colors, and were made in both plain and twilled weaves. A specimen is shown in plate 56*a*.

CEREMONIAL RUGS OR BLANKETS

Stevenson (1891) alludes to the use of a small blanket, which from his illustrations seems to be much like a double saddle blanket, in the ceremonial he describes. He does not say that the piece is made expressly for ceremonial use, nor to my knowledge do any of the authorities even hint that blankets of sacred or ceremonial character were woven. There is no such category of blanket, so far as I can learn.[17] The so-called *Yei* or *Yei-bichai* blankets must be disposed of in this connection, however. They are plain-woven fabrics, usually of the modified serape size so character-istic of modern Navaho weaving. The design is a representation of one or more of the Navaho divinities (*Yei*), male or female, with the ap-propriate attributes and accouterment (pls. 52*c*, 53). The blanket, in fine, is an adaptation to the loom of the ceremonial sand-painting; but I find no evidence that it was woven with ceremonial intent or used ceremonially. On the contrary, it seems to be more of an American than a Navaho de-vice, as will be seen.

James (139-140) has an interesting account of the furore which greet-ed the first appearance of the *Yei* blanket, about the beginning of the present century. The Navaho were shocked and outraged, he says, by the sacrilege of one of their weavers in reproducing sacred symbols and figures in a blanket which was put on display in a trader's store. "Councils were held over the reservation to discuss the matter, and the trader was finally

---

[16] I suspect this type to be quite recent: I recall none of bayeta, and the Ethnologic Dictionary does not name it. Mr. L. H. McSparron is my authority for calling it a distinct type, and he gave me its Navaho name.

[17] Mr. Ben Wetherill confirms this, verbally. He has spent his life among the Navaho, being the son of Mr. John Wetherill, pioneer Indian trader and guide of Kayenta, Arizona, and speaks their language as do very few Americans. He told me he has never heard of a blanket woven for ceremonial use.

commanded to remove the blanket containing the offending emblems from the wall of his office."

I have personal recollections of a woman, the wife of an Indian trader, who made *Yei* blankets, soon after 1900 and for years thereafter, near Farmington, New Mexico. Her daring was greatly admired, and the blankets were eagerly purchased as curiosities. She did a thriving business, turning out one *Yei* blanket after another on a pattern which eventually became monotonously standardized; one of her products is seen in plate 53. By common report, Navaho tradition held that a weaver who made such blankets would be stricken blind for her temerity, but this woman's sight seems never to have suffered and the suspensive interest gradually died.

The *Yei* blanket is becoming more and more common. Certain traders seem to encourage its manufacture because they can sell it for a good price by playing up its rarity and pseudo-ceremonial character. Evidently the Navaho themselves regard the *Yei* blanket much as we would consider a parody of the Bible, as something in bad taste. Its bad taste from the artistic standpoint is beyond question, and it will probably prove only a passing fad; for once the aura of mystery is dispelled nothing will remain but an awkward human figure in garish coloring, infinitely less attractive than the simple geometric patterns which are truly representative of Navaho textile design. Of late years, and probably under similar monetary inspiration, blankets embodying whole sand-paintings have appeared on the market. One is shown in plate 54. Like the *Yei* blankets, they are but an invasion of the temple by the money-changers, although often possessed of both artistic and ethnologic value.

SASHES (*sĭs*), GARTERS (*jănĕzhi*), HAIR-CORDS (*tsĭtl'ŏl*)

The various types of Navaho weaving previously considered are products of the vertical loom (for even the saddle girth is woven by vertical suspension) and are of tapestry weave, with only the weft apparent on the face of the fabric. The belt loom with its raised-warp effects is used in weaving various narrow, long articles such as the woman's sash or belt, the garters and hair-cord that once were a part of the native costume, and the carrier-cord for the cradle. Some of these are illustrated in plate 21. All bear a strong general resemblance, differing mainly in size as determined by their function. The method of weaving was described in Chapter 3. The use of these articles is dying out, and their production is dwindling in consequence; unfortunately they lack the stimulus of commercial demand, which keeps the Navaho weaver at her loom today.

PLATE 53

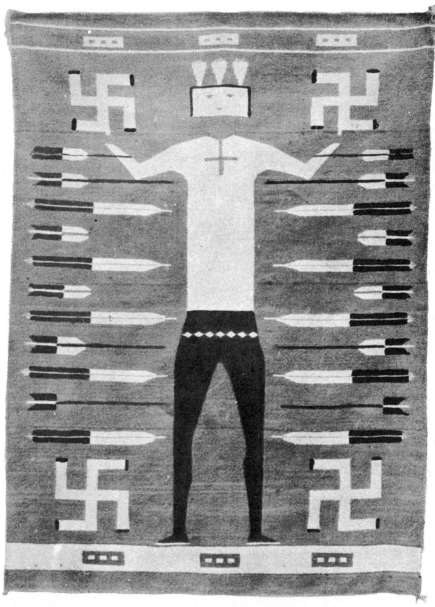

Yei blanket woven near Farmington, New Mexico, around 1910; about 48 x 60 ins. in size. Colors: black and white on red—all native wool, aniline dyes. Owner Mr. A. M. Amsden.

PLATE 54

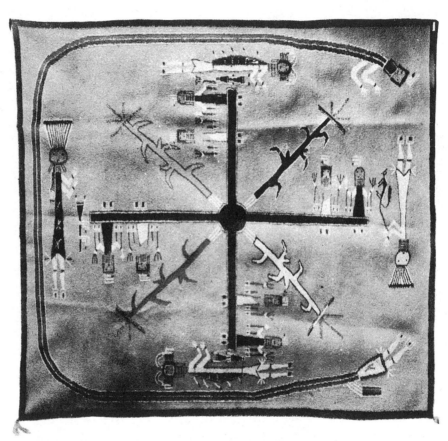

Sand painting blanket: **silnéole,** from the Night Chant. Size 66 x 69 ins., colors red, yellow, green, black, orange, white, on tan ground. F. K. Hinchman coll. Southwest Museum cat. 202L125.

Although a good copy of the sand painting, this specimen is not in any sense a ceremonial blanket. It was woven for sale, not for ceremonial use.

STOCKINGS OR LEGGINGS (*yistlé*)
According to the Ethnologic Dictionary (255-256):

Knitting is practiced by the Navaho to quite an extent. Like weaving, this, too, was originally borrowed from the Pueblo Indians. At present only steel needles are used in knitting, which are either purchased at the trading post, or made of wire or the ribs of an umbrella. These are broken to the proper length and slightly rubbed upon a stone to obtain a smooth blunt point.

Before steel and iron was available, knitting needles were made of wood, for which the slender twigs of . . . *Findlera rupicola*, or of . . .black greasewood, were used. Both are very hard and susceptible of a smooth, slick polish.

For knitting, blue, white and black yarns are used, and the present output of the knitting industry is limited to leggings and gloves. The latter are made with a separate thumb, although in late years some have also been knitted with all five fingers separate.

Leggings consist of long footless stockings, encasing the leg from kneecap to instep. At the top end a raised rim, about one-half to one inch wide, is knitted by using *left* stitches, that is, the yarn is passed from left to right instead of the usual way. This rim affords a hand grip, and also adds to the wear and tear in pulling on the legging. To distinguish the right from the left legging, and the inside from the outside, a line or ridge is knitted down along the outside of the leggings in relief, like a raised seam, by using *left* stitches at this point. At the lower end of the leggings a knitted or plaited wool cord is fastened, which passes under the foot below the instep, to keep the legging from working upward. The foot and lower legging is covered by the moccasin.

The stitch in knitting is closer and more tightly drawn than our own. Special care is paid to this feature to insure strength for long and hard usage.

Since leggings were always considered a part of the male attire (women have begun to wear them only in recent years) knitting was and still is mostly done by the men. The yarn leggings were not made or worn for riding purposes, for which they made leggings of leather or buckskin, and both were worn at the same time.

Pepper (1923) gives additional details apparently garnered at first hand:

> They use four needles to form the top and one to knit with. The name of the design on the side of the stockings, that is, on the outer surface, is *khi itoin*—the road that runs up the side of the legging. There is a form of stocking made with feet... Morgan [an informant] stated that a great many of the old women wore the white stockings whereas the blue and black ones were worn by the men. According to Mr. [Lorenzo] Hubbell the Isleta Indians used to make stockings with feet and then traded them with the Navahos. Stockings of small size, made for children, are called *yistle yazhe*.

A man knitting is shown in plate 55 and a pair of stocking-leggings in plate 56.

NAVAHO DRESS

Having reviewed in detail the old-time Navaho dress (for calico and overalls hold the field today) and noted the prime importance thereto of the loom, let us glance at the ensemble of tribal costume as it stood in the days when every family was its own tailor. First, then, a short description of the prehistoric or proto-historic costume of the days before looms and sheep, as told by the Navaho to the Franciscan Fathers of St. Michaels, Arizona (Ethnologic Dictionary: 457):

> The earliest Navaho costume was very meager and constructed of yucca and grass fiber. To obtain the pith the yucca leaves were boiled and pounded with a stone, then twisted and braided with mountain grass for such fabrics as the roof of the house, the mat for bedding, the leggings, shoes, and the blanket. This yucca blanket was occasionally braided with rabbit fur and as a rule provided with handles of the braided yucca on the sides and ends to better enable one in drawing it close to the body.

Later, this authority continues, the dress of the men became principally leathern (the women, one infers, passed directly from bast to wool in their clothing): a buckskin shirt, sinew-sewn, bartered from the Ute, with a fringed belt of the same material and buckskin breeches cut on a pattern evidently inspired by the Spaniard, with moulded legs and buttons down the side.[18] A shirt of four-ply buckskin and a helmet of the

---

[18] The Ethnologic Dictionary (457ff.) has drawings of these articles, none of which I have ever seen in actuality.

PLATE 55

Navaho man knitting. After Pepper 1923.

PLATE 56

a, Saddle girth, length 30 ins. Colors: white, red, green (both aniline). Southwest Museum cat. ACV163. No history.

b and c, Stocking-leggings. After Pepper 1923 .

same (pl. 57) were warrior's garb. The footgear of both sexes at about this period (say 18th century) is the leather moccasin.

Time passes, and the loom becomes the arbiter of Navaho fashion. W. W. H. Davis, who went as secretary to Governor David Merriwether on a treaty-making expedition among the Navaho in 1855, describes the change (411-412):

> They dress with greater comfort than any other tribe and wear woolen and well-tanned buckskin. The skin breeches come down to the knee, where they are met by blue stockings that cover the lower half of the leg; the breeches fit tight to the limb, and the outer seams are adorned with silver or brass buttons. The coat [19] reaches below the hips, with a hole at the top to thrust the head through and open at the sides; it is made of wool, woven in light colors, and is fastened around the waist by a leather belt highly ornamented with silver when the wearer can afford it. They wear numerous strings of fine coral, and many valuable belts of silver, and generally appear with a handsome blanket thrown over the shoulder in the style of a mantle.

Jonathan Letterman, Army surgeon at Fort Defiance in the same year, 1855, gives a more extended account of the native dress of the period (290), with which this chapter closes:

> The men clothe themselves somewhat differently. Some wear short breeches of brownish-colored buckskin, or red baize, buttoned at the knee, and leggings of the same material. A small blanket, or a piece of red baize with a hole in it, through which the head is thrust, extends a short distance below the small of the back, and covers the abdomen in front, the sides being partially sewed together and a strip of red cloth attached to the blanket or baize, where it covers the shoulder, forms the sleeve, the whole serving the purpose of a coat. Over all is thrown a blanket, under and sometimes over which is worn a belt, to which are attached oval pieces of silver, plain or variously wrought... The men, as a rule, make their own clothes. These articles constitute the only covering, together with the breech-cloth and moccasins, that are used. Many are seen who wear nothing but a blanket, and some in summer, nothing but the breech-cloth, and we

---

[19] [The native shirt is meant here, clearly, as it reaches just below the hips.]

have seen some with no covering but moccasins and a cotton shirt, when the mercury was below zero. The moccasin is made of buckskin, with a sole of raw-hide, and comes well up on the leg. It is fashioned alike for men and women. The latter wear a blanket fastened about the waist, and sewed up the sides for a skirt. The front and back parts being attached over either shoulder, a covering is obtained for the front and back portions of the body. The skirt comes down below the knee, about half way to the ankle, the leg being well wrapped in uncolored buckskin. . . As a general rule, neither sex wear any head-dress. . .

OUTLINE SUMMARY OF NAVAHO TEXTILES

A. Woman's dress
B. Man's shirt
C. Shoulder blanket
    Woman's
    Man's (chief blanket)
  Poncho
D. Serape
E. Saddle blanket
    Single
    Double
F. Saddle throw
G. Saddle girth
H. *Yei* blanket, sand-painting blanket
I. Sash, garter, hair-cord
J. Stockings or leggings

PART II
THE HISTORY OF
NAVAHO WEAVING

CHAPTER VIII

THE FIRST SHEEP

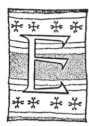VENTS that were to make loom-weavers of the Navaho moved rapidly after the dawn of the 16th century in the New World. Spanish settlement did not long remain confined to the islands of the West Indies where Columbus had planted his original colony in 1493, bringing in various European plants and animals, including goats and sheep. Florida, then thought to be an island, was the objective of the first serious attempts at conquest of the American mainland; but Juan Ponce de León's expeditions, beginning in 1513, met with stout resistance and gained no foothold. Pánfilo de Narvaez took up the task in 1527 with no better success, although his venture is memorable through the epic journey of four survivors of the Narvaez expedition—Cabeza de Vaca and his three companions, Dorantes, Maldonado, and the negro Estevanico—overland to the Spanish settlements in Mexico. These men traversed the southerly portion of the American Southwest and one of them was to guide an expedition into its very heart a few years later.

Meanwhile, in 1519, Hernán Cortés had landed on the east coast of Mexico, founded La Villa Rica de la Vera Cruz, burned his ships lest his men be tempted to return to them, and set forth overland to conquer the empire of Montezuma whose seat was in the Valley of Mexico. This effort was successful; Montezuma's capital became the City of Mexico, the nucleus of all Spanish activity in North America throughout the Colonial period. Colonization was pushed vigorously, farther and farther to the north and west; and when Cabeza de Vaca and his companions reached the present Mexican state of Sinaloa in 1536, they found fellow-countrymen living there. Scarcely a third of a century had elapsed since the first voyage of Columbus, yet the Spanish were already so firmly established in North America that they were giving ear to rumors concerning the mysterious territory to the north of their settled domain, and meditating further exploration and settlement.

FRAY MARCOS DE NIZA'S RECONNAISSANCE, 1539

Mendoza, Viceroy of New Spain, determined to know the truth about the northern country and its fabled Seven Cities.[1] He accordingly despatched Fray Marcos de Niza, a Franciscan monk of considerable experience in the New World, on a tour of reconnaissance. The negro Estevanico, or Esteban, the only one of Cabeza de Vaca's party except Dorantes to remain in New Spain, accompanied him as guide, and a number of friendly Indians went along as bearers of the cargo of presents or trade goods which every prudent explorer carried. This forethought probably saved the Friar's life, enabling him to buy his safety from his peddler's stock as he fled back to Mendoza with the report that was to determine the despatch of the Coronado Expedition.

The negro was sent ahead of the party and it was he who had the honor of being the first "European" to view a Pueblo village. In May or June, 1539, he reached Cíbola, the Zuñi settlements of present-day New Mexico. The first negro lynching in the annals of our country promptly followed. Fray Marcos, on learning of the event from Indian survivors of the advance party, was fearful of entering the villages, but contented himself with a view from a distant hilltop. Then he hastened back to the capital to report to the Viceroy that the Seven Cities did indeed exist, and he could testify that on the evidence of his own eyes one of them at least was a substantial and imposing settlement. The rumors of gold and jewels seemed more plausible than ever.

CORONADO'S EXPEDITION, 1540

The military force that Mendoza had determined to send northward if Fray Marcos' report justified the effort assembled in Compostela, on the Pacific Coast, in the early spring of the year 1540. Francisco Vasquez Coronado, Governor of the province of New Galicia, was captain-general of the expedition. Mendoza, who reviewed the force just before its departure, stated later that it comprised "about two hundred and fifty Spaniards on horseback—and about three hundred Indians, a few more or less." Other observers give quite different figures, but beyond a doubt the force was strong and well equipped.[2]

---

[1] The myth of the Seven Cities seems to have been a strange blend of European and Indian fantasy, nurtured by the thirst for gold and rendered credible by the unquestioned existence of much unexplored territory: might not there be another empire like that of Atahualpa in Peru or Montezuma in Mexico? Lowery, Chapter 5; Winship, Historical Introduction; and Bandelier 1883 and 1890, discuss the subject and the motives behind the expeditions of Marcos de Niza and Coronado. Lummis 1893 gives a vivid popular account of Spanish adventure in the Southwest.

Coronado's men captured the principal "city" of Cíbola—Hawikuh, now a ruined pueblo 12 miles southwest of present-day Zuñi—after a stiff fight with the inhabitants, on July 7, 1540, according to Winship. Within the village they found food in abundance: "corn, beans, fowls (turkeys) and fine white salt," but no gold. Fray Marcos, branded a deceiver by his companions, returned to Mexico in disgrace, but the forces he had set in motion were never stilled thereafter. Gold or no, there were souls to be saved and lands to be added to the dominions of Spain, and the expedition continued its march.

Pedro de Tovar was despatched with a small force to investigate the province of Tusayan, of which reports were given by the people of Cíbola. He spent several days in the Hopi villages composing this province, learning from the inhabitants of a mighty river to the westward. Returning to Cíbola, Tovar reported his discoveries to Coronado, who thereupon sent García Lopez de Cárdenas on a journey which resulted in the discovery of the Grand Cañon of the Colorado.

Hernando de Alvarado was sent eastward on a mission similar to that of Tovar. Passing Acoma on its high rock mesa [3] he pushed on to Tiguex, a village on the Rio Grande, near present-day Bernalillo. Hearing there were some eighty similar villages roundabout, he continued eastward and came to Cicuye or Pecos, the easternmost of pueblos and probably the largest of them all. Coronado with the main force soon joined Alvarado at Tiguex and the expedition went into winter quarters there, in the houses abandoned by the frightened inhabitants. During the winter the Indians captured a number of horses and mules—animals they had never seen before, just as they had never seen European sheep. [4] The winter passed in skirmishes and short tours of exploration, in the course of which the Spaniards found that they were indeed in a well-inhabited region. Villages of the Pueblo peoples were found at intervals of a few miles along the valley of the Rio Grande and its affluents from Jemez and Taos on the north, downstream in dwindling numbers to a point estimated by Castañeda as 130 leagues (about 350 miles) from the northernmost settlement.

---

[2] "The army left Compostela with 5,000 sheep and 150 cows of Spanish breed; these were the first that were brought into the country now forming the United States." (Hodge 1895: 227).

[3] The only pueblo which has been occupied continuously on the same site since 1540, authorities agree. Hodge 1895: 237; Kidder 1924: 40.

[4] Hernando de Alarcón, exploring the Colorado River from its mouth at about the time Tovar was at the Grand Cañon farther upstream, was told by the natives thereabouts that the strangers at Cíbola (Coronado's party) had with them "little blacke beastes with wooll and hornes," in Hakluyt's phrase as quoted by Winship: 405. Knowledge of sheep thus traveled far and fast, and we learn that black sheep were among the first introduced into the Southwest.

In the following spring the expedition set out on its bootless journey in search of Quivira, a reported rich province far eastward in the buffalo country, of which Coronado had heard tales while at Cicuye. They wandered long over the trackless plains, finding nothing but abundance of buffalo and a few semi-permanent grass-house villages of Indians, and in the end returned to the Pueblo country to pass the winter of 1541-42. Coronado was for returning to the Quivira region when spring came, but the army was disaffected and discouraged, poorly clad and equipped after its two years of wandering. The winter had been passed in struggles against the aroused and rebellious natives, and few members of the expedition to Quivira believed that the country held anything of sufficient value to justify further privation and danger. The return to Mexico was accordingly decided on and accomplished in the spring of 1542, *via* Cíbola and the general route followed on the outward march two years previously.

RESULTS OF CORONADO'S VISIT

Coronado's expedition accomplished little or nothing, yet was very important in several respects. It led indirectly to the colonization, half a century later, of the Rio Grande valley: to the establishment of the northernmost outpost of Spain in America—New Mexico. It brought Europe into contact with the Pueblo civilization, benefiting us today by the many accounts of the life and customs of the people in their strictly native state, which were given by members of the expedition on their return home. The first glimpse of a hitherto unknown people is the most precious of all, for everything it reveals is of truly indigenous character, whereas everything observed after alien contact has taken place must be weighed against the possibility of influence by that contact.

Coronado introduced European livestock into the Southwest, familiarizing the natives with those two animals in particular that were to alter their destinies so greatly in time to come: the horse and the sheep. Another result of the expedition, no less momentous perhaps, although of less fortunate character, was the enduring hatred of the Spaniard sown in the breasts of the natives by the brutal conduct of the invaders. Here began the long series of rankling insults and cruelties that culminated in the Pueblo Rebellion of 1680, that made the Mexican settler's possessions, even his family, fair prey to the Indian for many years after New Mexico had become a part of the United States. The sparks of the century-long guerrilla warfare that has flamed in the Southwest between native and invader were first kindled by Estevanico the Moorish negro: worthy emissary indeed of the great Christian power that had presumed to make the New World its appanage! Coronado's expedition contrived in many ways to fan the sparks into open flame, and from the time of its coming fuel was seldom wanting. The embers smolder still, for even today the Mexican is less welcome in some pueblos than the American.

A few of Coronado's followers remained behind. Friar Juan de Padilla, leader of the three missionaries accompanying the expedition, elected to return to Quivira with a Portuguese and several Indian companions; there he was later killed. Friar Juan de la Cruz remained at Tiguex, his life being taken less than a year after the departure of his companions. The third, Friar Luis Descalona, or de Ubeda, went to Pecos to establish the Christian faith there; and he, like the others, probably suffered martyrdom, although his fate is not recorded. A number of sheep were left with him, Castañeda says [5] (Winship: 535). Winship also records (401) that "many natives of the Mexican provinces stayed in the Pueblo country when Coronado abandoned it," a statement partly substantiated by Espejo who found at Zuñi three Mexican Indians who had come with Coronado more than 40 years before. Thus between the missionaries and the Mexican natives, the livestock strayed and stolen, and the arms and equipment that fell into Indian hands, a considerable leaven of European influence came into the native culture of the Southwest and found in varying degrees a permanent place therein.

NATIVE WEAVING

From the various accounts of the Coronado expedition as given by its members we can form a fairly complete and accurate picture of the pueblos and their inhabitants. Both villages and customs were so much like those of today that full description is scarcely necessary. Of particular interest to us is the question of weaving. Undoubtedly it was a common craft in most if not all of the pueblos, for references to it are frequent in

---

[5] Whether any of Coronado's sheep survived the 39 years that passed before Spanish sheep again entered the Southwest, to contribute to the Indians' flocks and herds of later times, is impossible to say. I think it quite likely. The Pueblo farmer, practical man that he is, would be quick to perceive the utility of an animal that could sustain itself on the natural vegetation of lands unsuited to farming; an animal which yielded useful wool and succulent flesh, and had the further advantage of being small, tractable, and easily sheltered against storms or invaders. On the other hand sheep, unlike swine (of which J. Frank Dobie gives an interesting account in his Vaquero of the Brush Country, pp. 34 and 35), would scarcely have the hardihood to perpetuate themselves in a wild state; hence any strays from the flocks could be counted as lost, and these first sheep and their issue may all have perished.

the various accounts. Castañeda, principal chronicler of the expedition, says of the pueblos of Tiguex that "the men spin and weave" (Winship: 521). Cotton was the usual textile fiber, as the numerous references clearly indicate; nowhere is there mention of woven woolens. Coronado in his letter of August 3, 1540, to Viceroy Mendoza, mentions that the people of Cíbola told him of Tucano (Tusayan) that "they raise much cotton there" (Winship: 562). Another chronicler confirms the statement, implying at the same time that at Cíbola cotton was not grown: "The villages [of Tusayan] are somewhat larger than those of Cíbola, and in other respects, in food and everything, they are of the same sort, except that these raise cotton" [6] (*Relación del Suceso,* in Winship: 574).

The Cíbolans did make use of cotton, however, for the narrative of Captain Juan Jaramillo of the Coronado expedition, as given in Winship (586), says in speaking of Cíbola: "They have square cloaks of cotton, some larger than others, about a yard and a half long. The Indians wear them over the shoulder like a gipsy, and fastened with an end over the other, with a girdle, also of cotton." The description of the cloak fits that found by Mr. Earl Morris in a prehistoric Pueblo grave in Cañon del Muerto, Arizona, as described in Chapter 2 herein; while the manner of wearing, down to the ultimate detail, may be seen among the Navaho today, as for example in plates 57, 69, 85, and is confirmed for the Pueblos by many drawings and photographs. Cotton was woven at Acoma, for there, according to the *Relación del Suceso* (Winship: 575), "they gave us cloaks of cotton;" and in the following paragraph the anonymous chronicler says of an unnamed pueblo on the Rio Grande that "they raise cotton." The loom is not described; we can only assume, on the evidence presented in previous chapters herein, that it was the vertical loom of the modern Pueblos and the Navaho, with a waist loom for weaving sashes and narrow kilts.

RODRIGUEZ AND ESPEJO, 1581-1583

For nearly forty years after Coronado's departure no European penetration of the Southwest is of record. Meanwhile the Spanish in Mexico were pushing northward in the central portion of the country, east of the Sierra Madre, and by 1580 mining outposts were in existence as far north as Parral in modern Chihuahua. From this region a small party under Fray Agustín Rodríguez in 1581 penetrated the Pueblo country by fol-

---

[6] Cf. Luxán: 91: "They say, however, that they obtain part of this cotton in trade from the province of Mohose (Moqui)." Bandelier says (1890 I: 37) that cotton was raised along the Rio Grande as far north as the latitude of Santa Fe, and his discussion of the whole question of clothing is excellent.

lowing up the Rio Grande—a route quite different from that taken by
Fray Marcos and by Coronado. They traveled extensively, generally con-
firming the accounts of the pueblos as given by the various chroniclers of
the Coronado expedition. The lower Rio Grande villages, beginning at
about the present town of San Marcial and extending northward at
lessening intervals as Tiguex was neared, had mantles of cotton in abundance, hence the people presumably were weavers.

Concern for the missionaries left behind by the Rodríguez party
prompted another expedition, that of Antonio de Espejo, who entered the
Pueblo country via the lower Rio Grande early in 1583. At the Hopi villages of Tusayan he was presented with four thousand cotton blankets,
"some colored and some white," Bolton records (165).[7] From the Espejo
narrative we glean a further interesting detail—that "the women (of the
Rio Grande pueblo region) wear cotton skirts, many of them being embroidered with colored thread;"—another custom which survives to this
day.[8] Hernán Gallegos, a member of the Rodríguez party, describes them
more fully (265):

> The men have their hair cut in the fashion of caps, so
> that they leave on their caps, I mean on the crown of their
> heads, a sort of skull cap formed by their own hair. Others
> wear their hair long, to the shoulders, as the Indians of New
> Spain formerly did. Some adorn themselves with painted cot-
> ton pieces of cloth three spans long and two-thirds wide, with
> which they cover their privy parts. Over this they wear,
> fastened at the shoulders, a blanket of the same material,
> painted with many figures and colors. It reaches to their
> knees like the clothes of the Mexicans. Some, in fact most
> of them, wear cotton shirts, hand painted and embroidered,
> that are very charming. They wear shoes. Below the waist

---

[7] From the various early narratives, one gets the distinct impression that the
Hopi were the most prolific weavers of all the Pueblo peoples—as they are known
to have been in later times, even unto the present day. According to Luxán (98,
102) Espejo's party was presented with 1400 blankets, together with "much spun
and raw cotton."

[8] Embroidery in aboriginal America was an art of high development, and apparently of wide diffusion. In Peru it reached a stage of great versatility, as shown
by Crawford 1916: 125, and O'Neale and Kroeber. The prehistoric Pueblos did embroidery particularly in their cotton textiles, using needles made of bone or wood,
or from a cactus spine or the tip of a yucca leaf. (Specimens of both embroidery
and needles are found in the P. G. Gates Collection in the Southwest Museum.) The
modern Pueblos embroidered their garments of cotton and of wool in elaborate
designs and many colors. The art has largely disappeared except among the Hopi,
who cling tenaciously to their ancient textile crafts.

the women wear cotton skirts, colored and embroidered, and above, a blanket of the same material, painted and worked like those used by the men. They wear it after the fashion of Jewish women. They girth themselves over it with cotton sashes adorned with tassels. They comb their hair, which is long.[9]

THE FOUNDING OF NEW MEXICO, 1598

Interest in the Pueblo region grew rapidly in Mexico, and several men of prominence there sought appointment as rulers and colonizers of this northern country. Some went so far as to set out and conduct extensive explorations without official warrant, but their parties were small and nothing of note was accomplished in this extra-legal fashion. The coveted honor was finally bestowed on Juan de Oñate, wealthy citizen of Zacatecas, in 1596; he was given supreme authority in the territory to be settled by his colony of "four hundred men, of whom one hundred and thirty had their families. For carrying baggage there were eighty-three wagons and carts, and a herd of more than seven thousand head of stock was driven on foot" (Bolton: 202). The caravan crossed the Rio Grande at the site of El Paso and reached in safety its destination, the pueblo of Caypa, christened San Juan, in the "province of the Teguas." Bolton continues (203):

> Oñate had already begun to visit the surrounding pueblos, and on August 11 work had been begun at San Juan on an irrigating ditch for the "city of San Francisco", the Spaniards being assisted by fifteen hundred Indians. On August 23 a church was begun and its completion was celebrated on September 8. Next day a general assembly was held of representatives from all the country thus far explored; rods of office were given to the chiefs, and the various pueblos were assigned to eight Franciscan missionaries, who soon afterwards departed for their respective charges. Thus was the province of New Mexico founded.

Oñate soon moved his headquarters to San Gabriel, now identified

---

[9] The words "painted" in this translation are probably a literal rendering of the Spanish pintado, which may mean dyed or colored as well as painted.

Villagrá, writing in 1610 of the Tigua Pueblos: "They dress in garments of cotton cloth, and the women wear beautiful shawls of many colors" (Canto XV); and of the Piro Pueblos: "The natives brought a great number of beautiful many-colored blankets" (Canto XV).

PLATE 57

a, Navaho warriors as seen by H. B. Mollhausen, well-known artist of several
early American exploring parties, about 1854. After pl. 23, vol. IV, **Reports of
explorations and surveys etc.**

b, Navaho dress about 1858, featuring plain stripes. Drawing by H. B. Mollhausen; after Ives plate VII.

Compare the shoulder blankets with plate 63a.

Map of the Navaho country as seen by Fathers Anastasio Dominguez and Silvestre Escalante, who in 1776 made a tour of exploration from Santa Fe to Utah Lake.

The "**Provincia de Nabajoo**" is outlined in heavy black and described as a region scanty in water and agricultural resources, but producing corn and vegetables in season, with sheep from whose wool (and from cotton as well) the Indians weave fine mantles with which they clothe themselves decently. "It is an Apache

nation, with the same language as the Gilas (western Apache), with little difference," the notice concludes.

The physical features, Indian pueblos, and Spanish settlements are located with accuracy and detail, although the archaic spellings make them hard to identify.

Copied from a photostat copy of the original in the national archives of Mexico by courtesy of Dr. F. W. Hodge.

PLATE 58

Chamita, at the junction of the Chama and Rio Grande rivers, site of the first Spanish settlement in the Southwest. Photo by Charles F. Lummis in 1891, from Lummis coll., Southwest Museum.

Cubero, a typical New Mexican village, with San Mateo (Mount Taylor) in the background. Ben Wittick photo, Wittick coll. Laboratory of Anthropology.

with Chamita, near the junction of the Chama River with the Rio Grande. Farms were established in the fertile valleys roundabout, among the Pueblo villages of the region. Santa Fe was founded about 1609-10. Colonization continued apace, and when the Pueblo Rebellion broke out in 1680 and swept every Spaniard from the land, some two thousand colonists and soldiers were established along the Rio Grande valley, from the vicinity of Santa Fe southward to El Paso. By 1693 Spain had reconquered her province of New Mexico and the native Indian was to have an alien master thenceforth to the present day. Further revolt in 1696 was quelled after bloody fighting.

The Pueblos never again gave serious trouble.[10] They settled themselves once for all into their old peaceful, hard-working routine of existence, pastoral now as well as agricultural; they became nominal Catholics, learned the Spanish language through force of necessity, and adopted the metal tools of the invader whenever these could be procured. The old native crafts of pottery-making and weaving were continued as before; and as time passed the spinners and weavers probably became quite oblivious of the fact that they were working with an alien substance—the wool of Spanish sheep—to the neglect of their own native textile fiber, cotton.[11]

---

[10] With a single exception, that of the Taos rebellon in 1847.

[11] There is no evidence that the Spanish horizontal pedal loom was ever adopted by the Pueblos. Why, indeed, should it be: an expensive, complicated affair, when their own native loom was so easily rigged, at such slight cost?

CHAPTER IX

EARLY NAVAHO WEAVING

HE Pueblo Southwest proved a lodestone to Indian as well as to Spaniard, and during about the same period. While Coronado, Espejo, Oñate, were marching northward to explore and colonize, Indian tribes from the north or northeast were moving down upon the mountain-bound plateau home of the Pueblos. This fact is not clearly of historic record, to be sure, yet as time passed and clashes between these two intruder peoples grew more marked and frequent, it became clear enough that the Southwestern situation was triangular to an alarming degree. Spaniard and Pueblo adjusted themselves to one another in course of time, only to find themselves beset by nomads who showed little respect to either. Coronado came upon an almost tranquil Pueblo land in 1540. His chroniclers mention vaguely a few non-Pueblo peoples, called "Querechos" after the name given locally to the inhabitants of the buffalo country to the east and later applied in a broader sense to any nomadic group, as "Chichimecos" was already being used in Mexico to designate a warlike people (Winship: 527, 580, 587-88). In later accounts the term figures more specifically, but still without any suggestion of these marginal wanderers as a dominant factor in the native population. Luxán, for example, mentions Querechos at war with the pueblo of Acoma, again in the "province of Moqui" (86, 87), and a "warlike mountainous people" living along the Little Colorado west of the Hopi villages (105).

More significant than these casual references are the omissions. Coronado met no Indians between the Gila valley and Cíbola or Zuñi, a region described at the time as the *despoblado,* or uninhabited country. Yet Benavides a short century later places "Apaches of Xila" in that general territory (42), and the Gila or western Apaches ever afterward made it their home. Where were they in Coronado's time? Espejo, like Tovar before him and Oñate after, met no Indians between Cíbola and Tusayan, where both Navaho and Apache later roamed. That is negative evidence of the absence of these tribes in the western territory in early historic times; but we have positive evidence of a similar situation in the east, at a time

later still. The Comanche of the western plains became a scourge of the
Rio Grande settlements in the 18th and 19th centuries, as we shall see.
Their advent is of historic record: Captain de la Serva tells categorically
of their first appearance in New Mexico in 1705 (Thomas: 57); and
Father Silvestre Vélez de Escalante wrote from Santa Fe on April 2, 1778,
to his superior, Father Juan Agustín Morfi (in Twitchell II: 269):

> Of the Comanches, if any information was had during
> the last century, it was not known until the present, when
> the Yutes [Ute] brought them to the pueblo of Taos. Today
> they govern nearly all of the plains and the buffalo country,
> which before the Yutes and the Apaches had ... And so, on
> the northeast, the east and the southeast they surround the
> kingdom, these Comanches; and on the north and northwest
> the Yutes, and from the west-northwest to the south, south-
> east are the Apaches.

The late Albert S. Gatschet told Dr. F. W. Hodge, after a study of
the Comanche language, that it was so nearly like that of the Shoshone of
the northwestern plains that he thought the two could not have been
separated more than two hundred years. Something similar could be said
of Apache and Navaho, linguistic cousins today and probably brothers in
a past not extremely remote. Their culture, too, is more of the plains than
of the Southwestern plateau. So, to summarize the point, we have much
to suggest that there were other new faces than Spanish in the Pueblo
country when the light of history first broke upon it.

For the Navaho, there is no reason to believe that they were encountered by any of the sixteenth century expeditions. Coronado entered
the Pueblo country at Cíbola and marched eastward to Tiguex and the
Rio Grande territory via Acoma. Subsequent expeditions reversed the
route (coming first to Tiguex by following up the Rio Grande from El
Paso) without changing its general lines; and it became almost traditional
to make the "grand tour" of the Southwest on a circuit roughly resembling
a thin, bent figure 8 laid on its side: the left-hand loop representing the
Zuñi and Hopi country, the right-hand loop the Rio Grande Pueblo
region, with Acoma as the central point where the loops meet. If anybody
pushed northward at any point along the circuit—toward the San Juan
river and the present Colorado-New Mexico boundary—the fact has
escaped notice. All accounts indicate clearly that the northernmost line of

pueblos marked the limit of Spanish exploration in the 16th century, and it seems proper to conclude that the Navaho were not encountered because they lived somewhere north of this line, where all but a few of them live today.

THE TRADITIONAL HOMELAND

Navaho tradition defines the homeland of the tribe quite as clearly, in general outline, as lines on a map, and Washington Matthews has recorded it all with his usual painstaking care in "The Navaho Origin Legend" (in Navaho Legends, 1897).

It is characteristic of a pantheistic folk to associate the outstanding physical features of its territory with the pantheon: Grecian mythology offers a familiar instance. In like manner is the Navaho country marked by points of major and minor importance in the legendry of the tribe. Each of the four cardinal points has its sacred mountain, the cosmic limit in that direction as seen through the mist of tradition. North is marked by a mountain (not surely identified) in the San Juan range of southwestern Colorado; South by Mount San Mateo, later called Mount Taylor, in the region of Laguna; East by a peak in the Jemez Mountains, thought by Matthews to be Pelado; West by the San Francisco Peaks, just north of Flagstaff, Arizona.

I have sought from many sources accurate identification of the four mountains marking the cardinal points, since Matthews is uncertain of two of them, and find general agreement that north is represented by Ute Mountain (or Sleeping Ute, Lazy Ute) in southwestern Colorado, east by Pelado, south by Mount Taylor, and west by the San Francisco Peaks. Those are the major points, the boundaries of the Navaho world as created by the tribal gods. Minor points are Hosta Butte, northeast of Gallup, New Mexico; Shiprock, in the northwest corner of the state; and *El Cabezón* (Spanish for the Great Head) between Jemez and Mount Taylor. *El Cabezón* is the head of a god, and the great beds of lava lying south and west of Mount Taylor are his blood (Matthews 1897: 221, 234).

Tradition is not fact, to be sure, but the identification of definite physical features with the origin myths of a people is sound evidence of passably long residence amid those features; hence there is no good reason to doubt that the Navaho occupied the region outlined above at a time remote enough to justify its association, plausibly, with the origins of the tribe.

TRIBAL BEGINNINGS

Of the character of those origins we have some interesting evidence through the patient researches of Dr. F. W. Hodge, who in a paper on "The Early Navajo and Apache" correlated Matthews' legendry of Navaho origins with his own broad knowledge of Spanish historical sources and drew a number of conclusions that seem eminently sound in the main. These will now be summarized and tested against other evidence on the same point.

The intermediate social unit among the Navaho is the clan. As with the Pueblos, the Navaho trace most of their clans back to a tribal accretion of alien groups or individuals, the founders of the clan. Hodge, taking Matthews' legendary accounts of clan beginnings, shows how successive groups from surrounding peoples joined the original (apparently small) tribal unit, swelling its numbers to the point of making the Navaho an ever-growing menace to the Pueblos roundabout. We have only the evidence of the tradition for the addition of Utes, of Apaches, of an unidentified Shoshonean group, and of various Pueblo units. But parts of the legend of Navaho origins have their roots in historic time and are subject to factual analysis.

Thus a Mexican clan, originating in a raid on a Spanish colony near Socorro, New Mexico, could not possibly have come into existence before the 17th century, for want of European settlement in that region. Similarly, Hodge shows that a clan group from the salt lake south of Zuñi is identifiable with abandonment, not long before Coronado came to Cíbola, of Marata, the Zuñi community on that spot, whose walls were found standing by Coronado's party. And the abandonment of Marata is almost of historic record, for Fray Marcos de Niza in 1539 talked with an old Zuñian—living in exile with a tribe farther south—who remembered Marata and thought it still inhabited!

Working backward from these known historic points, with the "age of an old man" as his unit of time measure, in accordance with the traditional Navaho method of reckoning, Hodge places the very beginnings of the Navaho tribe at about 1485 A. D. Matthews, working on legendary testimony without the aid of historical evidence, had carried the tribe back to "between 500 and 700 years ago, or seven ages of old men" (Hodge 1895: 223); that is, back to 1200 to 1400 A. D. Matthews' is a calculation based on the tribe's own version of its beginnings; Hodge's is revision of the same body of evidence in the light of historic factors that touch the story at certain points. Both lead very definitely to the conclusion that the Navaho tribe is of mixed ethnic character and of rapid and recent formation: a *parvenu* people like their ultimate conquerors, the Americans; and both calculations rest, in the last analysis, on the shifting sands of tradition.

There is, however, much more evidence pointing toward the conclusions just reviewed. The cliff-dwellings and abandoned pueblos of the Navaho country figure in tradition as ruins, formerly the abode of gods (Ethnologic Dictionary: 30); and we know positively, through archeological research checked and verified by the tree-ring chronology of Dr. A. E. Douglass (1929) that several of the most conspicuous ruins in the heart of the Navaho country—Pueblo Bonito and others of Chaco Cañon in particular—were inhabited as late as 1000 A. D., while others farther west, in Cañons de Chelly and del Muerto, date well into the 13th century. Inferentially, then, the Navaho came upon these ruins after the dates given.

The mixed physical character of the Navaho, as suggested by the legend of origins, is verified by the anthropological studies of Ales Hrdlicka (1900), who finds a great diversity of physical traits: so great, indeed, that everyone who troubles to observe the Navaho with more than cursory interest soon sees that the tribal physical types range from the squat solidity of the Pueblos to the tall, sinewy build of the tribes of the Great Plains.

Navaho culture reveals this same mixed character. On the ceremonial side it appears to have borrowed heavily from the Pueblos; its basketry is strongly Shoshonean;[1] its pottery, utterly un-Southwestern, and the earth-lodge type of dwelling or hogán, both greatly resemble those of the Mandan of the Plains; while weaving, the outstanding tribal craft, is Puebloan in its very essence. Language, it is true, fails to support the conclusion of Matthews and Hodge. Dr. Edward Sapir informs me that the Navaho speech is Athapascan of surprising purity, considering the obvious vicissitudes of tribal development. But we might remember in this connection that the Nordics and Latins who figure so largely in the American nation have changed our speech but little from that of England today; and that the language of a dominant people, history reveals, comes little scathed through tremendous changes in the social and ethnic structure. All in all, there is little evidence of tribal antiquity and homogeneity

---

[1] Most Navaho basketry of today is either Paiute or Ute (both Shoshonean tribes) with a foundation of three rods, but Weltfish says of the older type which has a two-rod and bundle foundation that it is the "only basketry of modern times which in all technical details duplicates the work of the ancient Basket Makers" (470). The Shoshonean character of Basketmaker material culture was first noted, I think, by Kidder (1924: 118).

in the Navaho, whether we view them in the light of their own traditions or in that of extraneous circumstance.

LOCATION IN EARLY HISTORIC TIMES

If the Navaho tribe grew rapidly from small beginnings, one would expect to finds its territorial strength in commensurate increase; and this in fact seems to be the case. There is good reason to believe the tribe centered in early historic times in the northeastern portion of its later broad domain, with the San Juan river marking its northwesterly limit and the foothills of the high mountains lying along the present Colorado-New Mexico boundary as a barrier to the northeast. Southward lay the chain of Pueblo villages of the Rio Grande valley, westward a vast empty area which the ambitious tribe was rapidly to make its own.

The very name Navaho has an association with this northeastern territory in the most generally accepted explanation of its origin.[2] Dr. Edgar L. Hewett (1906) points out that

> in the second valley south of the great pueblo and cliff village of Puye in the Pajarito Park, New Mexico, is a small pueblo ruin known to the Tewa Indians as Navahú, this being, as they claim, the original name of the village. The ruined villages of this plateau are all Tewa of the pre-Spanish period. This particular pueblo was well situated for agriculture, there being a considerable acreage of tillable land nearby—far more than this small population would have utilized. . . The Tewa Indians assert that the name "Navahú" refers to the large area of cultivated lands. This suggests an identity with Navajó which Fray Alonso de Benavides, in his Memorial on New Mexico published in 1630, applied to that branch of the Apache nation (Apaches de Navajó) then living to the west of the Rio Grande, beyond the very section above mentioned. Speaking of these people Benavides says: "But these (Apaches) of Navajó are very great farmers, for that is what Navajo signifies—'great planted fields.'

The word Navajo as a geographical term must have been well established in earlier times, for Gregg (I: 284), writing in 1844, speaks of the "ruins of Pueblo Bonito, lying in the direction of Navajo."

---

[2] Derivation from Spanish words (for the Spanish first used the name in writing) has been suggested: from nava, a plain, or navaja, a clasp-knife. But although the words fit the case nicely, the historical connection is hard to establish.

THE NAVAHO IN HISTORY

The first known historical reference to the Navaho[3] places them in the region whence their name is believed to derive. It is found in the *Relaciones* of Father Gerónimo Zárate-Salmerón, a history of Spanish activities in California and New Mexico between 1538 and 1626. The pertinent portion follows:

> When I said to these Hemez[4] that if there were guides I would gladly go to discover this nation. . . they replied that . . . (one had only to) go out by way of the river Zama (Chama) and that past the nation of the Apache Indians of Nabahó (our Navajos) there is a very great river (this was the upper course of the Colorado or Buena Esperanza) . . . and that the river suffices for a guide. And that all was plain with good grasses and fields between the north and the northwest; that it was fertile land, good and level, and that there are many nations—the province of Quazulas—the qusutas (Utas) and further inland another nation settled."

The geographic location of the "Apache Indians of Nabahó" is clear beyond question: it was between the Chama and the "very great river" that "suffices for a guide," which must be the San Juan, largest eastern tributary of the mighty Colorado.[5] North of this river lived the Ute— surely the "qusutas" of the old chronicler—with whom the Navaho have fought and traded for centuries.[6] The intervening country is as described, even today: "all plain with good grasses and fields between the north and the northwest."

Here, then, lived the Navaho when the light of history first fell upon them. The Ethnologic Dictionary (26 and 30) corroborates both the location of the tribe in early times and its antiquity as determined by Matthews and Hodge: "The Navaho still speak of a region, which they call *'dinetqa'* (*diné* country) and which their fathers occupied before

---

[3] The Apache, cousins of the Navaho through their common Athapascan linguistic affiliation, precede them in history by only a few years: Oñate mentions them in 1599 in a letter to the Viceroy of New Spain, locating them in "this eastern country" along with the people of Pecos. See Bolton: 212, 218, for the translated passage.

[4] [People of Jemez pueblo, who had told Father Gerónimo of a nation living to the northwestward, who spoke the ancient Aztec tongue. This nation may have been the Ute, distant linguistic kinsmen of the Aztec.]

[5] Despite Lummis, as just quoted, because the Colorado is distant, with rugged mountain ranges intervening. The only "very great river. . . past the nation of the Apache Indians of Nabahu" is the San Juan.

[6] "Ute River" was an old Navaho name for the San Juan, Mr. Earl Morris has told me.

they came to their present habitat. This region, according to their traditions, corresponds to the modern Jemez country and the Tewa country." The authors conclude that the tribe moved down the eastern slope of the Rockies and entered the Southwest some 500 years ago. For further confirmation we have the statement of Benavides (43-53) dating from 1630, that he founded a monastery at Santa Clara pueblo for the conversion of the Navaho; and the note by Hodge in the same work (243) that the Navaho caused the abandonment of Jemez pueblo about 1622, by their frequent raids. Luxán (86) tells of trouble between Acoma and the Querechos and it is possible that these were the Navaho, since Acoma is not far from the sacred mountain of the south, Mount Taylor. Zuñi and Hopi apparently were not molested until a later time,[7] although from early in the 18th century until the subjugation of the fractious tribe by American troops in the middle of the 19th, the Navaho were among their most dreaded enemies.

THE NAVAHO BECOME WEAVERS

We have seen the Navaho definitely brought into the historic scene by Zárate-Salmerón and Benavides early in the 17th century, but neither of these chroniclers indicates in any way that weaving was a tribal craft. In the case of Zárate-Salmerón little importance need be attached to this negative evidence, for he is concerned mainly with Spanish affairs.

Benavides, however, is in another situation; his Memorial is devoted largely to a description of the customs and the industries of the natives of New Mexico, and this subject is treated with sufficient thoroughness to assure mention of any activity important enough to serve as a descriptive detail. Weaving in particular is emphasized and lauded by Benavides when he speaks of the Pueblos, for the good friar is writing, in fact, a campaign document (as Bandelier remarked) designed to impress the high Spanish authorities, that they may be moved to support more generously the colonization of New Mexico and the conversion of its native peoples. He puts the Indians in their best light always, not forgetting to stress the economic aspects of his subject, with a canny appeal to avarice as well as to Christian zeal. The natural resources of the province are not overlooked, nor is the fact that every Pueblo household pays an annual tribute to the Spanish authorities of one *vara* (33 inches)

---

[7] An old Hopi man told Dr. F. W. Hodge that the Ute, not the Navaho, were the traditional enemies of the Hopi, clearly implying that the Navaho came later. Bancroft (201) has Navaho and Hopi in communication in 1692. Spier (1928) was told that the Havasupai first saw Navaho among them about 1860 (362 ff.).

PLATE 59

Bayeta poncho serape bought by Charles F. Lummis in 1889 from Martin Valle, governor of Acoma pueblo, who got it thirty years before from a Navaho war chief. Colors bayeta red, indigo blue, white. Size 55 x 72 ins. Weft count 13 warp and 44 (white) weft strands, both of these being native spun. The 2-ply bayeta weft is hardly finer than the native. Lummis coll. Southwest Museum cat. 547G2. Colorist: Mr. Clifford Park Baldwin.

Massacre Cave, Cañon del Muerto, Arizona. From the jutting cliff at the upper left the Spanish soldiers fired into the cave, which is hidden behind the mass of fallen rock slabs in the right foreground of the same view. Below is shown the interior of the cave, with bones of the victims still strewn about. The skulls were carried away as souvenirs years ago. The white dots on the overhanging ledge are marks of the Spanish musket balls. Photographs by courtesy of Mr. Earl H. Morris.

PLATE 60

A Massacre Cave fragment. Indigo blue and white stripes outlined in black, basket weave—in short typically Pueblo although its history is Navaho. The material is wool. Brooklyn Museum cat. 3830.

of cotton cloth. If the genteel and economically useful craft of weaving had been found among the Navaho, this shrewd propagandist would not have overlooked it, we may be sure; for he displays a particular interest in that tribe, devoting several pages of his Memorial to an account of his efforts to convert it to Christianity and to a description of its customs. Benavides mentions Navaho agriculture, describes the Navaho hogán, indicates that the tribe lives by hunting and is skilful at leather work (they made him a present of dressed deerskins). But of weaving there is not a word; so we may conclude that the craft was either non-existent or of slight importance among the Navaho in 1629.

Unfortunately for this study of Navaho weaving, the remainder of the 17th century is almost barren of available historical records. The Pueblo Rebellion of 1680 came as the culmination of a long period of friction between native and Spaniard and it undid nearly all that had been accomplished toward settlement and conversion. Every colonist was swept from the land during the twelve troubled years that followed, and most of the Spanish records within the province were destroyed. But we know that the Navaho took no stand in the conflict between native and invader. They used the war as a lever for their own ends, preying on the harassed Spanish forces and the hard-pressed revolting Pueblo communities with complete impartiality, and their flocks and horse-herds grew rapidly in consequence.[8]

The tribe grew as well during these troubled times. Many pueblos sent their non-combatants into the Navaho country for refuge when capture by the dethroned conquerors seemed the only alternative,[9] and numbers of these refugees were merged into the tribe. If the Navaho were not already weavers, certainly they had a golden opportunity of becoming such during the Pueblo Rebellion, with experts in the craft living among them, and their flocks growing rapidly. In the light of this situation (and bearing in mind that Spanish colonists with their European sheep had been in New Mexico only one century) it is highly probable that the Pueblo Rebellion established weaving among the Navaho, and that we may consider it a tribal craft from then onward.[10] Some beginnings may have

---

[8] Bancroft gives a brief account of Navaho activities during this period. See in particular pp. 201, 222, 223.

[9] Kidder (1920) describes ruins in Gobernador Cañon in northwestern New Mexico which show a jumble of Navaho and Pueblo house structures, and pottery characteristic of both peoples; concluding that they date from this period when Pueblo and Navaho lived for a brief time together.

It is known, too, that the Jemez fled to the Navaho in 1696, under Spanish pressure.

[10] There is a story—vaguely legendary—that the Navaho compacted with the

been made earlier, to be sure, but it would be rash to assume that a tribe of semi-nomadic huntsmen could—in the short space of a century—make the fundamental readjustments implicit in the pastoral mode of life and the practice of weaving. The sheep, like the horse, was predestined to become a dominant factor in the tribal life, making basic and far-reaching alterations in its pattern. This helpless little animal, supplying as it did the meat and the clothing of the tribe, moved into a position of economic dominion over its masters which altered the destinies of the Navaho nation for all time to come. An embarrassing hostage to fortune it finally proved to be, for when the Navaho were at last conquered and induced to live peaceably on a reservation as wards of the American government, it was the slaughter of their flocks that brought them to their knees in submission. Civilization conquered the Navaho not with the gun or the gospel, but all unwittingly, by means of the lowly sheep!

HISTORICAL RECORDS OF WEAVING

When research historians shall have laid before us more fully the mass of historical data on provincial New Mexico which is now buried in the archives of Spain and Mexico, we shall certainly find in it some reference to Navaho weaving in the early 18th century.[11] But for the present the history of this craft begins with a sentence found in a letter from Teodoro de Croix, Commander-General of the Interior Provinces of New Spain, to his superior José de Galvez, written February 23, 1780, and translated by Thomas (144) as follows:

> The Navajos, who although of Apache kinship have a fixed home, sow, raise herds, and weave their blankets and clothes of wool, might follow the good example of the Moqui. . .

Croix speaks from experience, not hearsay, for he was then in New Mexico, engaged in the task of adjusting (by armed diplomacy) the rebellious tendencies of the various native tribes to the colonial policy of

Hopi to teach them weaving. It does not ring true to the anthropologist, who knows that crafts and customs are generally diffused without such conscious and deliberate fostering. The practical American mind sees nothing shocking in the abrupt abandonment of practices hallowed by tradition and custom, in favor of new ones; but the Indian mind would certainly recoil from such a step.

[11] For example: Bancroft (247) has a promising reference to an official investigation of missionary affairs in New Mexico in 1745, at which "a dozen witnesses formally told the governor all they knew about the Navahos, which was not much." His information came apparently from "a manuscript in the Pinart collection." It must be said, too, that Hodge in Benavides summarizes various unsuccessful missionary efforts among the Navaho during the 18th century, but without mention of weaving (note 45, p. 268).

PLATE 61

a and b, Two Massacre Cave fragments. a is undyed, with brown and black alternating stitch by stitch in the narrow bands, on a white ground. b also is white, with a beaded black stripe above and three composite stripes showing black center outlined in reddish brown, probably native dye, and that bordered by very thin strips of red bayeta, 4-ply. Wm. Claflin Jr. museum cat. 6443.

c and d, Blanket fragments from White House, Cañon de Chelly. The Navaho often bury their dead in caves once occupied by the ancient peoples, and archeologists find fragments of their blankets scattered by burrowing rats. These have no date but are much like the Massacre Cave fragments dated 1804-05. c and d apparently from the same piece, with natural gray-white and brown-black wool stripes (broad) the latter flecked with yellow of native dye; darkest thin stripes a native red-brown, next darkest (medium width stripes) a native green. Peabody Museum cat. 89598.

PLATE 62

Blanket fragments from White House, Cañon de Chelly.* a has an original corner with its tassel at the upper left; colors natural brown-black wool with one stripe of indigo and two of native green at the corner tip. b all natural brown-black wool.

c has no history, but its resemblence to the ancient shoulder blanket of pl. 63 is striking. Natural rusty-black and white wool in alternate stripes of about one inch width is the material throughout. Selvage two cord, each three-ply, thread count 11 warp, 20 weft to the inch. Peabody Museum cat. 89598. Photographs by Mr. F. P. Orchard.

Spain on this northern frontier of its vast empire of the New World.

A task of heroic proportions it was proving to be, as Thomas makes clear. The thin line of Spanish settlements dotting the valleys of the Rio Grande and its tributaries from El Paso to Taos was completely ringed about with marauding and restive tribes. The Comanche menaced the entire western face of this fragile wall of *presidios,* missions, and homesteads. The Apache swung in a long curve across its southern and westerly exposures from the Pecos to the Gila, a constant menace to the northern settlements in the Pueblo territory and to the Sonora frontier (Spain's second line of frontier defense) as well. The Hopi province on the northwest corner of Spanish territory had made good its independence and was a constant source of irritation if not of open trouble. Northward—foes alike of the Hopi and the Spanish—lay the Ute; and between them and the Spanish settlements of the Chama valley, as we complete our circuit, were the Navaho, growing constantly bolder and stronger in their challenge to Spanish protection of the Pueblo villages whose spoliation was becoming a tribal custom. Of all these enemies the Navaho were to prove the boldest and the hardest to control in the century to follow. Unlike the Apache, who lay between the Spanish lines of frontier posts, they could never be hemmed in. At no time did Spanish or Mexican military strength feel equal to the task of surrounding them and pressing upon them from all sides at once.[12]

From the same work of Thomas upon the vicissitudes of Spanish rule in 18th century New Mexico we gain another interesting glimpse of the Navaho, this in 1785. The reference is to an expedition of military-diplomatic character by Spanish frontier officials to break up an alliance between Navaho and Gila (western) Apache. Thomas (350) translates:

> The interpreter on his part informed the governor that the Navajo nation has 700 families more or less with 4 or 5 persons to each one in its five divisions of San Matheo, Zebolleta or Cañon, Chusca, Hozo, Chelli with its thousand men of arms; that their possessions consist of 500 tame horses; 600 mares with their corresponding stallions and young; about 700 black ewes, 40 cows also with their bulls and calves, all looked after with the greatest care and diligence for their increase.

---

[12] A good contemporary account of the Indian menace to 18th century New Mexico is found in "Governor Mendinueta's Proposals for the Defense of New Mexico, 1772-1778," translated by Professor Thomas in New Mexico Historical Review, VI: 21-39.

This brief account is packed with information, as a short analysis will reveal. Seven hundred families of four or five persons in each make a tribal total of some three thousand souls; a goodly number, but perhaps not quite enough to justify the "thousand men of arms."

The tribe is well equipped with livestock, it will be noted, but horses are still more numerous than sheep at this early period, while cattle attain an insignificant total; but the Navaho never were cattlemen. Horses and sheep were ever their favorites. Cattle consume the pasturage needed for horses, but sheep can graze fat where those animals would starve.

The "five divisions" mentioned reveal a geographic extension much greater than that suggested by the 17th century references previously quoted. The tribe has progressed rapidly in its westward expansion, for Chusca (Chusca Mountains, evidently) and Chelli (Cañon de Chelly) are almost in Hopi territory. Zebolleta (near Laguna pueblo) and San Matheo (Mt. Taylor) with "Hozo" mark its southern extent. The latter evidently is *Ojo del Oso* or Bear Spring, where Doniphan made a treaty with the Navaho in 1846 (Chapter 11). It is at the present site of Fort Wingate, east of Gallup, New Mexico. Taking the San Juan river as the approximate northern limit and the Jemez region as the eastern, we have the tribal territory quite accurately defined as of the year 1785, and it shows little change today.

The next historical reference to Navaho weaving is quoted by Bloom (233) from the Spanish archives of New Mexico, document number 1335, as follows, the quotation being an excerpt from a letter from Governor Fernando de Chacón to Pedro de Nava, military commander in Chihuahua, written July 15, 1795:

> The Navajoes, whom you suspect may have aided the Apaches in their incursions, have since the death of their general Antonio been irreconcilable enemies, to such a degree that with us they have observed an invariable and sincere peace. These Gentiles are not in a state of coveting herds (of sheep), as their own are innumerable. They have increased their horse herds considerably; they sow much and on good fields; they work their wool with more delicacy and taste than the Spaniards. Men as well as women go decently clothed; and their Captains are rarely seen without silver jewelry; they are more adept in speaking Castilian than any other Gentile nation; so that they really seem "town" Indians much more than those who have been reduced...

PLATE 63

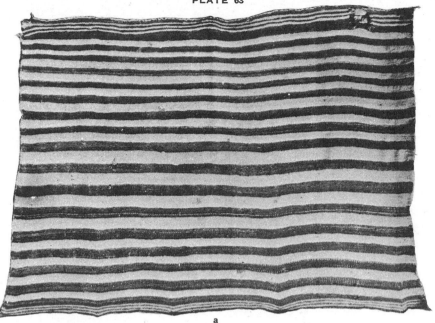

a

b

a, Old Navaho shoulder blanket. Size 66 x 48 ins., colors natural brown and white with a single strand of indigo blue. Found buried in a cave cist with the mummified body of a tall, spare man. His hair was tied in a hank and he wore deer skin leggings with woven garters, and a woven shirt. With the burial were buffalo and deer skins and the shoulder mantle or dress of Pueblo (woman's) type, black with indigo blue border in diamond twill, size 63 x 45 ins., shown in b; yet the man was Navaho, the burial in Navaho territory.

To assign these specimens to about the year 1800 seems no exaggeration in view of all circumstances.

PLATE 64

Two chief blankets from the Sitgreaves expedition of 1851. Sam W. Woodhouse, naturalist of the party in its explorations around Zuni, New Mexico, bought these two specimens and his son sold them to the Museum of the American Indian, Heye Foundation.

  a size 69 x 50 ins., cat. 11-8280; b 76 x 54 ins., 11-8281. Colors in each are broad stripes of black and white, narrower ones of indigo blue and red bayeta.

Advancing now to the year 1799, Navaho weaving is set forth as not merely a tribal craft, but an industry which is becoming an economic factor in the province. Don José Cortez, "an officer of the Spanish royal engineers, when stationed in that region," wrote then that "the Navajos have manufactures of serge, blankets, and other coarse cloths, which more than suffice for the consumption of their own people; and they go to the province of New Mexico with the surplus, and there exchange their goods for such others as they have not, or for the implements they need."[13]

Soon thereafter another reference appears, for which I am indebted to Dr. F. W. Hodge. It is found in Pedro Pino's *Exposición del Nuevo Mexico,* printed in 1812. Pino, who went to Spain in 1811 as a delegate from New Mexico to the Spanish parliament, wrote (41) of the Navaho that "their woolen fabrics are the most valuable (*apreciables*) in our province, and Sonora and Chihuahua (as well)."

Of these four earliest known references to Navaho weaving, each is more definite and emphatic than its predecessor. Croix in 1780 merely mentions the Navaho as weavers. Chacón in 1795 concedes them supremacy over the Spaniards in "delicacy and taste" in weaving. Cortez in 1799 makes it clear that the production of blankets more than suffices for tribal needs. Pino in 1812 categorically places Navaho weaving at the head of the textile industry in three large provinces: significantly ahead even of the Pueblo craft, which mothered that of the Navaho.

On abundant evidence, then, the Navaho had gained a recognized supremacy in native Southwestern weaving in wool as early as the opening of the 19th century; and down to the present day that supremacy has never been relinquished. The Hopi craftsmen may have shown more conscience and conservatism at certain times, but the Navaho women have proved the more versatile, imaginative and progressive, and the Navaho blanket has always been the favored child of that odd marriage of the native American loom with the fleece of European sheep.

---

[13] From "Reports of Explorations and Surveys," etc. Vol. III, Part III: 120. Mr. Frederic H. Douglas brought this reference to my notice.

A possible earlier reference to trade in Navaho blankets is cited by Bloom (232). It is from the correspondence of Governor Fernando de la Concha in 1791, Spanish archives of New Mexico, document no. 1176. Twitchell summarizes it (II: 339) as "new Navajo trade in peltries and fabrics, etc.", which Bloom says Concha initiated.

CHAPTER X

BAYETA—1800-1863

HE dawn of the 19th century found the Navaho firmly established, as we have seen, as makers of woolen blankets for barter with the Spanish no less than for their own use. Henceforth, then, Navaho weaving is to have an economic aspect of much broader scope than the tribal horizon. It is to enmesh the haughty and independent tribe ever more deeply in the web of alien affairs and fortunes from which as yet it stands so fiercely aloof, until a century later we shall find that the Navaho has all but abandoned the use of his own textiles in favor of American machine-made cloth, while the American (who meanwhile has become New Mexico's ruler) is demanding for his own use an ever-increasing output of Navaho blankets.

A series of factors and circumstances of widely diverse character attends the rapid rise of this obscure tribal craft which is eventually to become one of the recognized American industries. First came the loom, in the hands of the prehistoric Pueblos; next the introduction of sheep by the Spanish; then the Pueblo Rebellion of 1680-92, in which Spaniard and Pueblo unwittingly combined to foster weaving among the Navaho. Next link in this curiously diverse chain of Navaho economic destiny is a fabric, fresh from the Old World: a woolen cloth whose smooth, hard-twisted threads are to stimulate the Navaho weaver to such fine spinning and tight weaving of her own native wool as she would never have deemed possible; whose rich and vivid colorings are to serve as a spur to the development of native dyes of a hue worthy to stand beside them in the blanket whereof the shredded fibers of this European fabric (in what a strange reincarnation!) are the center and the inspiration. A fabric, this, which is to bring the Navaho woman to the full term of her patient skill and artistry, to win admiration and eulogy for her handiwork the world around, to command for it fabulous prices long after she has gone to her grave.[1] Its name is *bayeta,* or in plain English, baize. But the blunt

---

[1] Good bayeta blankets often sell for more than $1,000. To my own knowledge, $2,500 was once paid for a Navaho blanket of ordinary serape size.

English term seems unworthy of the romantic associations which cling to the Spanish word *bayeta*. It does less than justice, somehow, to the legendry and controversy that center in this fabric, to the strange blend of fact and fiction which, briefly, we shall now review.

BAYETA IN HISTORY

The prudent explorer when going among primitive peoples always includes in his equipment a few gewgaws and trinkets: beads, mirrors, effigies, knives, tinkling bells, perhaps; but by all means, a few yards of brightly colored cloth. Such inexpensive things are highly esteemed by uncivilized folk, and their value is far beyond that of the mere money which bought them before the expedition set forth. Fray Marcos de Niza, as we have seen, carried a store of trade goods upon his visit to the Seven Cities of Cíbola in 1539, and with them purchased his safety by placating a hostile Indian retinue as he fled back toward Mexico. Down through the days of Spanish conquest and colonization, of the Chihuahua Fair, the Santa Fe Trail, and the Atlantic and Pacific Railroad, such goods have been pouring into the Southwest. Missionary, soldier, peddler, trapper, Indian trader, have kept the stream flowing, and it flows today: a stream of gimcracks and small utensils, and bolts of cloth in brilliant colorings.

Stout flannel of deep red color was in especial favor with all concerned in this commerce in early days. It pleased the native greatly, for something with which to bedeck the person and minister to vanity as well as comfort filled a genuine if not a vital want. It lent itself perfectly to the exigencies of primitive transport, for it was light, compact, unbreakable, and immune to damage by heat and cold and dampness. In case of need it could be fashioned into warm clothing for the members of the party which carried it. All in all, a few bolts of baize were well worth their cost and the effort of carrying them, as every explorer knew. Not only in the Southwest, but everywhere in America, this fabric was finding its way into native hands throughout the period of European conquest, to be cut into squares and ribbons and used to embellish the clothing and accouterments of its delighted owners. Many of the articles thus ornamented are to be seen in museums and private collections today. By the weight and quality of the flannel and by the tone of its color, one may make a fairly accurate estimate of its age and provenience. The stout baize of a century ago is heavy, with thick warp and weft strands well spun and sturdily woven; its color is ordinarily a finely-toned, perhaps slightly rosy crimson, the hue of

PLATE 65

a

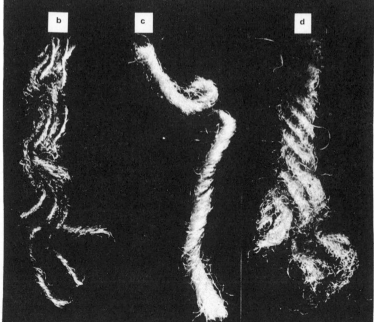

a, A flannel strip blanket, reversed twill weave, size 29 x 35 ins., colors indigo blue and white on a ground of scarlet strips of flannel. Mrs. C. Matthews coll. U. S. National Museum cat. 281491. Made probably in the eighties.

Bayeta (b) native (c) and machine-spun (d) weft strands. Enlarged 3½ times. Note that the native is all of a piece, the bayeta a loose bunch of threads but slightly twisted, the Germantown a tight spiral.

PLATE 66

A flannel strip blanket, plain weave, size 54 x 70 ins., colors indigo blue, native yellow and yellow-green stripes on a ground of scarlet flannel strips about ⅛ in. wide, having about the texture of a Turkish towel. The warp is of 3-ply machine-spun yarn.

This is Matthews' 1884 fig. 50b, and the catalogue description says old when bought, hence it probably antedates 1880. Mrs. C. Matthews coll. U. S. National Museum cat. 281466.

cochineal dye mellowed by years of service. The flannels of the last half-century, those sold by the established traders of modern times, are generally thin and sleazy by comparison, loosely spun and woven, their color the harsh scarlet of aniline dye. But red was the favorite color in all times and places, probably because it is the most conspicuous and showy. Good red flannel has never gone begging among the Indians.[2]

BAYETA IN THE OLD WORLD

Bayeta has been the Castilian Spanish equivalent of the English word baize for at least a century and a half.[3] It has variant spellings—*balleta, vayeta, valleta*—but the meaning has stood throughout as "flannel cloth, flexible and somewhat close-woven," to translate from the 1914 edition of the *Diccionario de la Lengua Castellana* of the Royal Spanish Academy, the Webster of Spain. The Encylopædia Britannica, 13th Edition, defines baize as a material which is "generally a coarse, woolen cloth with a long nap and is commonly dyed red or green." The derivation of the word is in doubt, according to this authority, being probably from its original color, bay (brown-red), possibly from the French *baie*, "as the cloth is said to have been originally dyed with Avignon berries." Historically, "the manufacture is said to have been introduced into England in the 16th century by refugees from France and the Netherlands."

Mr. James Strand, English correspondent of the *Textile World*, gives the following interesting summary of the origin and history of bayeta:[4]

> 'Hops, Reformation, bays and beer
> Came into England all in one year.'

This would appear to fix the rise of the bays or baize manufacture in England in the year 1536. The date has not been independently confirmed with precision, but in view of other information the broad accuracy of the fact in respect with bays seems probable. The Norwich "Book of Drapery" of 1570 names Bays first among local manufactures and in

---

[2] ". . . I saw the Jabesua [Havasupai] Indians well supplied with some pieces of red cloth. . ." (Garcés (1776) in Coues I: 340); and further: "These people go decently clothed, and are very fond of any red cloth of Castilla which comes from New Mexico" (p. 345).
   Bayeta to the Navaho is simply "red cloth"—nak'alchi (Vocabulary of the Navaho Language: 33).

[3] The second edition (1780) of the Dictionary of the Royal Spanish Academy lists the word as spelled here, adding that the cloth is ordinarily two varas (66 inches) in width.

[4] Through the courtesy of the editor of the Textile World and of Mr. Frederic H. Douglas, to whose inquiry Mr. Strand's statement was a reply.

1595 some 10,976 pieces of the goods were exported from
England. A passage in a communication of 1578 from the
Mayor and Aldermen of Norwich refers to "new inventions
of the strangers whereof the chiefest are bayes." The Norwich
goods of the period were in fact divided into Baytrie or
Bailtrie (bays) and Saytrie or Saietrie (Says) and a third sort
called Caugeantries. Bays were the specialty of the Norwich
Flemings; caugeantries of the Wallones; and says were more
or less common to both. Says were priests' cloths which from
the 14th century had been made in England, the manufacture having apparently arrived via Ireland from Catalonia,
Spain. About caugeantries it can be said that they appear to
have been fancy goods, for "mocadoes, currells, grosgrains,
velvets, turteins, and the like" were in this class. Baize is
generally held to imply cloth of plain weave and open texture, with a worsted warp and woolen filling, teased on one
side with a more or less long nap. "A Woollen Stuff, not
croisé, very loose made with the hair on one Side, a Kind
of Flannel very coarse" is the description given in 1742 in a
translation of the *Dictionnaire Universel de Commerce*. The
statement in Cole's Encyclopedia that the fabric was invariably dyed a bay color (whence the name) is contradicted
by the personal description given of a disguised priest who
made his way into England in 1582. James Lessmann, Franciscan friar, was tastefully attired in a "cloak of rat's colour
lined with green baize, the cape of tuffed taffeta, red and
blue. . . his doublet white and the stockings of his hose of a
bluish or murray colour." Thus there was a green baize even
at this early date and it is with green that the cloth is mainly
associated by those who know the fabric and its connection
with furniture. Green baize in England is the orthodox material for covering the bare wood of notice boards in clubs,
hotels and schools. Lawyers' offices of the old type invariably
had green baize covered doors and the stuff was used too for
covering screens and tables. Almost any green fabric or any
fabric for tables or doors is "baize" to an upholsterer and
what is called "table baize" in the furnishing trade is cotton cloth covered with a linseed oil mixture, plain, or printed
in colours. Upholsterers' workmen affect aprons of green

PLATE 67

b

a

Poncho **serapes** of bayeta in the traditional colors of indigo blue and white on a two-ply rose-crimson bayeta ground. a size 56 x 84 ins. The late Dr. Chas. F. Lummis called this his best; its thread count is 16 warp and 50 bayeta weft to the inch (good modern rugs count around 8 warp and 15 weft), its texture about that of heavy canvas. b size 54 x 74 ins. Miscalculation in the design is seldom found in such fine specimens as this (its thread count is 15 warp and 38 bayeta weft). Lummis coll. Southwest Museum cat. a 457G1, b 457G4.

PLATE 68

a, A Manchester bayeta. Collected in New Mexico in the 1870's by Mark W. Harrington, father of Mr. M. R. Harrington of Southwest Museum, who now owns it. Size 33 x 50 ins. colors black, white, and touches of (machine-spun) green on deep red bayeta.

b, Double saddle blanket or child's **serape**, size 32 x 46 ins., colors black, white, brown stripes, 4-ply red bayeta in ... and center stripes. Collected by Thomas S. Twigg (probably at Fort Laramie, Wyoming) in 1860. Museum of the

baize to a perceptible extent still and the fabric is the orthodox one in which to wrap framed pictures while they are
being carried from one house to another.

Baize is known also in another connection. An instance
of its use as lining has been given, and Defoe, writing about
1714, spoke of the cloth as "one of those of which the
Spaniards carry vast quantities to America." A Yorkshire
manufacturer giving evidence to a parliamentary committee
in 1828 mentioned that a great many cotton warp baizes had
been exported to South America for a long while. In course
of the same inquiry a Rochdale manufacturer stated that
domett, containing a great deal of cotton, had superseded
woolen baize. The supersession was not complete, for baizes
under the Spanish name of bayetas, dyed in bright colours,
are still shipped to South America from mills near Halifax,
Yorkshire, and in the Rossendale Valley, Lancashire, for
use as clothing. Bayetas, frizadas and pellons, as different
sorts of the goods are called, are a vanishing remnant of those
ancient times, serving at least to demonstrate the continuity
of trade history.

The origin of the name baize has never been satis-
factorily demonstrated. The suggestion has been thrown out
that its origin may be geographical and derived from Baiae,
near Naples, but in the absence of anything to link the goods
with the place the suggestion can at best be received as a
possibility, not as a fact.

BAYETA AND THE NAVAHO

The Navaho (possibly following Pueblo example) put bayeta to a
novel use, and thereby laid a foundation upon which an elaborate structure of romantic anecdote later arose. They raveled the cloth—perhaps
after it had seen service in its original state, as a thrifty means of using its
last threadbare remnants—and used it as a weft filler for their blankets.
The principal advantage and justification of this laborious practice was
the possession of a fine red color; for red, as we saw in the chapters on
Native Dyes, had ever been a problem to them.

Historical light upon this practice is dim indeed, but thanks to a
fugitive bit of history, we know that it dates back to the 18th century. In
1804 or 1805 a punitive expedition from the Spanish settlements of north-

ern New Mexico invaded Cañon del Muerto, great stronghold of the Navaho. The warriors fled, the non-combatants of the tribe living thereabout being sent into a high cave in the cañon wall for refuge. There all were killed by the Spanish, who found that the ricochet of their bullets from the stone walls of the cave spared them the peril and difficulty of seeking out the helpless refugees. Bits of the clothing worn by these unfortunates were found by explorers long after the tragedy, and in them occur thin stripes of bayeta: so thin, indeed, that they convey the mute suggestion of a material rare and highly prized.[5] Some of them are shown in plates 60 and 61.

There were no traders among the Navaho in this early time, so bayeta must have filtered into the tribal range in diverse and devious ways. Doubtless some of it came dishonestly enough, through the raids the Navaho made so frequently, but the greater part of the supply probably was obtained through trade: with the Pueblos,[6] who were at peace with the Spanish settlers and could thus obtain European goods easily; or with the settlements themselves, during the intervals of truce when the Navaho dared venture into Taos and Albuquerque and Santa Fe. Itinerant peddlers and trappers, too—Indian, Spanish, French, half-breed, even American—sometimes braved the perils of the Navaho predatory instinct and ventured along the outskirts of the tribal territory with goods to exchange for blankets or pelts.[7] So, one way and another, enough bayeta reached the Navaho to keep the best looms busy.

The old-time Indian traders and present-day blanket dealers who have been the chief perpetuators (and sometimes perpetrators) of the legendry of bayeta would have it that Spanish uniforms, stripped from the vanquished foe on the field of battle, were the true source of the bayeta in Navaho blankets. The story doubtless has a grain of truth, but scarcely more than that; Spain lost few soldiers in New Mexico, yet my own eyes have seen enough bayeta to clothe a company, while many times more has been destroyed by fire, wear, moth, and the various destructive agen-

---

[5] Mr. Earl H. Morris tells the story of the massacre (for which the cave was named Massacre Cave) in the National Geographic Magazine for September, 1925.

I have examined fragments of cloth from Massacre Cave in the private museum of Mr. Wm. H. Claflin Jr. at Belmont, Mass. Mr. Claflin himself collected them.

Brooklyn Museum also has a collection of Navaho objects from Massacre Cave —salvage from the tragedy.

[6] "These [The Hopi] are the masters of the nations [tribes], in the commerce they carry on, for the awls, dibbles, hoes, knives, leggings of red baize, and certain fabrics, which are found in the other nations, all issue from Moqui, whereto they come from New Mexico"—Garcés (1776) in Coues II: 464.

[7] Sabin (177) tells of a trip by Kit Carson in 1837 for trade with the Navaho.

PLATE 69

The **serape** as worn. Black Horse, prominent Navaho of the Fort Defiance region in early reservation days, wearing a **serape** of the times, evidently new. Photo taken probably in the eighties, photographer unknown, courtesy Signal Corps, U. S. Army.

PLATE 70

Cañon del Muerto, looking south toward Cañon de Chelly. Photo by J. K. Hillers about 1880, Southwest Museum coll.

cies which beset such relatively perishable objects as textiles. Another military uniform story attributes certain colors in old blankets to American army uniforms, and the phrases "cavalry yellow," "infantry blue," and "medical corps green" are sometimes heard. Here again, it seems to me, an oak of fancy has grown from an acorn of fact. Close scrutiny usually reveals that the fabric thus glorified is remarkable only for an oddity of color or for the faded hue of age. In my experience raveled fabrics other than red bayeta and its kindred strounding or flannel have been extremely rare.

The romanticists are fond of telling too that bayeta was a Spanish fabric. Lummis (who was never found tamely plodding in another's track) rose to yet greater heights and derived it from distant Turkey (1896) for no stated reason.[8] Bayeta did reach the Southwest via Mexico and Spain, and naturally enough, for the channels of trade in provincial New Mexico thus ran; but England was the place of manufacture, on the most reliable evidence.[9]

Even after New Mexico and the Navaho country had passed under American rule, Spain seems to have continued to send bayeta into the Southwest. Mr. C. N. Cotton of Gallup, New Mexico, who was an established trader among the Navaho as early as 1884, has told me that he recalls bolts of the cloth, wrapped in linen, with a label in Spanish mentioning Barcelona. Each bolt held about forty-five *varas* of material, as he remembered it. Lummis (1896) says the price paid by the Navaho buyer was six dollars a pound; Mr. Cotton pointed out that the price varied as conditions changed, but agreed that the cloth was very expensive.

Mr. Charles C. Pinckney, whose Indian trading career began in a store among the Navaho near Farmington, New Mexico, in 1886, has told me he sold bayeta (red only) until about 1890, when no more could be obtained through his customary sources of supply in the East. Matthews (1884: 376) had recorded even earlier that the bayeta of his time was coming from "eastern cities." Mr. E. H. Davies of Farmington, New Mexico, an Indian trader since 1905, told me a similar story: he tried to get bayeta in his early trading years at Westwater, New Mexico, north of the San Juan river, but the eastern supply house with which he dealt could not obtain the material. Evidently the American wholesalers were then dealing in domestic flannel, the aniline-dyed thinly woven successor

---

[8] Possibly the phrase "Turkey red"—but that is a color, not a fabric.

[9] The will of Don Diego de Vargas, conqueror of New Mexico after the Pueblo Rebellion, dated Santa Fe, 1704, disposes of certain garments of "scarlet cloth from England" and "cloth of England enough for a suit."—Twitchell I: 301 ff.

Bartlett (I: 330) tells how the Navaho "unravel fine scarlet blankets of English manufacture, the threads of which are then used in the weaving of their own."

to the ancient English-Spanish fabric, which was in turn displaced by Germantown yarn and aniline dyes for coloring native wool. But these events bear a date years beyond the heyday of bayeta, for little fine bayeta weaving was done after the Navaho were conquered and made reservation-dwellers in the decade of the 1860's, as told in Chapter 11.[10]

Welsh (22) speaks of "rolls of red flannel" seen in the trading tent of the late Lorenzo Hubbell in 1885, and Dr. F. W. Hodge in a note in the *American Anthropologist* (N. S. 6:4:543) tells of seeing bayeta in use by the Zuñi in 1889, and also in the store of the pioneer trader, Thomas V. Keam, at Keam's Cañon, Arizona, in 1897, when Keam informed him that it had been in stock for years with no demand. In 1884, says the government agent at Fort Defiance, "the Navaho weave about 10% of their own wool, besides buying much bayeta (an imported woolen cloth) which they tear into strips and use" (RCIA 1884: 134). Those two pioneers among Navaho traders, the late Lorenzo Hubbell and Mr. C. N. Cotton, could recall having sold bayeta until a still later time: Mr. Cotton told me he carried it as a regular trade item until about 1910, while Mr. Lorenzo Hubbell Jr. told Mr. Frederic H. Douglas that bayeta was made until about 1910, his father having disposed of his final bolt about 1920.

If genuine English baize was the subject of all of the above references, then I have erred grievously in bringing the bayeta period of Navaho weaving to a close with the conquest of the tribe and the beginning of reservation life in 1868. I am well convinced, however, that the use of the old name persisted long after the commodity designated had passed out of hand—that American textile mills and aniline dye vats were the source of much of the "bayeta" of these later years. I have samples of the "bayeta" of three decades ago, and in many specimens of Navaho weaving I have recognized this same material. It is thin and sleazy and altogether a cheap product if measured by the old standards. The nap is there, and the warp and weft of equal weight: but two threads together will not make one of

---

[10] This statement is mainly my own conclusion, based on the fact that only one or two of perhaps a score of fine bayeta blankets on which good historical data are available, were woven later than the sixties. I am convinced that the generation of weavers which arose after the exile of the tribe at Fort Sumner (Bosque Redondo), 1863-1868, never attained the high standards of its predecessors (this point is discussed in Chapter 11), so I have called the half-century between Massacre Cave and Bosque Redondo the "bayeta period." The reader will recall that "periods" of history are not strictly confined to the dates assigned to them, and so it is in this instance. Yet I have much evidence suggesting that most of the best bayeta weaving in existence today dates from the first half of the 19th century. Lummis (1896) agrees: "For it is nearly a generation since a Navajo blanket of strictly the first class has been created;" and Hollister (123): "The bayeta went into its decline about 1860, but did not pass entirely out of use until 1875."

the old. The color, too, is harsh and overly bright.[11] Hollister has a name for it (103): " 'squaw cloth', a coarse woolen stuff of many colors," which is sometimes known by the old name of bayeta, he adds.

Messrs. Pinckney and Davies, already cited, have told me another interesting detail concerning red flannel among the Navaho. Each mentioned that Army blankets of this fabric often fell into Navaho hands and were used in their own weaving. Mr. Davies (whose store at Westwater was really in Ute territory) recalled that the Ute had received an issue of these blankets from the Government soon after 1900, and had traded many of them to the Navaho.[12]

Bayeta, then, had successors of varying quality, as one would expect, for the commercial loom has always stood ready to accomodate every purse and taste; but a cheapening of the fabric down the years is quite clearly shown. Carrying this trend yet farther, cotton fabrics of late years have driven the woolens from their favored place in the Navaho economy, although I have never seen them used in the native weaving. Bayeta— using the term in the strict historical sense, to designate the old heavy baize of England—thus fell a victim to progress and invention, but it seems to have faded from the Southwestern scene so gradually that few were aware of its passing. Indeed, direct importation of English baize

---

[11] Mr. Wm. H. Claflin Jr. has a blanket of serape type in his private museum (cat. 24798) which Mr. Lorenzo Hubbell ordered made not long before the year 1910, to prove that the bayeta technic was not lost. It is bright-scarlet in color and very "fuzzy", although hard and tightly woven. If it is typical, a new bayeta blanket must have been an unlovely object, with bits of thread protruding everywhere. But to the best of my knowledge this specimen stands unique as the only pristine bayeta extant.

[12] I examined an Army blanket in the National Museum at Washington, and found it of distinctly better quality than the "trader flannel" of later years. The warp and weft were of equal weight, having about the thickness of the lead of an ordinary pencil. A single strand could have been used for weft in Navaho weaving, I thought. The blanket was loosely woven, hence would have been easy to shred or ravel. It bore a long nap on the face, and in all points greatly resembled the old bayeta. The color was a dark claret with a hint of brown—evidently a non-aniline dye, although it seemed more like one of the "red woods" (logwood, Brazil wood) than cochineal. The blanket weighed three pounds. This specimen (cat. 127982) was called an "old Ordance Department blanket", or "Artillery blanket, 1887. Cost $2.60." It measures 64 by 76 inches, and has the letters "U. S." woven in black in the center and a border stripe of identical color around all four sides, set back a few inches from the edge.

Another specimen in the same collection (cat. 201020) was much like the Army blanket just described, having the same dimensions, warp and weft of equal weight although lighter than the other, and the same loose weave, but lacking the nap of the older specimen. The color, a hard, bright scarlet, I thought was of aniline origin. In several points this specimen, evidently collected just before the year 1900, marked a greater departure from the old bayeta standards than did the other; a fact which is probably explained in large part by its later date. Yet its quality was far above that of specimens of red flannel of more recent date which I have seen.

was practised for years, some dealers calling this category of bayeta "Manchester" or "Huddersfield" from the place of manufacture (pl. 68*a*). Mr. Hubbell Sr. told Dr. Hodge, the latter recalls, that much of the bayeta of his time came directly from Manchester, England. Spiegelberg makes clear this detail of bayeta's varied history in the following quotation:

> This material in later years, 1850 to 1870, was imported by merchants of Santa Fe, New Mexico, at that time the largest supply point of the Southwest, first from Barcelona, Spain, and afterwards, an imitation of it (though in all respects as good as the original) from Manchester, England, and it is impossible for the best expert to detect one from the other. This flannel was not always of the exact same weight and shade of color, and hence the difficulty for many persons to determine the article (1904: 447).

When the United States took over the broad territory known as New Mexico, after the Mexican War of 1845-1848, it was inevitable that the channels of trade should alter their course. True, the Santa Fe Trail had become the principal trade route of the territory even before this change of political sovereignty; and the caravan trade with Mexico via Chihuahua (where a celebrated annual trade fair was held) was in proportionate decline. But American rule hastened the process, and American goods rapidly drove out those of Mexico and Spain. Bayeta seems to have held its own for several decades after the political shift, as we have seen, and might have held on longer still but for the growing use of aniline dyes (invented in England about 1856) and the inevitable Yankee tendency to manufacture something "just as good but cheaper." American-made flannel appeared on the shelves of the trading posts, more and more commonly. It was far inferior to bayeta in both color and quality; but it was cheaper, and easier to obtain. So the old-fashioned weaver who would still take the trouble to shred and re-twist a machine-made cloth to obtain a rich red weft material must perforce content herself with this. That many did so is attested by the existence today of blankets bearing a weft of red in which thin, loosely spun threads of a hard scarlet tone mock the smooth, thick, rosy-crimson fibers of the older and better material. "Bayeta" some blanket dealers call this American flannel, either ignorantly or with deliberate intent to delude the customer. Others, more discerning or more honest, use the term American bayeta. But it seems a cheapening of the historical bayeta thus to lump it with a baser fabric, and a needless increase of the confusion already reigning about the question.

WHAT IS A BAYETA BLANKET?

The foregoing pages should have made it clear that historically, bayeta is the old English baize of pre-aniline times. The Spanish introduced both material and name into the Southwest, and their conception of the matter should be binding upon us if we are to use their name for it. But the situation is by no means so simple, since the Navaho seized upon this fabric to tear it down and rebuild it in quite different guise. As applied to the Navaho blanket, the question of what constitutes bayeta has several complexities. It is agreed by all that a blanket containing only a little bayeta material may be called a bayeta blanket and sold as such: indeed, few if any blankets in existence are made wholly of bayeta, the general practice having been to combine native wools—generally using natural white, indigo blue, native black, and (much more sparingly) native green or yellow—with bayeta red. The bayeta content might thus be relatively small. Sometimes, though, the weaver in an excess of thrift seems to have spun native wool and bayeta ravelings together. Is this mixture entitled to bear the proud name? Not so, in my opinion; for bayeta in the best specimens is not re-spun (as is sometimes said), but merely re-twisted. That is, the weaver has taken the whole threads obtained by raveling, twisted them into a strand usually of two or three-ply weight (although I have seen as much as five-ply, each thread being very thin), and thus used them as weft. Now if she combs up the odds and ends of short thread remaining behind, and mixes this combing with native wool, she has produced a strand of essentially different character. Conceivably she might twist a bayeta thread with a spun strand of native wool, but I have never seen this combination to my knowledge; the colors would not blend as they do when the two materials are combed together.

Sometimes, too, the fabric was torn into narrow strips and thus used as weft filler. But these flannel strip blankets seem to date from the twilight of the bayeta period at their earliest, those I have seen being of poor quality and usually associated with Germantown or native yarn of aniline coloring. Two specimens are shown in plates 65*a* and 66, whereby it will be seen that these coarse unpatterned fabrics have nothing in common with the true bayeta blanket. They are odd and rare—but far from artistic or fine in workmanship.

Another question is whether blankets containing machine-spun yarn of vegetal coloring may be called bayeta blankets. I can see no room for argument here. Bayeta is baize and baize is a woven cloth, not merely a spun yarn. The two may be identical in quality, may indeed have lain in the same dye vat and have twirled on the same spindle back in England. But there is no reason to lump the manufactured cloth with the yarn which represents but a preliminary step in cloth-making. Mr. H. Schweizer of the Indian Department of Fred Harvey at Albuquerque, New Mexico, a leading authority on Navaho blankets, is careful to distinguish the old yarn blanket from the bayeta. He has pointed out, too, that the yarn, while quite as fine in color and texture, is much the rarer, hence should command a higher price. But yarn is prosaic—not to be compared with bloody Spanish uniforms and cloth from Turkey, in point of romantic association. Finally, should the cloth directly imported from England, the "Manchester" and "Huddersfield," be called bayeta? It is bayeta, as Spiegelberg said, except for not having passed through Spanish hands; and but for a tendency to be wine-colored or scarlet rather than crimson (in my observation), how are we to see it apart? I would call it a later bayeta, usually detectable by type of pattern if not by color or character.[13]

BAYETA COLORS

The experts in bayeta have always differed as to the colors which might properly bear the honored name of bayeta. Lummis, I believe, always insisted that true bayeta was red and red alone; and others of a romantic rather than a literal turn of mind have agreed. Hollister, for example, says (103): "The genuine bayeta was entirely of wool, dyed with cochineal, and presented the various shades of red natural to that dye." I must admit I have never (to my recollection) seen a material in Navaho blankets that I could confidently call old English baize, which was not of some color in the range between scarlet and red-brown. Yet James (27) admits other colors, as does Mr. Schweizer, to whom I have already referred as a sound authority, while a consideration of the historical aspects of the problem must lead one to the conclusion that the Navaho weaver might have used other colors, for the materials were not wanting. We know from various accounts that the imported woolen goods and clothing of provincial New Mexico were not exclusively red in color.[14] Red is the prevailing color beyond question, but it would be diffi-

---

[13] James in his chapter on bayeta (Chapter IV) obviously does not distinguish it from non-aniline yarn, nor the latter from the later, aniline-dyed Germantown. Thus he throws the point into delightful confusion; but his information on English baize and its dye-stuffs is good.

[14] Hodge in a note in Benavides (277) quotes from a letter written in Coahuila in 1689 an allusion to the request of the governor of an Indian village that the Spanish authorities give him "a piece of blue baize to make a shroud."

cult to defend the contention that it was the only one used. At any rate it cannot be denied that baize was made in different colors, green in particular having a strong association with the fabric, as Mr. James Strand, above quoted, makes clear. Dr. Hodge tells me he recalls having heard the late Lorenzo Hubbell in 1923 refer to dark blue (indigo-dyed) "Manchester bayeta."

PRODUCTS OF THE BAYETA PERIOD

Bayeta may be found interwoven with native wool in any of the old native garments described in Chapter 7 herein, but it has an outstanding association with one of them in particular, the poncho serape. This luxurious and expensive "overcoat" [15] made evidently for barter as well as for tribal use, for it is a Mexican type of garment—often was made almost wholly of bayeta, whereas most other garments had only stripes of that fabric in their composition. The *"Sarape Navajo"* (poncho or no) as Josiah Gregg called it, knowing it well for having lived in New Mexico in the decades of 1830 and 1840, was certainly the most expensive, celebrated, and characteristic Navaho product of that time, whether poncho or plain serape. Traditionally it had a background of bayeta red with horizontal striped patterns in blue (indigo) and white, sometimes a little yellow or green (both native). Plates 51, 59, 67, 76 show characteristic specimens of the type. The chief's blanket, the woman's dress and cape, the saddle blanket, children's blankets—all might have some bayeta figures in their pattern; but in the red, white, and blue serape bayeta reached its zenith.[16] So too did Navaho weaving: nothing ever cut from the tribal loom equals the finest of this type in every technical point of excellence.

ON DISTINGUISHING BAYETA IN BLANKETS

How does one recognize bayeta, after all this discussion? the patient reader may be asking. The question is almost equivalent to inquiring

[15] The late Dr. Charles F. Lummis, who from about 1888 onward collected the superb bayeta ponchos now in the Southwest Museum, has said that such specimens were worth fifty dollars or more when he first knew of them. Gregg, writing about 1841, says (I: 286) of the "Serape Navajo" that it "is of so close and dense a texture that it will frequently hold water almost equal to gum-elastic cloth. It is therefore highly prized for protection against the rains. Some of the finer qualities are often sold among the Mexicans as high as fifty or sixty dollars each." He also records (209) that the Mexican weavers of the province made an imitation of the "Serape Navajo" which brought as much as twenty dollars. Abert (36) mentions blankets worth $50 to $100—this in 1846-47; and Barreiro says (55) that "a Navajo serape is more highly prized than one of Saltillo, since the former is completely waterproof."

[16] Designs characteristic of the bayeta period are discussed in Chapter 14, which is devoted to a chronological analysis of Navaho design.

how the art critic recognizes a genuine Rembrandt, for the answer in each case is much the same: by a combination of qualities and characteristics, each to a great extent beyond cold and precise definition, each of such subtle character that the honest appraiser must occasionally confess a doubt.

Several tests are useful to a degree, but none in my judgment is a perfect touchstone. First of all, I look closely at the twist of the fiber under scrutiny, and I recommend that the reader examine with equal care the enlarged fragments in plate 65 which show the different aspects of raveled, native, and machine-spun wefts. The latter is easiest of all to recognize: it has a tight, even spiral trend in its multiple threads (yarn is of three- or four-ply, usually) that the eye detects readily. Raveled weft—whether bayeta, flannel, or other—nearly always is multiple-threaded, like yarn; but unlike yarn, it is not tightly and evenly twisted, shows no smooth spiral curl. Its individual threads ramble erratically in and out of the warp web, crossing one another at irregular intervals in a loose twist and having the appearance of lying almost parallel rather than of being twisted closely together. Native-spun weft bears a smooth fuzziness all its own, the individual hairs bristling out in all directions; and of course it is all of a piece, not multiple-ply as are the others. Only between heavy bayeta of one-ply weight and fine-spun native yarn is the difficulty of distinction sometimes acute. The interested amateur would do well to seek out a museum having authentic specimens of each of these types of weft, and practise himself in recognizing the peculiar characteristics of each.

Feel is another test, although to me it means little. Bayeta has a harsh, prickly feel, it is true, but an old, tight yarn feels much the same to my clumsy fingers, while even a native-wool weft that has seen service in sun and rain, or been much laundered in hard water, will assume this same brittle hardness to the touch. Yet the feel test is useful in conjunction with others.

Mr. John Wetherill, pioneer among the Navaho, has told me that he can always settle his doubts about bayeta by patiently searching along the surface until he finds a protruding short thread, which yields easily and comes away upon being gently pulled. The explanation lies in the process of raveling or shredding. Given a broad strip of cloth, raveling is all but impossible without cutting it into smaller strips, and this cutting produces short lengths of thread that are twisted in with the longer ones. The test is excellent, except that it distinguishes all raveled fabrics equally well, hence must be used as one among others only.

James, in his excellent chapter on bayeta (Chapter IV), mentions,

PLATE 71

Above, Fort Defiance, a contemporary drawing (made in the 1850's) by Lieut. Col. J. H. Eaton, reproduced in Drake I: 426 and Schoolcraft Vol. IV pl. 29. Photo from Signal Corps, U. S. Army.

Below, "Kit Carson's calling card," Mr. Will C. Barnes called this Carson inscription on the walls of Keam's Cañon. This photograph is from the P. G. Gates collection, Southwest Museum, taken about 1905 by A. C. Vroman. The inscription is self-dating, and the style of lettering suggests that Carson had a tombstone-cutter among his soldiers.

PLATE 72

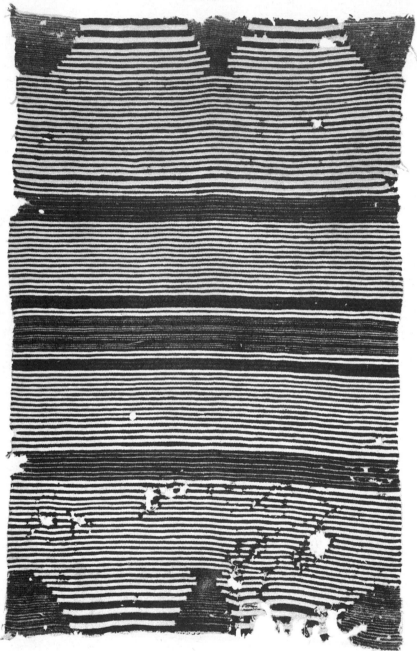

The Bartlett blanket, 1851, (see Bartlett I: 330). Size 32 x 50 ins., colors indigo blue, native black, green and yellow, 3-ply bayeta red, white, in narrow stripes.

John Russell Bartlett, U. S. Boundary Commissioner on the Mexican boundary survey under the treaty of Guadalupe Hidalgo, bought it from the Navaho and Peabody Museum of Harvard University acquired it in 1878. Cat. 14720. Photo by Mr. F. T. Orchard.

as criteria, burning and chemical analysis to determine the colorant, neither of which is practicable under ordinary circumstances. In this connection, however, I must mention that Dr. Spencer R. Atkinson demonstrated to me that a bayeta thread (the individual hair, that is) under a powerful microscope shows sharp bends or kinks at regular intervals, while a single native-spun fiber bends more gently and lazily; the reason being, we both thought, that machine spinning imparts a sharper twist than spinning by hand.

Color must always be considered; some make it their principal criterion. To my mind its chief value is in the elimination of fabrics of such harsh hue that they fairly shout "Diamond Dyes!", and in the detection of the later-day successors to bayeta: the raveled flannels which in their scarlet brightness always lack the mellow shade of the authentic old baize. Mr. Schweizer relies much on color, bearing in mind that the fame—and the high cost—of bayeta is founded in large part on the rich delicacy of its time-mellowed hue. He is a professional seller; but the buyer would do well to heed, and use this sound rule as well, for it is poor business to pay a large price for a blanket lacking in the patrician aspect of fine coloring.

In closing the discussion I would suggest one final rule for the would-be connoisseur: after a careful consideration of the various criteria of detail suggested above, consider the piece as a whole. Do not fall into the error of satisfying yourself on a single strand of weft, to find later that you are not pleased with the whole blanket. Study the pattern from a little distance: is it in good taste, harmonious and well balanced, accurately proportioned, well suited to the size and shape of the blanket? Are the lines clean and true, each unit figure well drawn? Be sure, in this connection, that the weaver has not fallen into the common error of miscalculating her space, and making the figures in one end either noticeably larger or smaller than those opposite; many good blankets fall short in this respect (pl. 67b). Next examine the texture of the piece to determine if the spinning is well and smoothly done, if the weaving is regular and even, the batten conscientiously applied to make a smooth, hard fabric. Beware of any shortcoming under any of these heads, for bayeta was an expensive fabric, entrusted only to the best weavers of the tribe: if the workmanship is amateurish or inartistic or hasty, it is not likely that bayeta was used.

Bayeta blankets are almost invariably of such high quality and artistry that the standards of art may properly be applied to them—and art, as everyone knows, is not easy to judge. That thought should be consoling as well as irritating, it seems to me, for the joys of the esthetic are all the more sweet for being hardly won: most things in life have a value or satisfaction in direct ratio to the pain or effort they cost us. Unless you are prepared to exercise and develop your judgment by careful observation and study of the best in bayeta (just as you would study the best in painting or sculpture), you will find little satisfaction in the possession of fine pieces, little justification for paying the high price they rightfully command. In short, if you are the type of collector who makes collection a fetish rather than a cultural satisfaction, you would better spend your money on postage stamps or old coins, and leave bayeta to its faithful devotees. They will not suffer it to perish of neglect, you may be sure.

BAYETA'S CONTRIBUTION TO WEAVING

It is generally conceded that progress in all lines of human activity alternately lags and surges forward as its various stimuli wane and wax. The bayeta period in Navaho weaving was one of rapid progress under strong impulsion. Bayeta in its (relatively) fine texture and its rich coloring set a standard of excellence that might never have been attained without it. Its employment in a product of the native loom was a high challenge to the woman bold enough to match her skill at spinning and dyeing against that of the textile experts of far-away England. Meeting this challenge successfully, as she did, the Navaho weaver at once brilliantly vindicated her adoption of the alien craft of weaving and set it upon the road to world renown. The bayeta period marked the high point, the "Golden Age" of Navaho weaving, for this rich fabric called forth the best in every phase of the craft—in spinning, dyeing, weaving, pattern creation. Only an expert could wed native wool and bayeta fiber in a harmonious and happy union. Only an artist could realize the full potentialities of such fine smooth wefts, such rich colorings, as bayeta afforded and inspired. And the Navaho woman responded to the stimulus, proved herself an expert and an artist—by grace of bayeta.

Almost a century has passed since bayeta was in its glory among the Navaho, and a time of discouragement to the old native crafts and customs it has indeed been; yet the young weavers of today recall (we may hope with pride) that their grandmothers raveled some sort of cloth bought from the white man, and fashioned it into blankets which were highly praised by Mexican and American alike, and were eagerly sought by Indians of a score of tribes, far and near. They know, these girls and young matrons who have been forced through the bewildering experience of Government boarding schools and automobiles and motion pictures, that they are the heritors of a good and worthy tradition. If all inspiration has faded from that dim memory, then truly is Navaho weaving in sorry plight, for a handicraft without traditions soon falls victim to the machine. But if only a spark remains of this old pride (and I am sure of that, at least) with only a tithe of the old-time skill, yet must we be grateful to bayeta and hopeful for the future of the craft for which it did so much.

PLATE 73

Chief Manuelito. Born in 1821, he signed the treaty of 1868 at Bosque Redondo, led the first Navaho police (1872), headed a delegation to Washington (1874), died in 1893. One of the two scars on his chest he boasted was inflicted by Kit Carson, whom he successfully eluded with a band of his followers. Photo from Wittick coll. Laboratory of Anthropology, probably copied by Wittick from an unknown photographer.

PLATE 74

a

b

Two chief blankets from Carson's Navaho campaign. a size 56 x 42 ins., colors black, white, indigo blue, bayeta red.

b size 73 x 46 ins., colors black, white, indigo blue, native yellow (in short stripes) and bayeta red. U. S. Hollister coll. American Museum of Natural History cat. (a) 50.1/4425, (b) 50.1/4429.

Both, according to the catalogue, were brought to Colorado in 1864 by one of Carson's guides.

CHAPTER XI

TAMING THE NAVAHO—1863-1868

ANUS, the two-faced god of ancient Rome, would have been an appropriate diety for the Navaho of the early 19th century. The tribal countenance of this time has two markedly different aspects, and in the accounts of contemporary observers we find high praise and scathing blame strangely intermingled. Weaving was in its most brilliant stage, the bayeta period, and the fame of the Navaho blanket grew like young corn in summer. That was the smiling aspect of Janus, and for it we may thank the women of the tribe. His sinister side is seen when the activities of the men are scanned, and we find that while the women sat peacefully at home plying spindle and batten to the ever-growing glory of their craft, the warriors were no less intent on a reputation in their own right. They were out pillaging the communal lands and herds of the Pueblos and the isolated farmsteads and small villages throughout New Mexico.

Thus did it come about the native resident shuddered at the very name which to the visitor from the United States called up a pleasing image of pastoral bliss and honest industry; and if one asked a chance acquaintance for an opinion of the Navaho, the tone of the reply would depend greatly on whether that person had just bought a blanket or lost a herd of sheep. But the men managed to ravel the tribal repute much faster than the women could spin it, and it was generally agreed throughout the Spanish settlements of the Rio Grande valley, from Taos on the north down to sun-baked Socorro, that the Navaho were the foremost scourge of a land that knew its scourging well. Scarcely a chronicler of the period, from Zebulon Pike in 1805 to "El Gringo" Davis in 1857, neglects to pause a moment in his narrative and curse the raiding Navaho, active on a front extending from the Hopi villages of Arizona to the Comanche country in Texas.

And just as the weavers of the period were encouraged and stimulated by the warm reception given their vivid and durable blankets by Mexican and American visitor alike, so were the raiders favored by the political fortunes of the time. Of the growing tension between Spaniard and Anglo-Saxon they of course knew and cared little. Free as wild antelope and simple as children, they had yet to learn that the world is a large place, filled with tribes of white men who fight among themselves like tribes of Indians. So slowly did this lesson penetrate the Navaho mind that the new tribe known as Americans had them crushed and utterly beaten almost before they had convinced themselves that any serious harm lay in these handfuls of ruddy-faced soldiers who were continually riding into their country, alternately to intimidate them with threats of extermination and to wheedle them with promises of gifts and protection—always in the name of a chief known variously as "President" and "Washington". The Navaho heard much of this chief in the parleys his fighting men were always so willing to hold. A great believer in talk he seemed to be: treaties were his solution for every trouble, with much big talk about peace and friendship. That was probably because his soldiers obviously did not know much about the country, or about Indian fighting, or because Big Chief Washington was afraid to lead his own war parties against the powerful, swift-riding Navaho. These boastful, talkative Americans were no more to be feared than the Mexicans who had been living on the borders of the Navaho country for so many years now, or than the fainthearts known as Pueblos—tribes of farmers at heart who were no match for fighting men. None of the three was a real menace to Navaho freedom, being rather a welcome annoyance, adding a fine thrill to the roving, marauding life; and what a great life it was, raiding the Pueblos and the Mexicans for livestock and women, and parleying with the Americans for presents! Boom times were these for the Navaho, ending—as such times do—with a crash that set their world to ringing.

EXIT SPAIN

New Mexico fell just short of three centuries under Spanish rule. Francisco Vásquez Coronado, the explorer, seized the territory for Spain in 1540 and his priests at once set about its Christianizing; Juan de Oñate, the colonizer, began its settlement in 1598, and Diego de Vargas, the conqueror, definitely established Spanish sovereignty after the bloody events of the Revolt of 1680. With the 19th century revolt charged the air again: in 1810 Mexico declared its independence of Spain, and remote New Mexico had another master before it fully realized that such great changes were even in the air. But the first regime of independence in

Mexico was not a successful affair, and it was not until 1824 that our distant northern province began to notice a sensible change in its fortunes. In that year it rose to the dignity of statehood in a territorial merger which included Chihuahua and Durango, with Chihuahua City the capital of this splendid political creation. Durango, jealous of Chihuahua, objected to the arrangement; so New Mexico was cast adrift as a territory later in the same year. In 1836 came a new constitution for the Republic of Mexico, and New Mexico was made a department in a sweeping political gesture which fixed neither eastern nor western limits to its extent; and as such it continued until the American occupation of 1846 came as the forecast of a permanent change of sovereignty which was to offer the erstwhile forgotten province the honor of figuring again as a territory, then as a state once more. New Mexico is the original "football of politics"; it has been everything, some things twice.

These changes of political stature and complexion meant nothing to the free and belligerent little nation living in the rugged, barren country lying between the San Juan and the Rio Grande, on the northern borders of Spanish America. The Navaho may have noticed that raiding was more profitable and less risky than it used to be, with their Mexican neighbors deep in politics and the Americans creeping in over the Santa Fe Trail to add a new element of uncertainty to the complexion of the times. At any rate they were at their raiding best during this time of political change. Bancroft (Chapter XIV) records a treaty of peace with them in 1823, with trouble again in 1825 (comment enough on the durability of treaties!) and "continued hostility" in 1840-41. Prince (232) tells us that Juan Bautista Vigil, last of the Mexican governors of New Mexico, made campaigns against the Navaho in 1823, 1833, 1836, and 1838, and summarizes the situation with the words, "all through this period, down to the final overthrow of the Navajoes long after the American occupation, there existed an almost constant condition of warfare with that powerful tribe." The Navaho had boasted that they let the Mexicans live on only because of their usefulness as shepherds to the tribe, and the taunt seems scarcely to have been an exaggeration of their power. New Mexico was under their thumb and they bore down where and when it pleased them. But events were shaping themselves to relieve the pressure.

THE UNITED STATES STEPS IN

General Stephen Watts Kearny occupied Santa Fe with American troops in August, 1846, as one of the strategic moves of the Mexican war.

He learned quickly enough that his problems of conquest and pacification included an enemy within an enemy, for later in the same year he instructed Colonel Alexander W. Doniphan, already on his way to occupy Chihuahua, to give some attention to the Navaho situation. Major William Gilpin of Doniphan's command accordingly led two hundred men marching up the Chama valley, down the San Juan river and up the Little Colorado, cautiously circling the Navaho territory in a maneuver that must have proved surprising to its occupants. Doniphan with his main force went meanwhile to Albuquerque, down the Rio Grande to the mouth of the Rio Puerco, and up that stream to Ojo del Oso (Bear Spring) where New Fort Wingate later stood. There the two forces joined and a treaty was signed with a number of Navaho who had been gathered in for the occasion.

The treaty of Guadalupe Hidalgo in 1848 ended the war with Mexico and gave the United States clear title to a territory larger than the original thirteen colonies, plus certain moral obligations toward and in connection with some 120,000 Indians [1] in various stages of civilization and social unrest, of whom about one-fourth were in New Mexico alone. The obligations have proved a source of embarrassment and expense down to the present day, and the end is still beyond vision. Some appreciation of their existence, if not of their serious character, is shown in the appointment of an Indian Agent at Santa Fe as early as the year 1849. James S. Calhoun was the appointee, he who became territorial governor in 1851. He advocated a system of reservations and agencies for Indian administration— the Navaho to have an agency at Zuñi—and his report of stock losses by Mexican farmers, due to Indian raids (289), is eloquent of a situation calling for more strenuous measures than a distant federal government, already preoccupied with the problem which was leading toward the Civil War, was ready to take.[2]

Doniphan's treaty of 1846 aged rapidly and to little purpose, with Navaho raids more frequent than ever. One Major Walker made a sally against them in 1847, going as far as the mouth of Cañon de Chelly with a force of volunteers; and in 1848 Colonel E. W. B. Newby replaced the treaty with another after an "expedition" under his lead had plunged madly into the Navaho deserts and come out almost without firing a shot. In 1849 came Major John M. Washington who marched from Jemez

---

[1] Bancroft: 459.

[2] Bartlett (II: 398) says the Assistant Marshals of the United States report stock stolen by Indians in New Mexico in 1846-50 at: 453,293 sheep; 12,887 mules; 7,050 horses; 31,581 cattle.

to Cañon de Chelly, where a "lasting peace" was concluded with the Navaho thereabout. The latter turned over some stolen property and captives, and agreed to make a larger delivery at Jemez thirty days later. Washington jogged on happily to Zuñi, and on his return to civilization he learned that the Navaho, instead of going in repentance to Jemez, had raided Santa Fe!

The "lasting peace" lasted almost two years: 1851 found Colonel E. V. Sumner leading the American Army's perennial tour of the Navaho territory and giving his followers an extra thrill by marching ten miles into Cañon de Chelly, greatest of Navaho strongholds. As usual no serious accidents marred the perfect enjoyment of the outing, and Sumner reported the Navaho "completely overawed." The Americans did gain an important tactical advantage from this junket, by establishing Fort Defiance—first military post in the Navaho country—in 1852.[3]

Fort Defiance had its dampening effect on Navaho activities for a time (aided by a judicious distribution of goods to the spoiled tribe), but in 1857 a negro servant was killed and warfare resumed its desultory round. In 1860 the Navaho attacked Fort Defiance but were repulsed, and a retaliatory sortie rather carried off the honors of the affair by killing many of their horses and sheep. Again the Americans had scored a point— one that was to prove very useful in later actions of the same sort. The Navaho, as usually they did when they found themselves in a tight place, sued for peace; diplomacy had become almost a recognized profession among them, and they understood its uses. It was the year 1861, and Indian affairs were giving way to graver matters in the military mind. So the small war was concluded with a treaty while the larger one got under way on the distant Potomac.

CARLETON AND CARSON

Fifteen years the American army had controlled New Mexico, and the mythical Swiss navy could hardly have been less effective. The Indians ran riot—Navaho and Ute on the northwestern frontier, Comanche and Kiowa on the eastern, Apache to the south and west.[4] Now came another

---

[3] This date has been variously reported from 1851 to 1853, but Backus, the first commandant, says (210) the fort was begun in 1851 and finished in 1852.

[4] "The record of murders committeed annually by them [the Navaho] is truly frightful. In the range of their depredations, which extend through some of the most densely populated districts of the Territory, there is scarcely a neighborhood but what has lost some of its most valuable citizens by their hands. . . Its number will extend to nearly three hundred for the past eighteen months."—Supt. J. F. Collins in RCIA 1861: 124.

menace: the Confederate invasion under General Sibley swept through the Rio Grande valley, captured Albuquerque and Santa Fe, and drove on toward Fort Union, nerve center of Federal military strength for the whole Southwest. The hour was at its darkest, the proverbial hour "just before the dawn." The lowering skies cleared when the Confederates were routed at Apache Cañon; but day really broke for troubled New Mexico when Brigadier General James H. Carleton was appointed department commander. His first report to the War Department shows him a man of action:

Headquarters Department of New Mexico,
Santa Fe, N. M., September 30, 1862.

General: I have the honor to inform you that I relieved General Canby in command of this department on the 18th instant, and he left this city for Washington, D. C. four days afterwards. I find that during the raid which was made into this Territory by some armed men from Texas, under Brigadier General Sibley, of the army of the so-called Confederate States, the Indians, aware that the attention of our troops could not for the time be turned toward them, commenced robbing the inhabitants of their stock, and killed, in various places, a great number of people; the Navajoes on the western side, and the Mescalero Apaches on the eastern side of the settlements, both committing these outrages at the same time, and during the last year that has passed have left the people greatly impoverished. Many farms and settlements near Fort Stanton have been entirely abandoned.

To punish and control the Mescaleros, I have ordered Fort Stanton to be reoccupied. That post is in the heart of their country, and hitherto when troops occupied it those Indians were at peace. I have sent Colonel Christopher Carson (Kit Carson), with five companies of his regiment of New Mexican volunteers, to Fort Stanton. One of these companies, on foot, will hold the post and guard the stores, while four companies mounted, under Carson, will operate against the Indians until they have been punished for their recent aggressions. The lieutenant colonel, with four companies of the same regiment, will move into the Navajo country and establish and garrison a post on the Gallo, which was selected by General Canby; it is called Fort Wingate.

I shall endeavor to have this force, assisted by some militia which have been called out by the governor of the Territory, perform such service among the Navajoes as will bring them to feel that they have been doing wrong.

I am, general, respectfully, your obedient servant,

James H. Carleton,

Brigadier General, Commanding.

Brigadier General Lorenzo Thomas,

Adjutant General, U. S. A., Washington, D. C.

Carleton's method of bringing the marauding Indians to feel that they had been "doing wrong" is stated with his characteristic simple vigor in his instructions to his right-hand man Kit Carson, Colonel commanding the First New Mexico Volunteers, dated at Santa Fe, October 12, 1862:

All Indian men of that tribe [Mescalero] are to be killed whenever and wherever you can find them. The women and children will not be harmed, but you will take them prisoners, and feed them at Fort Stanton until you receive other instructions about them. If the Indians send in a flag and desire to treat for peace, say to the bearer that when the people of New Mexico were attacked by the Texans, the Mescaleros broke their treaty of peace, and murdered innocent people, and ran off their stock; that now our hands are untied, and you have been sent to punish them for their treachery and their crimes; that you have no power to make peace; that you are there to kill them wherever you can find them; that if they beg for peace, their chiefs and twenty of their principal men must come to Santa Fe to have a talk here; but tell them fairly and frankly that you will keep after their people and slay them until you receive orders to desist from these headquarters; that this making of treaties for them to break whenever they have an interest in breaking them will not be done any more; that that time has passed by; that we have no faith in their promises; that we believe if we kill some of their men in fair, open war, they will be apt to remember that it will be better for them to remain at peace than to be at war. I trust that this severity, in the long run, will be the most humane course that could be pursued toward these Indians.

There were rumors of another Texan raid, and it was no time for half measures. Treaties, moreover, had lost their novelty—and the new department commander was no treaty-maker in any event. Twenty-five years of service as an Army officer on the western frontiers had taught him a number of things about Indians. He knew that the Navaho in particular had been spoiled by too many treaties, too much empty talk and hollow threatening. They had a lesson coming—a lesson long delayed by the timidity or the ignorance of Carleton's predecessors in office—and he (with Kit Carson's expert help) would see that they learned it well. There was no thought of revenge, no impulse of cruelty, in either mind. These two men had the hard common sense to draw the inevitable conclusions of their long experience with Indians. They fully understood the evil, they knew the only remedy; and with the cold precision of surgeons they went to work. Carleton's view of the situation is well stated in his letter of September 6, 1863, to the Adjutant General at Washington:

> The purpose now is never to relax the application of force with a people that can no more be trusted than you can trust the wolves that run through their mountains; to gather them together, little by little, on to a reservation, away from the haunts, and hills, and hiding places of their country; and then to be kind to them; there teach their children how to read and write; teach them the arts of peace; teach them the truths of Christianity.

And then? This frontier Indian fighter who has been accused of ruthless cruelty in the handling of his difficult problem, continues in a vein of surprising idealism:

> Soon they will acquire new habits, new ideas, new modes of life; the old Indians will die off, and carry with them all latent longings for murdering and robbing; the young ones will take their places without these longings; and thus, little by little, they will become a happy and contented people, and Navajo wars will be remembered only as something that belongs entirely to the past.

THE NAVAHO ROUND-UP

The outcome of an expedition led by a Carson and directed by a Carleton could never for a moment have been in doubt. By February 1, 1863, the general was able to report to Washington that the Mescaleros were completely subdued:

> I have now three hundred and fifty of that tribe at Fort

Sumner and *en route* thither. These comprise all that are left of those Indians, except a few who have either run off into Mexico or joined the Gila Apaches. I shall try to settle what have come in on a reservation near Fort Stanton, and have them plant fields for their subsistence the coming year.

The reduction of the Mescaleros was but one phase of the task Carleton had set himself and chosen the famous scout to conduct in person. The Navaho offered a harder problem, for their territory was larger and more difficult to invade, while the tribe was well provided with livestock for food, clothing, and transport, and could make a long resistance.

Elaborate preparations were made for the Navaho campaign, scheduled to begin July 1, 1863. Fort Stanton had been reoccupied, Fort Craig strengthened, and (Old) Fort Wingate established. The last-named was garrisoned by four companies (some 300 men) of the First California Infantry Volunteers, who were to have "at least two companies in the field all the time." Carson was ordered into the Navaho country with his regiment of First New Mexico Volunteers, his total force being 27 officers and 709 men, of whom 260 were unmounted, as revealed by Carleton's order of June 15, 1863, which constituted the force.[5] A new military post, Fort Canby (near present-day Ganado, Arizona), was to be his headquarters, and there large stores of military supplies were gathered.

The orders for the Navaho campaign were identical with those guiding the Mescalero operations which preluded it, except that the Navaho were given until July 20 to surrender themselves and join the captive Mescaleros at Fort Sumner. After that date all men capable of bearing arms were to be killed, all women and children held as captives; crops were to be destroyed, livestock either taken for military use or slain. A bounty of one dollar for each sheep and twenty dollars for every sound horse and mule stimulated Carson's volunteers to look sharp and sweep clean. Garrison commanders throughout the department of New Mexico were ordered to scour their respective territories for Navaho and Apache bands, for it was soon seen that the round-up was scattering the Indians far and wide. The commander at Fort Wingate was instructed to destroy all crops within a radius of seventy miles of his post. And so throughout the summer and fall of 1863 the whole military resources of New Mexico were bent to the task of making either a corpse or a prisoner of every

---

[5] This order is printed in full in the 1867 Report of the Joint Special Committee, source of the various Carleton quotations herein given. It should settle definitely the question of numbers engaged, which have been variously reported.

Navaho then living. The Ute joined the hunt for their own personal reasons and profit; and so many citizens of New Mexico went Navaho-hunting that the Governor had to call them off by proclamation in May, 1864.

Carson marched his command directly to the Pueblo Colorado,[6] where Carleton had ordered him to establish Fort Canby.[7] The post established, he left it with a garrison force and himself took the field. His reports tell of a series of "scouts" throughout the late summer and fall of 1863. Wherever Navaho might be, there rode Carson and his men, covering the whole broad sweep of desert country lying between the Little Colorado and Cañon de Chelly. Zuñi and the Hopi villages lay within the area and Carson visited them both. Each had been suspected of aiding the Navaho, so the Colonel deliberately made them take the role of enemies of that tribe by sending out warriors with his scouting parties. He gave them fair warning that aid to the foe would bring destruction of their villages; this Carleton had solemnly promised the Zuñi, "as sure as the sun shines." The Ute had declared themselves long since, and were happily applying the Carleton policy to their traditional enemies. A very good policy they found it, except that Carson (on orders from Carleton, and against his own judgment) would not let them keep captives they took, for use as slaves or for sale to the Mexicans. They might keep livestock, however, and Carson noticed that their interest in the campaign languished when they had accumulated all the animals they could well manage. Like the Navaho, they were accustomed to fight only for plunder; but they made efficient scouts and spies, and Carson complimented them highly in his reports from the field.

Chasing small parties of fugitives, capturing livestock, destroying crops, Carson rode up and down the western frontier of the Navaho. He fought no pitched battles, stormed no fortresses, and the work seemed a costly effort from which little good was coming. Carleton encouraged him: "As winter approaches you will have better luck." He could be patient as well as fiery; and small bands of Navaho were already coming in voluntarily, destitute and half-starved.

Winter came, with heavy falls of snow to drive the fugitives down

---

[6] A small stream tributary to Leroux Wash, and thus to the Little Colorado. See map inside cover.

[7] Apparently nothing remains today of this temporary fort. Nobody at Ganado could tell me its location or anything about it—but it must have been there or thereabouts, for the ancient ruins known as the Pueblo Colorado are two miles upstream (pl. 79).

PLATE 75

a

b

Two chief blankets of the Bosque Redondo period. **a** size 76 x 56 ins., colors black, white, indigo blue stripes with red bayeta figures. Collected by Thomas S. Twiss in the 1860's, presumably at Fort Laramie, Wyoming, this (if the history is accurate) is the earliest known chief blanket to depart from the traditional pattern of plain stripes. Museum of the American Indian, Heye Foundation cat. 10-8457.

b size 72 x 52 ins., colors black, white, indigo blue, and bayeta red (short stripes). Bought in Colorado some time before 1870 by Wm. Stanley Hatch and sent to Edward Trowbridge of Cambridge, Mass. Wm. Claflin Jr. museum cat. 24799.

PLATE 76

A pre-Bosque **serape**. It came into the present owner's family in 1860 at Santa Fe, New Mexico, with the signs of several years of careful use already upon it, hence may easily antedate the fifties. This specimen is not for sale, and I withhold the owner's name to spare him the importunities of collectors; anyhow it is destined to a museum, where all such fine pieces should lie forevermore. Size 48 x 67 ins., colors indigo blue (rather streaky), ivory-white and rose bayeta. Thread count variable, averaging 13 warp and 35 weft to the inch.

from their mountain retreats, and the general back in Santa Fe urged a move long planned—the invasion of Cañon de Chelly, where the Navaho had always felt themselves secure. So on January 6, 1864, Carson with 14 officers and 375 men moved upon this tremendous chasm of red sandstone, into which previous expeditions against the Navaho had glanced timorously and then retreated in haste, lest its sheer walls prove a death-trap. He did not enter it at once (Carson had learned years ago that he who takes fewest chances lives longest, in frontier warfare) but divided his forces into two parties and sent one along each rim of the chasm to reconnoiter the depths below. The plan was to join a third detachment, Company H of the First Cavalry, New Mexico Volunteers, under Captain Albert H. Pfeiffer, which had been sent direct from Canby to reconnoiter the eastern opening of the north branch (now called Cañon del Muerto) of the cañon. The parties on each rim advanced to within sight of the eastern mouth, but no sign of Pfeiffer's party was seen. Puzzled, Carson turned back to his camp, and there was the missing contingent! They had traversed the cañons from east to west, a distance of some thirty miles, with Indians harrying them constantly from above, and ice on the stream in the cañon bottom making progress painfully slow. Not a man was lost, however, for the very height of the cañon walls—more than a thousand feet for much of the distance—kept the enemy from doing any severe damage. It was a bold move, nevertheless, for the Navaho might have hemmed them in or laid a successful ambush in the little-known depths of the great chasm. Pfeiffer knew neither their strength nor the character of their stronghold when he plunged into it and staked all on his ability to win through.

Company H had found few Indians on its march—but might there not be more fugitives in the south branch? Captain Asa B. Carey took the company and marched through Cañon de Chelly from the west, while Carson and the command waited shivering in the base camp. Carey had less trouble and better fortune than Pfeiffer, for a large group of Navaho surrendered to him without a struggle, and "that night I counted 150 full-grown Indians in my camp, besides many children," he says in his report, as reprinted in Sabin.

The cañon invasion determined the success of the round-up. Even the *ricos,* the wealthy stock-owners of the tribe who thought they could retire with their herds to the lofty Chusca Mountains and escape American capture, saw that their enemy would go anywhere to get them, while the humbler tribesmen beheld their last refuge taken away. To all the dread

truth came plainly home: nowhere on earth could they hide themselves away from Kit Carson's men. "We have shown the Indians that in
no place, however formidable or inaccessible in their opinion, are they
safe from the pursuit of the troops of this command; and have convinced
a large portion of them that the struggle on their part is a hopeless one,"
Carson wrote to his commander on January 23, 1864. Death, capture,
starvation, surrender: those were the alternatives. Most of the tribe chose
surrender, and all through the spring of 1864 Forts Canby, Defiance, and
Wingate did a thriving business in Navaho prisoners en route, via Los
Pinos on the Rio Grande, for the new home of the tribe at the Bosque
Redondo, near Fort Sumner on the Pecos. A count made the next year
showed a total of 8,491 Navaho assembled there in the distant Mescalero
country.

Fort Canby was abandoned in August of 1864. The troops were sent
into Arizona on an Apache campaign, Carson going to the Bosque Redondo for a time, later on a successful expedition against the allied Comanche and Kiowa on the western plains. Pressure on the Navaho was
continued relentlessly, however, and in March of 1865 Carleton was informed by a "chief" who had been sent back from the Bosque to persuade
others to surrender that only six small bands were left. Largest of these
was that of Manuelito, sometimes called the "last great chief of the
Navahos," comprising about one hundred persons in very poor shape. But
these few die-hards caused little trouble; the Navaho as a free people had
ceased to exist.[8]

Carleton and Carson had performed a highly successful operation, removing the offending organ bodily and with scant loss of blood, for the
casualties on either side were not high.[9] But would the patient recover
and return to normal health? That problem, unhappily, could not be
solved by their special type of skill. In truth, their work was done. Carleton had charge of the Navaho throughout their captivity, it is true, but
his military mind like his military machine proved utterly unadapted to
the problem that now arose: a problem in psychology, in sociology, in
economics, in government. It was doomed to failure; not only for being
imperfectly understood and grossly mishandled, but for resting on the old
false premise that the red man can be made like the white man. So the
great human drama of Bosque Redondo moves into its second act, of

---

[8] Manuelito surrendered in October, 1866.

[9] "Less than fifty Navaho killed" says Cheetham (393), who evidently speaks
from the official record. Army losses were much less.

PLATE 77

Serape of the Bosque Redondo period; size 49 x 72 ins., colors indigo blue stripes out-
lined in black, white bands. This specimen has no Navaho history; it is strongly
Puebloan in type, as witness the warp fringe and the unbound edge. Lieut. G. K.
Warren presented it to U. S. National Museum in 1866. Cat. 1891.

PLATE 78

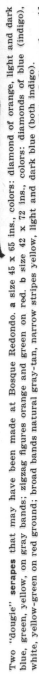

a

b

Two "dougie" **serapes** that may have been made at Bosque Redondo. a size 45 x 65 ins., colors: diamond of orange, light and dark blue, green, yellow, on gray bands; zigzag figures orange and green on red. b size 42 x 72 ins., colors: diamonds of blue (indigo), white, yellow-green on red ground; broad bands natural gray-tan, narrow stripes yellow, light and dark blue (both indigo).

Both blankets traded to C. A. McGregor at Fort Reno, Oklahoma Territory, between 1875 and 1880 by Plains Indians who said they got them from the Navaho, who "made them in that country", this suggesting Bosque Redondo. Although they antedate 1880 beyond question, I cannot escape the conclusion that the scarlet red in each and a metallic blue-green (badly faded) in a are aniline. Americans at the Bosque could have supplied such dyes even at this period, for the first American dye factory dates from 1864.

which the scene is laid in a vast barren valley which ten thousand un-skilled and unwilling hands are expected, somehow, to transform into a farm.

BOSQUE REDONDO

The Bosque Redondo—part of a reservation forty miles square, with Fort Sumner in its center—proved no Promised Land, and the "children" who were forcibly led forth from their wilderness to people it clamored unceasingly to be led back again. In its new home the transplanted tribe found itself sharing the bottom-lands of a broad bend in the Pecos river with some four hundred Mescalero Apache who were there first and considered the place rightfully their own. It was Carleton's plan to develop farming in the irrigable portions (estimated at six thousand acres) of the locality and make both tribes self-supporting, contented and peaceful tillers of the soil. The Navaho were accordingly set to work digging ditches and breaking ground for planting. The work did not please the formerly free-roving Indians; neither did its monotonous, unmilitary character appeal to the soldiers in charge of this curiously socialistic experiment in civilization by fiat of military government. It required no Delphian oracle to foretell that matters would not run smoothly in the new colony, but only a daring imagination could have conjured up all the miseries and disappointments that actually came to pass.

Man and nature seemed in league from the outset to defeat Carleton's solution of the Navaho problem. Man's part was a feud of increasing bitterness between the civil and military authorities of the federal government—between Matthew Steck, Superintendent of Indian Affairs in New Mexico under the Department of the Interior, and General Carleton, military commander of the territory. Carleton, having by military tactics provided the hungry mouths to feed, expected Steck to help with the feeding. The military were fighters, not Indian guardians, was his attitude: he had carried his campaign to a successful end and spoiled the Navaho for war, now let the Indian Service foster their career in the arts of peace. Steck, however, saw matters differently. He had never favored the removal of the Navaho from their homeland (although he did believe in the reservation-and-concentration policy) and he had no appropriation, no provision of any sort, for assuming the sudden burden of eight thousand helpless, starving souls. Carleton had started this mess, let him clean it up. Steck campaigned so actively against the Bosque plan that a controversy arose involving the whole territory of New Mexico and the honor and

glory of the Departments of War and Interior at Washington, until
finally a special committee from Congress journeyed to the scene of dispute and took reams of testimony on whether the Indian Service should
be under the one or the other Department, whether Indian tribes should
be packed about the country like traveling minstrels or settled on reservations in their own territory.[10] All of which helped mightily to feed and
clothe the destitute Navaho!

Carleton made heroic efforts to meet the situation and his disgruntled
soldiers worked like Trojans. Thirty miles of irrigation ditch was dug, two
thousand acres of land plowed and planted to wheat, corn, beans, by
the season of 1865. But there can be no harvest with nature unfriendly:
every crop planted in the years 1864 to 1867 was a failure. Sometimes it
was insects, again drought; or again, a flood in the Pecos, or lashing
winds or unseasonable cold. The land seemed cursed and all went wrong.
The water (slightly alkaline, even the most ardent pro-Bosqueists admitted) sickened men, killed livestock (the Indians said), and poison weeds
killed more. Starvation and want were never beyond sight, with rations
habitually short and unpalatable; for the Navaho found it hard to ac-
custom themselves to wheat flour, the staple of diet. Wood was difficult
to find (fancy a Navaho grubbing up mesquite roots!), and the captives
shivered through bleak winters in flimsy shelters of brush and canvas,
while the Comanche and Kiowa raided their dwindling flocks and herds.

Mescalero and Navaho never realized Carleton's fond prophecy that
the two, being racial cousins, would merge into one people. They fought
and bickered continually, and when the entire Mescalero contingent of
nearly four hundred souls silently left the reservation one night in November, 1865, the Navaho were too hopeless to rejoice. They got the
Mescalero lands—but to what good, if nothing came to harvest? In the
spring of 1868, utterly discouraged and demoralized, the Navaho planted
almost nothing, determined at last to meet fate unresisting (although
their agent suspected they were preparing a secret desertion). At last it
was clear that the Bosque Redondo experiment had failed: the Navaho
would not become farmers and the Government would not maintain them
in idleness.

The Government gave in. Lieutenant General W. T. Sherman and
Colonel S. F. Tappan came out from Washington in May, 1868, as peace

---

[10] Both were arguments of long standing, each Department having an immemorial conviction that it could handle Indians more effectively than the other.
Until 1849, when the Department of the Interior was created, the War Department
had charge of Indian affairs.

commissioners to negotiate with the Navaho for their removal to a reservation in the old tribal territory. Both parties were in a tractable mood after so much suffering on the one side and so much costly experimentation on the other, as General Sherman indicated in the following letter to Senator John Sherman, his brother:

Fort Union, New Mexico, June 11, 1868.

Dear Brother:

I have now been in New Mexico three weeks along with Colonel Tappan, peace commissioner, for the purpose of seeing the Navajos, and making some permanent disposition of them. . .

We found 7200 Indians there, seemingly abject and disheartened. They have been there four years. The first year they were maintained by the army at a cost of about $700,-000, and made a small crop. The second year the cost was about $500,000, and the crop was small. Last year the crop was an utter failure, though all the officers say they labored hard and faithfully. This year they would not work because they said it was useless. The cost has been diminished to about 12 cents per head a day, which for 7000 Indians makes over $300,000, and this is as low as possible, being only a pound of corn, and a pound of beef with a little salt per day.

Now this was the state of facts, and we could see no time in the future when this could be amended. The scarcity of wood, the foul character of the water, which is salty and full of alkali, and their utter despair, made it certain that we would have to move them or they would scatter and be a perfect nuisance. So of course we concluded to move them. After debating all the country at our option, we have chosen a small part of their old country, which is as far out of the way of the whites and of our future probable wants as possible, and have agreed to move them there forthwith, and have made a treaty which will save the heavy cost of their maintenance and give as much probability of their resuming their habits of industry as the case admits of. . . (Thorndike: 318-319).

So on June 1, 1868, another Navaho treaty took its place in the long series. This one, however, thanks to the severity of Carleton and

Carson, was to be more than a scrap of paper. It was drawn to encourage farming (for the men must be kept busy somehow), with free implements and seeds, a tract of land (not over 160 acres) to each head of a family wanting it, and a small clothing allowance yearly for ten years. It provided for schools as needed, one for every thirty prospective pupils. Fifteen thousand sheep and goats were to be bought for the tribe (in fact, 30,000 were bought); and they were urgently needed, for the Navaho agent in 1868 estimated that the exiles on returning to their old home had only 1,550 horses, 940 sheep, and 1,025 goats: less than half an animal for every person, if we take the agent's estimate of the population at 8,000 souls.

The conquered Navaho set forth from the Bosque on June 18, 1868, and on November 1 of that year Agent Dodd at New Fort Wingate formally assumed charge of "7,111 Navajo Indians, viz: 2,157 under 12 years of age, 2,693 women, 2,060 men, and 201 age and sex unknown." The Navaho were home again, a sadder and a wiser tribe.[11]

AFTER-EFFECTS

The effects of this violent and complete disruption of Navaho life are beyond calculation. As long as a Navaho remains upon earth the epilogue of Bosque Redondo will be still in the playing, for this episode of five years duration turned the stream of tribal history into a new channel for all time to come.

Bosque Redondo was a military conquest, and very much more: it was the utter subjugation of as free a people as could be found anywhere within or upon the horizons of civilization. No mere change of political sovereignty was at stake as in the wars between western nations, no transfer of nominal allegiance from one state to another, with only a brief disruption of the accustomed routine of living. Bosque Redondo was a moral holocaust, as devastating to Navaho civilization as were the barbarian invasions of the Dark Ages to ours. It destroyed their material prosperity—but that was soon recovered. It abolished their freedom—but even that was of less consequence than its greatest result, which was a silent inner transformation: the destruction of this remarkable people's morale, of its audacious, unbounded confidence in itself. The transformation is epitomized in the spectacle of a nation of barbarian nomads accustomed to ride far and free, fearing nothing on earth and hearkening to

---

[11] The diminished number (from 8,491 at its highest) is due to desertions rather than deaths. The hospital records of Fort Sumner, printed in the 1867 report, reveal no high mortality.

PLATE 79

RUINS. PUEBLO COLORADO CREEK, CANADO.A.T.

Probable site of Fort Canby. Carson was ordered to establish this temporary fort "at the Pueblo Colorado," meaning presumably at the prehistoric ruins bearing that name, which are shown here as a low mass of crumbled stone walls on the banks of the Pueblo Colorado creek or wash. Photo by Charles F. Lummis in 1891. Lummis coll. Southwest Museum.

PLATE 80

89620

Issuing rations at Fort Defiance under the treaty of 1868. Probably one of the later issues—the last was in 1879. Most of the figures in the foreground are wrapped in machine-made (Oregon City type) blankets either issued or sold by traders. Photo from Signal Corps, U. S. Army, photographer unknown.

no lesser voices than those of the tribal gods, meekly shouldering the hoe at the beck of an alien master. To most Indian tribes civilization has come in assimilable drafts. To the Navaho it came as a rushing flood, tumbling their whole world topsy-turvy. From a freedom almost idyllic they were plunged into a perpetual semi-servitude, in just five years.

But we must not over-sentimentalize the effects of Bosque Redondo, for two strongly corrective facts are established beyond question. The first is that the Navaho merited heavy punishment for their cynical disregard of the lives and property of their neighbors, Pueblo and Spanish; and five years of bitter exile is not an inhuman retribution for two centuries of rapine and murder. The second is that the Navaho deliberately threw themselves in the pathway of a relentless force, the westward march of European civilization, and came off very well in the end. No longer free, they are a nation still: larger, wealthier, more secure, than ever before. They have weathered a crisis that proved fatal to many a tribe—that of final adjustment to the conquering American. If that inevitable clash was a brutal shock, Navaho arrogance must be held equally responsible with American rigor. Both parties may with reason deplore the event and rejoice at the outcome; for here, as so often elsewhere, history is justifying at its leisure an act of seemingly intemperate haste and severity.

In its effect on the dominant tribal craft of weaving, the conquest of the Navaho is especially marked. The destruction of most of the tribal flocks of course reduced activity at the loom almost to a standstill, while the troubled and uncertain times of that fateful decade of the eighteen-sixties had no beneficent influence on a craft which is preeminently a sedate and peaceful one.

It is a natural law that everything living upon earth moves through constant slow change, first toward its apogee and always toward its extinction. The institutions and activities of a society show the same tendency, and the upward curve of any of them may be bent downward without a moment's pause in the ceaseless movement of its own infinitesimal flux. Weaving is one of the ancient crafts of mankind, one that has repeated many times over the life story of the individual man: hesitant childhood, vigorous youth, fecund maturity, decline into senescence, perhaps total extinction; but always, it may be in another time and place, there is rebirth and the cycle in motion again. And the transition from one to another of these stages is not necessarily the inexorable march of a natural force (as old age creeps upon man), but more frequently the sudden upshot of an apparently remote and unrelated circumstance. Such an event was Bosque Redondo in the life cycle of Navaho weaving. It marked the passage from brilliant, self-reliant maturity to uncertain, dependent old age. It fixed—definitely and for all time, beyond reasonable doubt—the high point of achievement in this craft, and swung downward in a decline which for being gradual has been none the less constant, a curve that went sweeping proudly upward for at least a century before.

Certain definite factors in the decline are clearly discernible, although one cannot put into words the subtler phases by which degradation creeps into the practice of a craft of such large artistic content as that of weaving in the hands of the Navaho.

The conquest brought many changes in Navaho life which bore directly on the loom. It destroyed the old unthinking freedom, killed the joyous, prideful spirit in which fine blankets were woven and worn before Government-issue clothing set a lower standard of tribal dress, and the gaudy figures of cheap calico conveyed a feeling of discouragement to the over-modest weaver. It brought in the resident trader with his cheap cotton twine to provide a warp, ready-spun, in place of the stronger native wool warp of earlier times; with his Germantown yarns as a quick substitute for bayeta, and his aniline dyes to displace the native colorants of infinitely finer tone. It set an alien master (and often of the least worthy)—figuratively—beside every loom in the land, to tell a sensitive, talented, and artistic weaver how to make a blanket that would have a proper barbaric appeal to an intruding white man; to impose the dictates of a selfish instinct of gain upon an artist immensely superior to her instructor except in her simplicity and helplessness. It opened a door, in short, through which flowed that mediocre flood of frontier civilization and petty officialdom from which the Navaho by a sure instinct had hitherto held themselves aloof. And as regards the Navaho blanket, the conquest of the Navaho commercialized that article for all time to come. Hitherto it had been woven as a garment for one of the tribe, and tribal standards had been at stake in its every stitch; now it was to be made, more and more as time passed, as a floor rug for a distant, alien woman, bought for her for a pittance by an unresponsive trader whose sole interest was in making a profitable sale. The conquest of the Navaho made the blanket a rug, made a journeyman weaver of the Navaho artist in wool. Is it any wonder that the blanket of pre-Bosque times is an utterly different thing from the rug of today?

PLATE 81

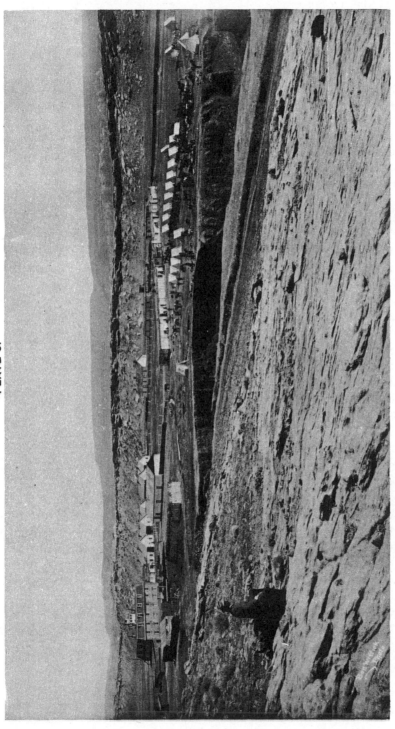

Fort Defiance about 1890. Most of the buildings date from years before the agency was established. Wittick coll. Laboratory of Anthropology.

PLATE 82

An early bordered pattern. Navahos at Fort Defiance in 1873, photo by T. H. O'Sullivan of the Wheeler Survey, 1873. This is the earliest bordered pattern of record; it is meandered, not straight as in later times. Munk Library coll. South west Museum.

CHAPTER XII

BLANKET TO RUG
THE TRANSITION PERIOD—1870-1890

E COME now to the stage in the history of Navaho weaving that witnessed the gradual transformation of the blanket, an article of clothing for the Indian, into a rug, an article of furniture for the American. Politically it is a time of peace; nowhere has the Navaho shown greater intelligence than in his implicit acceptance of the lesson of Bosque Redondo and the absolute sovereignty of the United States of America. Only fools, it is said, make the same mistake twice. The Navaho has been no fool. One sharp experience taught him the new rules of the game of living and he has respected those rules, in letter if not in spirit, ever since they were so forcefully brought to his notice. In his case particularly, discretion has proved the better part of valor—powerfully aided, it is true, by the fortuitous circumstance alluded to by General Sherman in the letter quoted in the previous chapter, that the Navaho country was not likely to be needed for American settlement. Fortunately for the tribe it has not been needed. Certain lands along the San Juan were once coveted by white settlers and an attempt made to dispossess the Navaho; a similar attempt was made by the Board of Supervisors of Coconino County, Arizona, a few years later; and again, a persistent belief in valuable mineral deposits in the Carrizo Mountains threatened to open a small area to American exploitation. But the minerals were not found, and the Navaho reservation has grown steadily in area [1] to keep pace with a constant tribal increase in numbers [2] and in wealth.[3]

The fortunate Navaho enjoys almost undisturbed the barren freedom of his ancestral domain. His tribal range is from Jemez, as of old, to the Little Colorado, a considerable gain westward. On the north he has crept a bit beyond the old barrier of the San Juan, for the Ute is no longer there to dispute the passage. Southward he ventures little farther than the Santa

---

[1] From 5,200 square miles in 1868 to 19,913 today. Successive RCIA will supply details of growth to the reader interested.

[2] 8,181 in 1869, at first distribution of annuity goods under treaty of 1868, to 40,858 in 1930.

[3] 30,000 sheep in 1870 to 1,370,000 sheep in 1931.

Fe railroad; no hardship, for he never had attempted to go much beyond Fort Wingate and Cebolleta and the old military road that linked them before the iron track was laid. Even the railroad has conformed to Sherman's prophecy and left the Navaho territory unriven.

Within this broad extent of country as yet uncoveted by the conqueror the Navaho leads a life closely approximate to that of old. Sheep and horses are still his main preoccupation and source of wealth, the hogán (to the horror of hygienists) is still his home. Established traders furnish the American goods—clothing and staple groceries—which have fixed themselves in the tribal economy, and provide a steady and sure outlet for his wool, pelts, and native rugs. Of late years, oil revenues have proved a new source of income. Government has developed new water supply and improved old, it has bettered (for commercial purposes) the quality of his sheep and their fleece, and it has stood ready in emergencies, as during the drought of 1894-95 and the severe winter of 1931-32, to feed him and his animals. Officials, educators, reformers, have proved only a mild annoyance at their worst, good friends at their best. All in all, civilization has been forced on the Navaho only in very mild doses, after the heavy purging of Bosque Redondo; and he has shown his gratitude by an exceptional record of good behavior.

THE FIRST TRADING POSTS

As viewed from the vantage point of today, the circumspection with which the white man has penetrated the Navaho country is laughable. Literally for centuries, the proud, all-conquering European nibbled timorously at the edges of this area which today occupies three counties on the map of two states, with all the caution of a Da Gama eying darkest Africa. Spain would gladly have settled the fertile valleys of the San Juan and its tributary streams of the northern frontier had the Ute and the Navaho been willing. But her colonists and soldiers found it sounder strategy to content themselves with the Rio Grande valley, her priests and missionaries took heed of the experience of Fray Alonso de Benavides and his unsuccessful mission for the Navaho founded at Santa Clara pueblo in 1622. "Nabajó" bespoke all the terrors of the unknown. When the New Mexican ventured within its borders he went armed and in force. Far from thinking seriously of settling there, he was glad to get out with a whole skin; and he would sooner set out alone for Mexico City than for the San Juan river or Cañon de Chelly.

When New Mexico became American territory through the Mexican

War the Navaho country began to lose its fearsome repute. Military expeditions marched through and around it every year or two, as we saw in Chapter 11. Forts were established on its southern borders: Defiance in 1852, Old Fort Wingate in 1862, New Fort Wingate a few years later. Still there was no thought of settlement; and until Kit Carson's campaign of 1863-64 and the subsequent establishment of the reservation, the Navaho's traditional domain was respected as enemy territory. Law halted on its borders and force alone ruled within.

Meanwhile the American was creeping upon the Navaho from another side, from the north. The persecuted Mormons who fled to the shores of Great Salt Lake in the years following 1846 sent a long arm southward and planted small colonies in the valley of the Virgin and its tributary the Santa Clara, not far from the Colorado River. Soon they were crossing that difficult stream, sending missionaries among the Hopi [4] and giving presents to the Navaho who would block the trail to the villages of that people. Cordial relations were fostered by a policy of avoiding bloodshed whenever possible. In consequence the Mormon elders on the north went peacefully among the Navaho at the very time that tribe was in open warfare against every alien living southward.

After Bosque Redondo and its chastening lesson, peaceful penetration of both fronts became easier. The Mormons established a trading store at Lee's Ferry on the Colorado in 1874 (Little: 129).[5] In that and the year following they were colonizing the Moenkopi and the adjacent Little Colorado valleys (Little: 110, 134)—west even of the Hopi villages, but in territory already overrun by the fast-spreading Navaho. Trade between Mormon and Navaho became a routine affair, and Little (134) quotes Hamblin as saying of the Lee's Ferry store in the years 1874-75 that "the Navajoes carried on quite an extensive trade with our people, principally in exchanging blankets for horses." The era of the trading post had dawned, and Navaho blankets were a recognized article of exchange. They were freighted to Salt Lake City along with the wool and hides bought; the trader paid twenty-five cents a pound for blankets, Mr. Joseph Lee recalls.

Lee's Ferry appears to have been the first trading post devoted pri-

---

[4] Jacob Hamblin led the first party in 1858, making frequent visits thereafter, as told by Little. In 1858 he took them a present of $60 worth of goods consisting of "wool cards, spades and other articles" (Little: 64). This reminds me that General Carleton is quoted in the 1867 Report of the Joint Special Committee as sending a quantity of wool cards to the Bosque for the use of the Navaho there.

[5] Hubbell (24) says that John D. Lee was at Lee's Ferry when he stopped there in 1872, but gives no hint of the existence of a trading post.

marily to the Navaho trade, but the sutler's stores of the army posts, Forts Wingate and Defiance, were exchanging American goods for Navaho even earlier, laying the foundation of that commerce which was destined to grow so rapidly in decades to come. I find little in the published accounts to throw light on the first traders' stores, but three pioneers of the movement have helped me with their personal recollections and to them I am largely indebted for the following information.[6]

The late S. E. Aldrich of Whittier, California, had the longest Southwestern experience of the three; he was soldiering in New Mexico in the early seventies, and in 1882 he entered the trading business. Mr. Joseph Lee is another; he went to Tuba City (of the Moenkopi colony) in 1879 and has lived thereabouts, engaged in Indian trade, ever since. Mr. C. N. Cotton, now of Gallup, New Mexico, is the third. He was the partner of that prominent early trader, the late J. Lorenzo Hubbell at Ganado, and later a wholesaler (the first one locally, I believe) at Gallup. Mr. Lee's recollections cover the Mormon area which I have called the northern front, while Messrs. Cotton and Aldrich speak of the growth of the trading business with the authority vouchsafed only to men who may rightly be classed among its founders.

By the middle seventies two more traders have entered the scene. The late J. Lorenzo Hubbell vouches for one in an article of reminiscence written shortly before his death in November, 1930. This was "a Mr. Coddington, who operated a trading post at Fort Wingate" (Hubbell: 26). Mr. Hubbell worked for him before venturing out on his own. Messrs. Aldrich and Cotton both recall very dimly the other as "Old Man" Leonard, trader at Fort Defiance, who about 1875 moved to the site of the present Ganado, Arizona, and bought out Stover and Crary there. Thomas V. Keam, like Mr. Aldrich an ex-soldier, was Leonard's successor at Fort Defiance, these gentlemen both say.[7] Leonard was soon to have a neighbor in his stand on the Pueblo Colorado wash, where Fort Canby stood for just over a year in 1863-64. Hubbell in 1876 left Mr. Coddington and established himself three miles upstream from Leonard, at a point which as nearly as I can determine is the exact site of Fort Canby—the spot

---

[6] Supplemented by the written record wherever possible. Dates are apt to be only approximately right in this account, for it is hard to think back fifty or sixty years with perfect accuracy.

[7] Keam was with Carleton's California Volunteers on their march to New Mexico in 1862. After discharge he became a Government interpreter, later a Special Agent of the Office of Indian Affairs. In 1882 he settled at Keam's Cañon (see map), later selling his property there to the Government and retiring to his old home in Cornwall, England.

where the Pueblo Colorado or "Red Village" ruins stand.[8] This territory was not included in the reservation as first established, and Hubbell homesteaded his land. The agent at Fort Defiance in his report for 1876 mentions one licensed trader on the reservation—evidently Keam, Leonard's successor at Fort Defiance.

Hubbell bought out Leonard after two or three years (hence about 1879) and moved down to the Leonard stand, now Ganado. The former owner went into the cattle business and disqualified himself for further immortalization in this record. In 1884 or 1885 (Mr. Cotton is certain of the later date, but the earlier has been reported) Mr. Cotton became the partner of Hubbell at Ganado.[9] There he remained until in 1894 or the following year he moved to Gallup and started the wholesale business which until recently occupied him continuously since its establishment.

Meanwhile others had opened trading stores among the Navaho. Thomas V. Keam in 1882[10] had taken up a homestead and opened a store at the cañon which now bears his name. It was really in Hopi territory, but got Navaho trade as well. In the same year Mr. Aldrich entered the trading business. With J. W. Bennett he established a store at Manuelito,[11] on the new railroad line and almost due south of Fort Defiance. Later in that year Bennett sold his interest to Elias S. Clark, who subsequently became an attorney at Phoenix, Arizona. Bennett was owner of the store at Houck's Tanks which he had bought from its founder about 1880.

Business going well at Manuelito, the partners promptly branched out. A temporary store was established in Washington Pass, northeast of Fort Defiance, with Clark in charge and Charles Hubbell, brother of J. Lorenzo, as an employee. Welsh visited it in 1884, describing it thus:

> Toward three o'clock in the afternoon we came to the trading-tent of Messrs. Clark and Hubbell, two young men,

---

[8] I say the exact site because Carson was ordered by Carleton to establish Fort Canby "at the Pueblo Colorado," evidently meaning at the ruin itself, which is some three miles above Ganado.

[9] He had come west with the railroad in 1882, having been the first telegraph operator at Wingate station.

[10] The date has been variously reported, but Culin in his obituary notice of Keam gives 1882. Culin knew Keam well and may be considered familiar with the point. See American Anthropologist, N. S. 7: 121. Furthermore Agent Sullivan of Moqui Agency writing in August, 1881, mentions Keam as post trader at Ft. Defiance. In the following year the agent mentions Keam's ["Kearn's"] Cañon, indicating that Keam had moved there in the meantime.

[11] Named for the prominent Navaho, commonly known as "Chief Manuelito." A man named Brown was living there and doing a small trading business when the partners arrived. They bought him out.

the former from the state of Maine, the latter of Mexican and American parentage, who have just started what promises to be a successful trading-post among the Navajos. These gentlemen received us with cordial Western hospitality and spared no pains to make us comfortable. Their improvised store consisted of a large tent securely fastened by cords and staples, so as to be capable of resisting the violent winds to which this country is subject. The undivided compartment of the great tent served as a place of business, a kitchen, and a sleeping-room. Across the front part of the tent a rough counter had been erected, backed by a high line of shelves, on which were piled rolls of red flannel, calico, cans of preserved vegetables and fruits, bags of coffee, sugar, and all the heterogeneous collection of goods suited to attract the eye and supply the wants of a semi-savage people. In front and behind the tent, huge bags stuffed with the wool of Navajo sheep, that had been received in trade from the Indians, lay waiting departure for the East. Trotting in over the plain from various directions came, singly or in small parties, Navajo men and women carrying bags of wool behind them and ready to do business with the traders. Others within the folds of the tent leaned reflectively across the counter, meditating with the slowness characteristic of Indian deliberation upon the nature and extent of their purchases. A scene so animated and varied could not but give pleasure to one in any degree appreciative of the picturesque.

Certain Navaho objected to this store for some superstitious reason and Major D. M. Riordan, agent at Fort Defiance, promised the owners a troop of cavalry if necessary to protect them, Mr. Aldrich recalls. The trading tent in the Pass proved but a temporary venture. It was abandoned soon after Welsh's visit, about 1885 Mr. Aldrich thought, and a store opened at Sehili, farther north (pl. 85*a*). This point appears on the General Land Office map of Arizona as spelled above, although other spellings are of record. It is on the upper reaches of the stream which flows through Cañon del Muerto—the stream through which Pfeiffer's cavalry splashed and floundered on an icy January day of 1864, when the Cañon was invaded.

Archie Sweetland bought out the Clark interest in both stores about 1886, and in 1889 he became sole owner of Sehili, which he abandoned about 1890. Deep snow (for it is mountainous country thereabout) forced the Navaho to move out during the winter to find forage for their animals, making this a poor trading stand.

Mr. Aldrich in 1890 launched a new venture, a store at Round Rock some twenty miles northwest of Sehili, on Lukachukai Creek. Henry (Chee) Dodge, well known interpreter and later a man of much tribal influence and wealth, was his partner there for a time, Government regulations requiring a resident owner or partner at every store and Mr. Aldrich being at Manuelito. Not long afterward Mr. Dodge located near the present Crystal store, then unknown. Mr. Cotton bought the Round Rock store some ten years after its establishment, and it has gone through various hands but is still in active trading. A minor venture of Hubbell and Cotton was the establishment in 1886 of a temporary store at Chinle, later an important trading center, with John Bohn in charge, Mr. Cotton recalls. This venture lasted apparently less than a year. The next store at Chinle, that now owned by Camillo García, was built by William Stagg several years later. Ben Wittick photographed it, year unknown, when S. E. Day was its proprietor (pl. 85*b*). Joe Wilkins, a freighter for the Manuelito store for years, started the post at Crystal around 1890. He sold it to J. B. Moore about 1897, says James (205); and Moore from there launched the style in rugs known now as the Two Grey Hills. The latter store, across the Chuska Mountains from Crystal, also was started by Wilkins, upon his sale of the Crystal stand.

Those are the principal stores of the interior territory to 1890. Along the railroad both isolated stores and settlements were springing up constantly. Mr. Aldrich has named several for me and they are worth putting on record, for all got some Navaho trade and helped to spread the new gospel of the white man's ways. And their very multiplicity should bring conviction of the swiftness with which new things among the Navaho displaced the old.

The Lynch brothers, one of them named Hugh, were trading at Navajo, Arizona, about 1881. This was the farthest west of Navaho stores along the railroad, for the tribal territory ended thereabouts. George W. Sampson (Samson?) was established at Sanders, nearby, in 1883; and it was about 1885 that Billy Weidemeyer settled at the spot the Franciscans were later (1898) to make known as Saint Michaels. It was called La Cienega. During this period Cook's Ranch, opposite Manuelito, was a stopping point for westbound travel by road, but it was abandoned soon after the Atlantic and Pacific Railroad reached it.

Nearer Gallup (rapidly becoming the principal railroad point for Navaho trade, although Manuelito for a few years outdid it) was Stover with another partner, not the Crary we have already noted, at Defiance station. They sold out to a man named Smith (small chance for fame has he!). After a hiatus in his proprietorship during which some Arkansas gentlemen tried unsuccessfully to manage the troublesome Indian clientèle while he lolled in California sunshine, he returned thereto, gambled with his customers by way of enlivening business, and by them was killed. The same Sampson or Samson we saw at Sanders established a store at Rock Springs, just north of Gallup, about 1887. Charlie Fredericks was at the Navajo Church, the mighty red sandstone cliff eight miles east of Gallup, around 1890, with a limekiln and a small trading store. In 1889 the agent at Fort Defiance mentioned (RCIA 1889: 256) "thirty-odd traders who surround the reservation at different points." The same report of the following year spoke of nine traders on the reservation (RCIA 1890: 162). Thus the stage was set for the new era of Navaho weaving, the era of the rug.

GENESIS OF THE BLANKET TRADE

The Indian trader (among the Navaho) is just that—a trader. Instead of selling goods, as does the merchant in American communities, he exchanges them. Money has never held the place on the Navaho reservation it occupies elsewhere. To this day few Navaho will accept checks, or even Government currency—and they care little for gold. Money to them is silver; and silver is money not for its exchange or token value, but for an intrinsic value the Navaho can appreciate much more fully than the white man: it is the ingredient of silver jewelry. Jewelry is quite as much a medium of exchange as money. Every trader today has his pawn book and his pawn rack, attesting the common practice of accepting silver and turquoise, coral and shell, in lieu of cash. "That necklace is worth fifty sheep," the trader will tell you. "Sell it? Wouldn't think of it! Old Klah will be around to redeem it when wool season comes." Wool season witnesses a procession of Indians bearing bags and blankets stuffed with wool, to be exchanged first for the family jewelry in pawn, then for the groceries and clothing and knick-knacks only the trader can supply. Money circulates among the Navaho today, but business formerly was done almost wholly by barter: white man's goods on the trader's shelves for everything Indian the white man could use, with the newly built railroad off southward ready to haul it away to market. The Navaho had little

PLATE 83

A weaver of 1873. She and the boy wear striped native garments and the piece in the loom also is striped—no figures in evidence. Photo taken near Fort Defiance by T. H. O'Sullivan of the Wheeler Survey. From Signal Corps, U. S. Army.

PLATE 84

Freighters. Five blankets are shown, none with bordered pattern. Mr. C. N. Cotton identified the driver as J. Lorenzo Hubbell, the picture being without historic record. If he is right Hubbell's apparent age would date this photograph in the early eighties. Courtesy of Mr. C. C. Pierce.

enough to offer: sheep, wool, pelts, dressed deerskins—scarcely anything else. But some one of the early traders had an idea. Why not blankets?

Nobody could deny that the Navaho made a good, honest blanket. The neighboring tribes were well aware of the fact—the Apache, Ute, and many more remote or lesser peoples; and even the Pueblos, who had been great weavers in their time, were relying on Navaho blankets more and more. The Mexicans (meaning, to be precise, the descendants of the old Spanish colonists) had been patrons of the Navaho loom since men's memory ran, and every American who was an old-timer in the country owned a blanket or two—for use as a lap-robe, a bed blanket, or an extra cloak in rough weather. Cowboys would have nothing else as a saddle-blanket. Now why couldn't the market for Navaho blankets be enlarged beyond its local orbit, made to include the people back East who had as yet no idea that the savage western Indians were quite civilized craftsmen in their way? The trader would profit doubly, getting a percentage on the goods exchanged to the Navaho for the blanket, as well as on the sale of the blanket to the white man. Later it was discovered that the idea held promise of a third source of gain: the trader could sell the Navaho certain materials needed in weaving, such as dye, spun yarn, cotton twine for warp, then trade for the blanket, and sell it on the market—three transactions, three separate profits. If one man thought of all that, his portrait, crowned with laurel, should be over every trader's doorway. One man probably did not, but Messrs. Hubbell and Cotton in their store at Ganado were certainly among the pioneers of this ingenious plan for sharing with the Navaho some of the advantages of American methods. I suspect that some prescience of success in this new partnership of weaver and trader may have prompted Mr. Cotton's decision to leave Ganado for Gallup, to become a wholesaler instead of a retailer in the Indian trade. At any rate, he worked vigorously on the problem of creating a market for Navaho blankets "back East." He got hold of a mimeograph outfit and directories of various eastern cities, and proceeded to circularize the "whole country," as he put it in conversation. He featured three grades of merchandise. First came the rugs, the better specimens of blanket being put into this category (possibly to Mr. Cotton goes the honor of another brilliant thought in this series—that of selling blankets for use as rugs). Next grade was the saddle blanket, third the coarse shoulder blanket known among traders as "dougies" [12] (pls. 34, 37, 46, 47, 69, 77, 78). Saddle blankets cost the trader seventy-five cents each, shoulder blankets (the

---

[12] Di-yu-ge, Navaho for a soft, fluffy weave: Ethnologic Dictionary: 244.

serape type, that is, which the trader soon came to know as bed blankets) two dollars. Mr. Cotton says he loaded up, foreseeing a better demand and higher prices when his mimeographed message should have done its work.

The demand, apparently, duly came. From the various annual reports of the agents at Fort Defiance we get fragmentary statistics telling the story of a rising market for the ancient and honored *"serape Navajo,"* now about to become a rug.

References to the economic phase of Navaho weaving occur early in the reservation period, even before the establishment of trading posts could have influenced the craft. Thus in 1873 Special Agent D. Gould wrote that "the manufacture of the well known Navajo blanket is a source of considerable profit to them, by providing them with the main portion of their clothing, by sale, and by trade among the Mormons of Utah Territory, and other tribes of Indians" (RCIA 1873: 274). The agent at Fort Defiance reported in 1880 that the Navaho in that year sold 800,000 pounds of wool and manufactured 100,000 pounds additional into blankets, adding that "the reputation of the Navajo blanket is wide-spread, and a considerable trade is carried on by the Navajos in the sale of their blankets with other Indian tribes and traders" (RCIA 1880: 131). Thus early the trader was a factor in the commerce, it will be observed: just twelve years after Bosque Redondo. In 1882 the agent noted the increased demand for blankets after the coming of the railroad in that year (RCIA 1882: 129); and his successor in 1885 wrote that "the trade of their fabrics with the whites, Mexicans and neighboring Indians furnishes them with a considerable revenue;" also that "a large fancy blanket requires weeks, often months of patient toil, and is worth from $25 to $100" (RCIA 1885: 156). Plate 82*a* shows a blanket woven at about this period, that we may surmise belongs to the "large and fancy" category.

The Fort Defiance incumbent of 1887 [13] gives us an unusually large crumb of information in his report of that year (RCIA 1887: 172):

> An important item of manufacture is the Navajo blanket. There were made during the year about 2,700 blankets, of large and small pattern, ranging in price from $1 to $100 each. Fully two-thirds of this number were sold and traded for goods. About one-fourth of this number were

[13] Twenty different men held the post of agent at Fort Defiance between the years 1868 and 1898—an average tenure of office of eighteen months. To one who can read between the lines, the whole tragi-comedy of Indian administration in earlier days is epitomized in that brief statement of fact.

PLATE 85

a

b

a, Sehili trading post, or as Ben Wittick spelled it, Tze-he-lih. S. E. Aldrich, one of its founders, identified the stout man seated beside the little girl as Archie Sweetland, proprietor after Aldrich withdrew. Sweetland took over the store about 1886 and abandoned it about 1890, thus dating the photograph. Eight blankets are shown, none with bordered pattern. Courtesy Laboratory of Anthropology, Wittick coll.

b, An early trading post. The present Garcia store at Chinle, photo by Ben Wittick about 1890, when Mr. S. E. Day was proprietor. It is still in active business. Wittick coll. Laboratory of Anthropology.

PLATE 86

A Saxony yarn blanket. Size 58 x 81 ins., colors dark and light blue and green, red, white; cotton warp. Given to O. H. Browning, Secretary of the Interior 1865-1869, and in his family until bought by the Indian Arts Fund. Laboratory of Anthropology, cat. T-175.

what is known as fancy blankets, ranging from $4 to $100 in price, according to size, quality, and style. These blankets are much prized and sought after by hunters of Indian relics and curiosities. The time occupied in weaving a large-size fancy blanket is from two to three months. The other blankets are of a cheaper and coarser grade, and valued at from $1 to $5. Of the latter they sell and trade a large number to the Apache and Ute Indians, who seem to prefer them to the Government blanket for actual wear.

This account makes it clear enough that the bulk of Navaho output at this time was the "dougie" type—the coarse, soft, striped-pattern blanket useful in so many ways, whether as garment or article of bedding: the type of blanket shown in plates 34, 37, 46, 47, 69, 77, 78. The fancy blanket, we may be sure, was either of Germantown yarn or of wool colored with the new aniline dyes, of which more is said a few pages farther along. This type evidently was prized for its oddity rather than for utility; it was collector's material, often made to order. Two types then are clearly in the picture of this transitional period in Navaho weaving. One is the old traditional shoulder blanket, strongly Pueblo in general character (perhaps because the Pueblo type is somewhat simpler in pattern and more loosely spun and woven than the usual Navaho specimens, and the tribe at this period was still impoverished and crushed from the bitter experience of Bosque Redondo); it was truly a blanket, but was destined soon enough to grow thicker, larger, heavier—to become a rug.[14] The other type has fewer native characteristics still. Its garish colors are aniline, its pattern less and less typically Navaho as time passes, its size and shape anything the white man may see fit to order or feel able to afford. These two types soon merge into one: the hard, heavy, colorful Navaho rug of the modern period. From about 1890 onward most Navaho textiles (except the smaller saddle blankets, women's dresses, saddle throws, pillow-tops) are of this type. In general size and proportion they are reminiscent of the "dougie", which is itself related to the poncho serape of more opulent and independent days; but there is little other resemblance to these older types.[15]

---

[14] The cowboys, best early American customers of the Navaho loom, demanded a larger blanket than the strictly native "dougie", which measured about 40 x 70 inches, Mr. Cotton told me, for more comfortable sleeping on chilly nights. Hence they were among the first to foster that enlargement of the Navaho blanket which finally produced rugs of full living-room size, of which specimens are seen in pls. 90, 91b.

[15] The persistence of the traditional sizes in Navaho weaving may be ascribed

In 1890 we get our first estimate of the cash value of Navaho weaving. The agent for that year reports a total output valued at $40,000, of which $25,000 was sold, $15,000 kept for tribal use (RCIA 1890: 162). About two blankets (or rugs) of every three are now woven for the market, on the basis of this estimate. Nine years later, year 1899, Mr. Cotton, now at Gallup in the wholesale trading business, is quoted as estimating the blankets shipped out in that year as worth about $50,000 (RCIA 1899: 157). Navaho weaving is becoming truly an industry; but these figures are pale by 1913, when F. H. Abbott, Secretary of the Board of Indian Commissioners and one who should know, estimates the total sales at one-half million dollars (Abbott: 27-28). Ten years later, 1923, Lindquist (277) gave total value as $750,000 annually, with 5,500 weavers at work. By 1931 the estimates reached the million mark (Burge as quoted herein, Chapter 15); and there we may well stop. But before leaving the topic let us glance backward and do a bit of figuring: we find that since the first reported estimate of annual sales value—$25,000 in 1890—the increase has been just forty-fold in forty-one years.

COMMERCIAL YARNS

The phenomenal growth of the Navaho weaving industry was due not alone to the efforts of the pioneer traders and dealers. Aniline dyes must be given a large measure of credit, for the laborious processes of native dyeing could never provide enough color for a million dollars' worth of blankets in a single year; and along with aniline dyes, the influence of commercial yarns must be considered; they came even earlier.

Always, Navaho weaving has had the benefit of materials directly attesting the superior textile skill of the white man. First it was bayeta, machine-spun and vegetal dyed in colors the Navaho could never equal. Then as the lumbering caravans of the Yankee trader flowed into New Mexico along the Santa Fe Trail, a rival to bayeta crept into favor; it was manufactured yarn, vegetal dyed like bayeta cloth, but ready for the loom without the tedious process of raveling and retwisting. We know that yarns were used in Navaho blankets as early as the eighteen-sixties

---

in part at least to the fact that convenience as well as custom prescribes certain sizes of loom as most easy to rig and to operate (the reader will not have forgotten that a new loom is made for every blanket, thus avoiding the complete standardization of size we find in the Mexican textiles produced on the permanent—European type—loom); and not only easiest to work, but best fitted to the favorite weaving implements of the operator—batten, shed rods, and heddle rods, which in length should match the width of the loom. These implements, like the loom poles (another standardizing factor) are used over and over, and weavers have different sets, large and small, for rugs of different sizes.

(see plate 1), and it is quite probable that they came in a decade earlier. I have been told that these early yarns came from Germany, imported mainly by German Jews who were refugees of the revolutionary movements which swept Europe in the middle of the 19th century. Certain it is that many of the names associated with the heyday of the Santa Fe Trail suggest such origin. On display in the State Historical Museum at Santa Fe, for instance, is an old photograph of the five Spiegelberg brothers: Willi, Emanuel, S. J., Levi, and Lehman; and the caption explains that they were established as traders in Santa Fe in 1846. In later years other similar names become familiar: Bernard Seligman, who came to Santa Fe from Germany in 1856;[16] Jake Gold, early Santa Fe merchant, called the first Indian curio dealer; Abraham and L. Staab, who came to the United States in 1858, to Santa Fe in 1860.[17]

SAXONY

Saxony then was the principal woolen center of Europe; America had few such manufactures; so it was natural that these German expatriates should foster the sale of Saxony yarns in their new territory. The name Saxony is still used to designate blankets embodying that old yarn— much rarer, and often finer, than bayeta.[18]

Mr. Cotton suggests that yarns were imported to the Southwest primarily for sale to the Pueblos, for use in their ancient art of embroidery; and it is true that the peaceful Pueblos offered a better market than the elusive marauding Navaho of pre-Bosque days. Mr. Jesse L. Nusbaum had told me that he had heard "from old-timers," I believe, that Bosque Redondo was a strong factor in the introduction of yarn to the Navaho. This story, entirely plausible, has it that the Navaho being on the one hand deprived of their native wool in their exile, and on the other pressed to make blankets as souvenirs for their soldier captors, turned to yarns— presumably supplied by the soldiers from their canteens or trading stores— and there made many of the old yarn blankets like that of Chief White Antelope (pl. 1) [19] and the serape shown in plate 86.

[16] Read: 783.
[17] Read: 785.
[18] Along with Saxony, one hears also, on dealers' or collectors' lips, the term zephyr. Mr. Abbott Stevens of North Andover, Massachusetts, a woolen-mill owner, assures me that this is not a recognized trade term but apparently a catchword or selling term with no definite meaning. It is used, apparently, to designate a yarn of finer quality than the ordinary Germantown, for Mr. Stevens said it suggested to him a fluffy yarn, loosely spun.
[19] Compare Beadle (273) in 1879: "At the Fort [Wingate] officers who wish an unusually fine article furnish both 'chain' and 'filling.''

These early yarns are quite recognizable after some experience by their general softness of color, silkiness of texture, and—most definite of all criteria—the fact that they are nearly always of three-ply weight; the later Germantown is usually four-ply.[20] These facts I have determined beyond all question by careful examination of many specimens. Generally the style and color of a blanket will tell at a glance whether it is of three- or four-ply material, close examination seldom failing to confirm the decision. Few are the blankets made entirely of vegetal-dyed yarn, but little figures and stripes of this fabric appear far more often than one realizes—unless one makes a practice of looking closely at the material—in blankets of the period 1860-1880. The colors I have found most common are red and green. Not all of these pre-aniline yarns have the silky quality of Saxony. Some are coarse as the cheaper yarn of later times and are probably the immediate predecessors, made in America, of the yarn next discussed.

GERMANTOWN

Germantown is the American aniline-dyed successor to the European vegetal-dyed yarns, named for its seat of manufacture, Germantown, Pennsylvania. It came into use among the Navaho about 1880 and for perhaps thirty years was highly popular. It has a strong association with cotton warp, the ordinary wrapping twine of the trading post, which the Navaho liked to use because it saved so much trouble in spinning and gave so fine a warp string. Traders and dealers stamped out the use of cotton warp as detrimental to the wearing qualities of the blanket, but I have noticed that the best old Germantown pieces often have it; and it is found commonly in the cheap pillow-tops today.

Germantown too has died out of favor, and few textiles of modern make embody it. It was expensive, costing ten times more to the pound than native wool; its brilliant colorings proved a temptation the color-starved weaver could not always resist, and blankets of Germantown are often too flamboyant for most tastes; and finally, it merely added to the problem of disposing of the annual Navaho wool clip by diverting a cor-

---

[20] One hears occasionally of "split yarns," yarns the weaver has carefully split in two by raveling, presumably to secure a finer strand. I have never seen any to recognize, although I have a small Germantown saddle throw with a fringe of two-ply, but what of three-ply yarn? I suspect that "split yarns" are either the fine three-ply yarns, tightly woven, of the early yarn days, or else a retwisted strand, perhaps a late bayeta. Given the difficulty of the splitting and the fact that unsplit yarn makes a finer strand than all but the best of native-spun, the practice seems to me to have little to recommend it. The term may be a dealer's or collector's inspiration, unfounded in fact.

PLATE 88

ne essence of Germantown. Chosen for color illustration as an example of the possibilities of German-
wn yarn in good hands. Note that each corner is treated differently, and that the weaver has yielded
udgingly to the vogue for borders. Size 33 x 52 ins., colors as shown, weft all 4-ply Germantown, warp
ading-store cotton.

Without history, it may safely be dated at about the year 1900 on various points of internal evidence.
wner Mrs. Edward H. Angle. Colorist Mr. Clifford Park Baldwin.

PLATE 87

Two early yarn blankets (3-ply) date and colors alike proclaiming them pre-aniline although they are not of Saxony. **a** size 29 x 25 ins., colors: stripes of red, yellow, blue, white; figures of white, yellow, blue bars. Owned by Mr. C. B. Cosgrove and in his family since 1873.

   b size 57 x 41 ins., colors cherry red center and crosses (set in blue), with green meandered lines. Collected by Governor W F. M. Arny in 1872, labeled "Pueblo Indians, N. Mex." U. S. National Museum cat. 11316. This is the earliest dated meander known to me.

PLATE 89

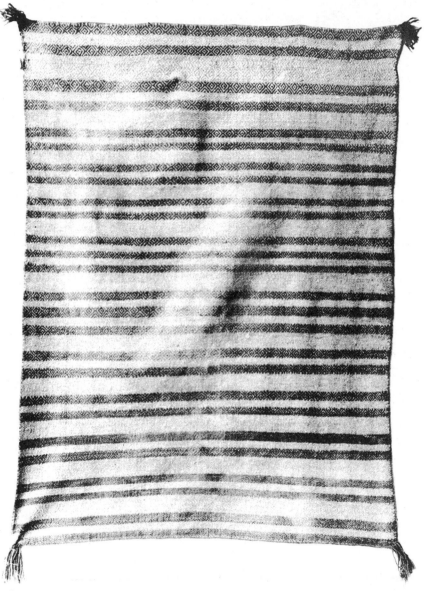

Early Germantown. Double saddle blanket, size 30 x 40 ins., colors red and green, in the 5-unit diamond weave: earliest example of this weave known to me. Washington Matthews coll. U. S. National Museum, cat. 129956. Figure 48 in Matthews 1884, hence woven before that year.

responding quantity of native wool from the loom.[21] Plates 16, 52a, b, 88, 89, 112, show Germantown specimens.

ANILINE DYES

When W. H. Perkin in 1856-57 made the manufacture of artificial dyestuffs commercially practicable he became (at some years removed, to be sure) one of the great arbiters of Navaho economic destinies. The first American dye factory was built in 1864, and a tariff went into effect the same year. By 1870 aniline dyes were in general use. They reached the Navaho country at about the same time as Germantown yarn and cotton warp, around 1880. James, who had the advantage of being much closer to this period than the present writer, says (48) that "Mr. B. F. Hyatt, who was the post trader at Fort Defiance, introduced aniline dyes and taught the Navaho women with whom he traded how to use them. Mr. Cotton wished to do the same at Ganado, but Mr. Hubbell objected, foreseeing what afterwards actually occurred—the deterioration of the quality of the work. . . In the winter of 1886-87, however, Mr. Cotton had his way and he succeeded in having one of the great dye manufacturers put up, ready for use, a quantity of aniline dyes. He instructed the weavers how to prepare them and then encouraged them in the making of various and individualistic designs."

Mr. Cotton has told me of this early step toward the use of aniline dyes, recalling that the firm of Wells and Richardson of Burlington, Vermont, was the manufacturer of these first package dyes, later to become so popular under the trade name of Diamond Dyes. Other brands have invaded the field, some of the wholesalers having their own, but the little paper envelope of powder—dye and mordant combined—still reigns supreme. It has only to be thrown into boiling water (yes, envelope and all, often enough) and the wool boiled in the solution until the color seems right. The process is simple, the dye inexpensive, and the color strong and abundant—if not always of a tone to please the fastidiously color-conscious. Lately, a hue and cry has risen against this cheap package dye which has caught so many unsophisticated tourist eyes (and sold so many Navaho rugs!) with its gaudy tints limning bold, simple patterns. Its muddy hues to many are offensive, and experiments are in course that may end its long vogue; but of this more is said in Chapter 15. Whatever its fate, for good or ill, the packet of colored powder that needed only boiling water to re-

---

[21] A further discussion of Germantown, from the standpoint of design, will be found in Chapter 14.

lease its flood of color has been the keystone of Navaho weaving for a round half-century. Some say famous, others infamous—but all agree that it *made* the Navaho rug.

SUMMARY OF THE TRANSITION PERIOD

The chaotic twenty years following the return of the tribe from Bosque Redondo are hard to whip into ordered clarity for the benefit of a reader perhaps bewildered by the multiplicity of changes and the paucity of information concerning them. Stripped of all useless detail, however, the high lights of the period emerge clearly enough.

With the establishment of the Navaho reservation in 1868 the isolation of the tribe was broken and the American government undertook a deliberate (although not openly declared) campaign of economic dominance as an adjunct to the mailed fist so recently shown its new wards. Clothing was distributed yearly over a period of ten years, it will be remembered. Thus the loom was deprived of its prime function, thrown almost into disuse, as the Navaho learned to depend on the Yankee machine for their clothing.[22] That was one of the shrewd points of Government policy. Another was the encouragement of established traders. They seized upon the outmoded loom quickly enough, taught it to weave rugs for the white man's taste and purse; and again the loom figured in the growing economic vassalage of the prostrate tribe. It happened (we cannot blame the Government for this) that cheap dyestuffs had just come into use: aniline dyes. These the trader assiduously planted in the heart of the new industry, along with commercial yarns and cotton twine. Obviously, the trader's advantage lay in selling the materials of weaving rather than encourage the Navaho to provide their own.

The demand for rugs grew steadily, fostered as it was by many shrewd and zealous minds. Grew too the Navaho demand for American goods, temptingly displayed on every trader's shelves. So the tribe was molded, quickly and easily enough, into that hybrid, pathetic object, the reservation Indian. Even so, the Navaho was lucky: the white man coveted his weavings, not his land. The Navaho found his little niche in the American scheme and dropped quietly into it. His sheep and his loom enable him to play the new game of living the white man's way. The provident barrenness of his country preserves it unto him. A great pity it all is, some will say, thinking of what might have been. A great blessing rather, when we

---

[22] The annuity distribution of 1872, for example, comprised clothing worth $40,000 and "other goods" only $14,000 (RCIA 1872: 53).

PLATE 90

Hubbell store at Ganado, Mr. Hubbell seated in foreground. The Staples rug, largest known to me, is in the right background. Twelve blankets are visible, only one bordered. Photo taken in the late nineties, Wittick coll. Laboratory of Anthropology.

PLATE 91

a

b

a, A carpet yarn specimen. Chief blanket, size about 72 x 60 ins., colors black, white, blue, red. The material dates it early 20th century. Museum of Northern Arizona cat. 590-2833.

　b, A large rug, a Hubbell specialty. Size 11½ x 16 feet, colors black, gray, white. Probably woven about 1910. Displayed in Southwest Hall, Southwest Museum, cat. 267G1. Gift of Dr. Granville MacGowan. Photo by Frashers, Pomona, Cal.

think of what surely would have been except for Spanish sheep and Pueblo loom, barren hills and valleys, trading posts and fancy rug patterns and Diamond Dyes. Say what you will, the Navaho has been lucky from start to finish.

CHAPTER XIII

THE RUG BUSINESS—1890-1932

HE amazingly high figures of annual sales reached in recent years by the Navaho rug were not attained without striving and struggle. Troubles crept into the new industry early in its youth, for something of the frenzied character of a "boom" soon developed in weaving circles. The conjunction of a sharply increased demand with the sudden freedom from the old restricted range of color brought by aniline dyes, seems to have robbed the weavers for a while of their better judgment. They set out to make bigger and brighter blankets with a vengeance. The white man wanted a large, heavy blanket, highly colored, for use on the floor of his hogán, did he? Nothing simpler; and the excited weaver set herself to piling the wool into her enlarged loom without proper cleaning, spinning, or dyeing. Her color combinations were as eccentric as her workmanship was sketchy; and today, when you see a large, coarsely-stitched and loosely spun rug, with a bold pattern of diamonds or checker-boards or jagged meandered lines done in a half-dozen colors including the purple, you may be fairly confident it dates from this "boom" period of about 1890-1900, when aniline dyes were a novelty and commercial demand an intoxicating stimulus. Time has dealt gently with most of the survivors of this esthetic debauch, and many of them are really attractive rugs today; but in their lusty youth they were coarse and shaggy and eye-affronting beyond belief. Many of them, too, have a cotton warp—an excellent criterion of age for the collector's use.[1]

The more conservative of traders and dealers of course saw the dangers springing up and set out to eliminate them. Purple dyes were banned absolutely, cotton warp frowned upon, better workmanship demanded. Lorenzo Hubbell interested himself particularly in patterns, Mr. Cotton has told me, having the artist E. A. Burbank make color paintings of all the old Navaho designs and figures he could find and using them as models for his weavers' guidance. When a pattern proved popular with

---

[1] When in doubt between cotton and wool, apply the match test described on page 93.

buyers, the fact was noted and weavers encouraged to follow its general style.[2] Thus crept in that tendency toward standardization of pattern, with the white man's preferences consecrated in such items as the border and the use of isolated geometric figures in the field thus enclosed—for the Navaho seldom or never employed these graphic devices in earlier times, as the reader will have suspected if he has observed closely the illustrations in this book.

Another strong factor in steadying the wavering course of the infant industry was the Fred Harvey Company, concessionary of the eating-houses and news stands of the new railroad which is now the Atchison, Topeka and Santa Fe.

A vigorous partisan of the new Navaho rug, Harvey featured it on news stands and in train sales along the entire route of the railroad. In 1900 Fred Harvey and the Santa Fe jointly established the Indian Building at Albuquerque (and later the Hopi House at Grand Canyon) now known by travelers at home and abroad. Navaho women weaving blankets in this building afforded an opportunity to travelers to get first-hand knowledge of the craft, thereby arousing the interest of millions. Soon after the establishment of the Indian Building at Albuquerque Fred Harvey contracted with J. Lorenzo Hubbell (Mr. Cotton being then in Gallup) to take his entire output of good or best quality blankets, agreeing on definite prices for certain sizes coming up to certain standards of weave, colors, and design. These prices, seemingly being somewhat higher than those prevailing in some other quarters, at first caused much adverse comment. But Fred Harvey insisted that the business needed greater stability of price and standardization of quality, and that his was the only intelligent course. Some dealers would sell mediocre rugs too high, cheating the customers; others would sell fine rugs too cheaply, cheating the weaver and themselves.[3]

Among the abuses of the early years was that coarse, heavy type of

---

[2] "In his office at Ganado, Arizona, John Lorenzo Hubbell has scores of blanket designs, painted in oil, hung upon the walls, and they present a most surprising and wonderful combination. These are designs that have been found to be pleasing to purchasers, and when a special order for a blanket of a certain design comes in, the weaver is shown the picture of the one desired. She studies it a while, takes the wool provided, or herself prepares it, and then, with such slight variations as she is sure to introduce, goes ahead and makes her blanket."—James 125.

In a photograph of the Aldrich store at Manuelito I noticed a dozen large drawings of rug patterns hung from the ceiling for visiting weavers to see.

[3] Time has proved Fred Harvey right, for today traders have almost uniform prices. Dealers' prices may vary somewhat, but the Navaho rug is in some degree both curio and luxury, and these lines of goods are notoriously variable in price scales.

machine yarn which Hollister (127) calls carpet yarn, saying that the Navaho in Arizona have lately been weaving many rugs of this material. I have seen only a few specimens of the fabric, one of which is shown in plate 91*a*; and inquiry among many persons of long experience with Navaho weaving proved fruitless until I tried the Indian Department of the Harvey Company. There I learned that years ago a "certain trader" at Flagstaff as well as Gallup had introduced in his stores a yarn made of coarse wool costing about half the price of Germantown. "Kemp Blankets" he called these heavy hair-like rugs made of it; and the name has the merit of frankness, for kemp is a hair, peculiar to diseased sheep and fleeces of low quality. The carpet yarn blanket or rug,[4] then, is one made of this low-grade yarn. It has the superficial appearance of Germantown, the colors being identical in general effect, but is very much harder, coarser, and heavier.

The Harvey Company fought carpet yarn as it did Germantown and cotton warp; apparently with especially good effect, for the use of this material seems to have been confined to a brief space of time, soon after 1900, and specimens of it are rare today.

The Harvey Company at about the same time spiked another incipient abuse of Navaho artistry—a very flagrant one—when a rug factory brought out a rug with Navaho designs and sent the Company a sample consignment. The shipment was accepted and paid for, and the samples hung in the various Harvey stores with big placards telling what they were. Nothing more was heard of this pseudo-Navaho rug.

Fred Harvey fought cotton warp and Germantown yarn from the first, labeling specimens of the latter, "This yarn is not Indian spun." The aim was to make and keep the Navaho rug an honest and genuinely Indian piece of merchandise, one that could be sold year after year to a satisfied and constantly growing public. When one considers that thousands of eastern residents were journeying yearly to California, the value of the Harvey sponsorship of the new rug becomes apparent. One may safely say that no other dealer had a fraction of the public following that the nature and extent of his business brought to Fred Harvey.

Another and to my mind a most important activity for which dealer and buyer alike—the collector in particular—may thank Fred Harvey is the buying up of old blankets, the pre-aniline, truly Navaho blanket which the new rug was supplanting so rapidly. Few museums and im-

---

[4] Mr. Aldrich and his wife and son recalled selling this yarn in their store at Manuelito, soon after 1900. It was listed in the wholesaler's catalogue as goat-hair yarn, costing a bit less than Germantown.

portant private collections are without fine old specimens that have passed through his hands. He saw the value of this outmoded article when others less discerning were casting it aside for the new, and I think it no exaggeration to say that Fred Harvey has saved from destruction thousands of worthy old specimens of Navaho weaving. The vision and initiative of Mr. J. F. Huckel, Vice President of the company, and Mr. H. Schweizer, veteran manager of the Indian Department, have brought to the Fred Harvey Company the honor of being a staunch and enlightened protagonist of Navaho weaving, old as well as new.

REGIONAL STYLES AND SPECIALTIES

Navaho weaving has always been in part an alien craft; indeed, its most urgent stimuli have come from without the tribe: Pueblo loom, Spanish sheep, English baize, German yarns, American dyes. Beside these dominant influences, fundamental and widespread enough to affect the entire craft, are others of more local character. Of them, naturally enough, we know less; but we do know that a Spanish influence on both design and color is clearly discernible in many blankets, notably the "slave blankets" presumably woven by Navaho captives in Spanish hands, that some of the Navaho made blankets for trade to neighboring pueblos, after the loose-woven, plain-striped Pueblo style; that others catered to the partiality of the Ute for bold patterns in black and red. In truth, the commercial aspect of Navaho weaving is no new thing. In Chapter 10 we noted the great popularity of the *"serape Navajo"* of a century past. Chief blankets have been found among tribes of the distant Great Plains.[5] Apache, Pueblo, Ute, were all customers of long standing; and to this day the Navaho attend annual *fiestas* at Jemez and Laguna, trade fairs at which they exchange blankets for such Pueblo specialties as pottery, dressed skins, turquoise. Always the Navaho has had many neighbors and customers, white and Indian. Proximity fostered demand, and it would have been poor business not to cater to local taste to a reasonable degree. In the years that followed the establishment of the reservation in 1868, the American has busily surrounded and mingled with the Navaho. His whims are the dominant ones; and he is responsible for a number of parochial developments in the native rug industry.

---

[5] Plates 48, 75, 78, 98, 100, 102, 106 herein show blankets collected among other tribes than the Navaho. Hollister (49) mentions the predilection of the Shoshone for them. Mallery (283 and fig. 238) interprets Lone Dog's Winter Count, Sioux tribe, as recording that in 1853-54 Spanish blankets were first brought to the country. The drawing, figure 238, strongly suggests a chief blanket.

Hubbell of Ganado was the leading innovator of the early days of the Navaho rug business. Long before the twentieth century had rounded its corner he was producing "made-to-order" rugs for the eastern market. Mr. R. T. F. Simpson has told me how he copied two of the Hubbell favorites of the late nineties, a long narrow rug, all native, popular for porches, and the well-known "Moqui pattern"—the old Hopi blue-and black-striped background pattern with bold Navaho figures (generally in red and white) superposed (see pls. 16, 93). It was generally woven of Germantown and many are the specimens extant today, which the expert recognizes immediately by the poisonous purplish cast of the blue stripe—a mockery indeed of the rich indigo blue of the authentic type.

Large rugs (pls. 90, 91*b*) were one of Mr. Hubbell's specialties. He had weavers experienced in the special problems attendant on the production of rugs ample enough to cover the floor of an average room. They were financed by special arrangement, payments being made on account as the work progressed, for few weavers could afford to wait six months or a year for their money. Such rugs were not woven indiscriminately for the market, but as special orders, and few are to be seen today. Plate 91*b* is one of this type, although not certainly known to be from Ganado.

The Hyde Exploring Expedition was another dominant figure in this early-day field of the new rug. Founded in 1893 by two wealthy brothers, B. T. B. and Fred Hyde, it set out in 1896 to build up an extensive business in Indian goods. The late George H. Pepper, to whose work in native dyestuffs that portion of this meager study owes so much, was an employee, and he seems to have led the Expedition on a crusade against the evils of the time in Navaho weaving. His own words best convey his deep conviction (1903: 10):

> What a commentary on our vaunted civilization. Primitive weaving in progress while aniline dyes in a nearby receptacle contaminate more wool. Hideous colors concealing a sister disgrace in the form of cotton warp. Fat envelopes within reach that need but the tearing of an end and lo the white man's dye is ready. And such dyes! Like a plague they have swept across the Navajo land, breeding contagion wherever they went, and, like leprous discolorations they have marred the face of one of nature's children.

Cotton warp and Germantown yarn were opposed no less vigorously, while the colors green and purple were strictly forbidden in all rugs destined to bear the tag of the Expedition. These measures were in accord with the best ethics of the time, for Hollister, about 1903, notes (108) that "there is a tendency on the part of traders to induce the Navajos to return to the old-time methods, and also to insist that when mineral dyes are used they shall be only of the best quality."

Although it maintained curio stores in both New York City and Phoenix, Arizona (publishing a magazine, *The Papoose,* in New York in 1902-03), the Expedition's center of activity was Pueblo Bonito, the famous Pueblo ruin in Chaco Cañon in the east-central portion of the Navaho reservation. Here Pepper conducted extensive excavations [6] financed by the Hydes and scientifically sponsored by the American Museum of Natural History of New York; and here he made those experiments with Navaho native dyes to which his published works herein quoted pertain. The Expedition's trading store at Pueblo Bonito was one of an incipient chain that eventually totaled nine, the aim being to control Navaho weaving at its very source. Other stores were at Manuelito on the railway west of Gallup, at Thoreau, shipping point for Pueblo Bonito, and at Farmington on the northern border of the reservation. Accumulating stocks dictated the opening of retail outlets in Boston, Philadelphia, New York City, and at Paul Smith's in the Adirondacks. Special exhibits were made at various popular eastern resorts. Thus many thousands of rugs were sold, Mr. B. T. B. Hyde told me just before his death in July, 1933, while back at Pueblo Bonito his brother Fred kept a corps of weavers at work on rugs of old pattern. The Benham Indian Trading Company took over the Hyde retail interests, operating the shop in New York City and later moving to Los Angeles, California. This firm no longer exists.

The Hyde Exploring Expedition was short-lived, and its influence on the nascent rug industry is hard to appraise. It did much ardent propaganda in the East at a time when the market for Navaho rugs was still in the making, for good or ill; and for that reason if no other its name should be immortal in this small corner of history.

CRYSTAL AND TWO GREY HILLS RUGS

A trader who distinguished himself by his activities in behalf of better quality in rugs was J. B. Moore, who had the store at Crystal, New Mexico, from some time in the nineties until 1911-12. Seeing that improper scouring of the native wool was one of the greatest faults, he sent quantities of wool to eastern mills for scouring and carding, then had it dyed

---

[6] See his report of the work in Anthropological Papers of the American Museum of Natural History, vol. XXVII (1920).

PLATE 92

An early bordered pattern. Only by an effort did the weavers bring themselves to making the plain-stripe borders of the modern period; all early borders are figured. Photo by A. C. Vroman, P. G. Gates coll. Southwest Museum, taken about 1905.

PLATE 93

The "Moki pattern" popularized by J. Lorenzo Hubbell in the early rug days (see pl. 17). This specimen is of earlier times, for on the authority of Mrs. Mamie Wittick Maxwell, daughter of the pioneer photographer Ben Wittick (whose historic negatives she recently gave to Laboratory of Anthropology) it once belonged to Manuelito (pl. 73). Her father knew the blanket well.

Size 52 x 72 ins., colors: alternate bands of indigo blue and black, whence the pattern gets its name, with figures in bayeta red, white, blue, two shades of green, both 3-ply machine-spun. Mrs. Philip Stewart coll. Laboratory of Anthropology cat. no. 26.

under his supervision in colors selected by him, and by the best weavers made into rugs patterned after his own ideas. The result, as might be expected, was a product of high technical excellence and excessive sophistication in design. James illustrates in color several rugs inspired by Moore or his successor, J. A. Molohon & Co., in his figures 203, 217, 228-234 inclusive, and a mere glance at them reveals the drastic alteration of design by such traders as these. Moore was an energetic man, selling his rugs by mail directly to the consumer, and his successor for years continued the business along the lines already established.

One no longer hears mention of the Crystal rug, but several traders with whom I have talked credit Moore with the inspiration of a regional type that persists to this day—that known as the Two Grey Hills rug. In its best form this type has no dyed colors, being made in the natural colors of white and black, and their combination (in process of carding) which is a gray; Moore evidently popularized gray in Navaho weaving.[7] The pattern is of the sophisticated, intricate Crystal type, generally with an elaborate meandered border. Of late years aniline color has been added, first a mild yellow, later reds and browns, but the characteristic involved pattern and the high quality of workmanship persist. Specimens of this type are the subject of plates 94 and 95.

Two Grey Hills is the site of a trading post some fifty miles southwest of the Government agency at Shiprock, New Mexico, on the San Juan river. It is about equally distant from Crystal, and the lofty Chuska Mountains lie between. Yet the Moore influence has seated itself in this locality, aided by the intelligent coöperation of several traders roundabout no less than by the fact that this region is one of the most favored of nature of the entire Navaho country. Its neighboring mountains, lofty enough to be heavily forested, assure a rainfall much greater than the average for the reservation; so with water and pasturage assured, and wood and game abundant in the mountains, the Navaho thereabout have become a sort of local aristocracy. They are permanently settled, moving only up to the mountains and down again with the seasons; they have means, and leisure, and considerable of the ancient pride of craftsmanship.

[7] The earliest gray of reliable date known to me is in a "dougie", possibly Hopi, collected by Thomas V. Keam and displayed at the World's Columbian Exposition, Chicago, in 1893: U. S. N. M. 168240. I have seen gray in blankets that I thought could date back to the preceding decade, but never prominent in pieces of obvious pre-aniline character. Hence I suspect the trade of having encouraged (or at least not having discouraged) the use of gray throughout the reservation period, as a means of using black wool in a light color. Some sheep have naturally gray wool, so this color may have been used in all times—but the early traders gave it a social status, as it were.

Here the Moore tradition flourishes today, traders backing it with hard cash as well as kind words,[8] and this small corner of the reservation has a widespread reputation as the home of the best of modern Navaho weav--ing.[9]

The Moore method of improving weaving is being followed to some extent today by the Shiprock Trading Company, which for years has been one of the outlets of the Two Grey Hills rug. Some years ago Mr. Fell, Superintendent of the Pendleton Mills, makers of the widely popular Pendleton blanket, visited Shiprock. Noting the poor quality of most of the rugs being made, he investigated methods and expressed surprise that the product was not even worse, the addition of merino strains to the local breeds of sheep producing a fine, knotty wool difficult to control by the old primitive hand methods. Mr. Fell took home samples of the wool with the thought in mind of selling the traders a carded wool which their weavers would be able to spin more successfully. As a result, Messrs. Bernard and Drolet [10] of the Shiprock Trading Company are now experimenting with a long staple wool provided by the Pendleton Mills in quantity lots, carded and dyed ready for spinning. A Swiss dye of high quality is used (for one of the weak points of the dyes sold to the Navaho has been their mediocre quality), the dyeing alone costing about twenty-five cents a pound of wool. In the warehouse I was shown several large cartons of this prepared wool in white, black, blue, orange, yellow, red, two grays, two browns. Its great superiority in both quality and color to the native product is seen at a glance, and in the hands of an expert it yields a strand of almost machine-like smoothness and fineness.

Such artificial stimuli to a native American industry as these we have been discussing have both bad and good aspects. Among the bad may be listed the white man's dominion over an art-craft whose entire charm has always lain in its individually native character; when Navaho weaving shall have become merely American hand-weaving, its Indian appeal will have fled. Not helpful, if not especially pernicious, is the importation of

---

[8] Mr. T. D. Seymour, formerly of Chinle, told me he has paid eight dollars a pound for Two Grey Hills rugs when the best of the others brought only two dollars and a half. This type has a recognized higher value than all others.

[9] Much credit is due Mr. W. T. Shelton, who as agent at Shiprock in 1909 started the annual Shiprock Fair, an event which has been a potent force for excellence in weaving. Mr. Shelton also was active in improving the quality of Navaho sheep, being one of the pioneers in this neglected field of reform, discussed farther on. After many years dormant, the fair was revived in 1932 by Superintendent E. A. McCray.

[10] From Mr. Sam Drolet I received this information, both he and Mr. Bruce Bernard according me many courtesies.

PLATE 94

A Crystal rug, from J. B. Moore, Crystal, N. M. Size 43 x 62 ins., colors black and white figures on red ground. Denver Art Museum Cat. RN12.

PLATE 95

Another Crystal rug. Size 38 x 60 ins., colors gray center panel, black border band, black and white figures. Both this and pl. 94 were woven in the nineties. Denver Art Museum cat. RN13.

wool among a people whose main dependence is the sale of wool: a "coals to Newcastle" situation that certainly cannot claim the sanction of economic law. On the other hand, there certainly is one large measure of good in these reforming efforts: they set, maintain, and compensate a high technical standard where without them the trend has been fairly constantly downward to the detriment of all concerned. As Mr. Drolet pointed out to me, their imported wool, unspun, is less of a white man's product than Germantown yarn; and if a woman neglects the fleece of her own flock for theirs, she gets a financial return sufficient to compensate her sacrifice. Here again we face the question of costs and returns. Navaho weaving is an industry, and industries must be self-supporting or they cannot long endure. Navaho wool will go whither the demand is greater, the reward higher—to the market or to the loom.

THE PROBLEM OF WOOL

It is self-evident that a Navaho blanket can be no finer than the wool of which it is made, and in the fabrics of different grades and periods we find fleeces of widely divergent quality, from coarse goat hair to silkiest merino. The Navaho of course were alive to this factor of quality in wool, exercising a conscious selection of material according to its intended use. Goat hair occurs most frequently in the warp strings of common blankets, especially in the "dougie" serapes of early reservation days; and in this same function dark wool—undesirable elsewhere because of its color—is often found. The coarser portions of the sheep's fleece went into the commoner's garments, which blushed not for a roughness of texture or a dullness of color the patrician bayetas of the wealthy tribesman would never have tolerated; and the longest, whitest, silkiest of the fleeces were kept carefully apart for weaving into shoulder blankets or poncho serapes, or perhaps a fine saddle-cloth to set off the brass and hammered silver of the horseman's gear. By no casual chance is fine wool usually found in the best-woven and most attractive blankets. The Navaho knows wool, but unhappily for the general average of Navaho textiles, he does not know how to safeguard its quality in the breeding and care of his flocks. He neglects to segregate ewes and rams, shears his helpless animals in all seasons, provides them scant shelter, meager rations, bad water. Except for a continual flow of new ovine blood into the Navaho stock its quality would have gone very low indeed during the two or three centuries of its existence.

The Navaho did not know it, but in fact the sheep he stole from

Pueblo husbandman and Spanish colonist back in the 17th and 18th centuries were of the finest blood of the Old World. The Spanish merino of this period was famous for its abundant, silky fleece; so famous, indeed, that the King of Saxony in 1765, against strong popular opposition, brought into his kingdom 200 Spanish merinos. Twelve years later he yielded to a general demand for more, and great was the disappointment of all good Saxons when the King's emissary could obtain only 110 of the 300 he was charged to bring back.[11] Saxon wool soon was preeminent in Europe; Saxony by 1848 had become a sheep-fold, with twenty-five million sheep feeding a textile industry employing twenty-five thousand workers.[12] It was at about this period that the Westphalian traders recently come to Santa Fe from Germany brought into the Southwest the first manufactured yarns. Soft, lustrous, beautifully colored with the finest vegetal dyes of the period, they were sought as eagerly as bayeta, woven alongside the silkiest of the Navaho fleeces into some of the choice blankets of the fifties and sixties: [13] Spanish merino fleeces both, for the yarns were of Saxony and in commerce they bore its name, as we have seen.

Throughout the long period of Spanish and Mexican dominion over New Mexico the Navaho flocks throve and increased. Pasturage was plentiful, for the small tribe roved a wide territory even then, and constant raids brought in new blood of the same merino strain. Whether the fleeces maintained their high quality is doubtful; handling of a large number of old woolens, both Spanish New Mexican and Navaho, makes me believe silky fleece was the exception rather than the rule. At any rate there was coarse and fine, black as well as white, liberally besprinkled through the flocks of both peoples, when the Navaho had a stroke of luck, well disguised. Their bitter decade of the sixties, Kit Carson and Bosque Redondo, left them with few sheep and with no heart to go out and steal more. But the treaty of 1868 provided for the purchase and distribution of 15,000 sheep and goats, and in 1869 30,000 sheep and 2,000 goats were distributed (Matthews 1897: 7), so the Navaho herds got a new start and with a different blood. Mr. Robert C. Prewitt, merchant of forty years' experience in the Southwest, told me he read in some old Government source that the sheep furnished under the treaty were Kentucky Cotswolds.[14] I have never found this statement, but Mr. B. I. Staples had a

---

[11] Browne: 259-261.

[12] Encyclopædia Britannica, 11th edition, article "Saxony".

[13] The supreme example of this type known to me is the White Antelope Blanket shown in plate 1. Another is seen in plate 86.

[14] As this book goes to press an effort is being made to induce the Navaho to reduce the number of their sheep and goats from 1,400,000 to 600,000.

similar recollection and I think it correct.[15] They were, at all events American sheep; and American sheep crept steadily into Navaho sheep-folds from then onward. Three years later 10,000 more were brought in as part of the annuity distribution of that year under the treaty of 1868 (RCIA 1872: 296). The Government's wholesale efforts seem to have ended here, and the mixture of American and the last vestiges of ancient Spanish strains has been the characteristic Navaho sheep of the last half-century. Inbreeding and poor forage (for the Navaho range supports far too many grazing animals) lowered the general quality constantly, and today, the old-stock Navaho sheep is a lean, hairy animal, goat-like, whose long carcass will not fatten, whose kempy wool brings only the lowest of market prices after shearing only four or five pounds to the animal.

Various Indian agents have for years wrestled with the problem of better Navaho sheep, a pioneer among them being Superintendent W. T. Shelton during his tenure of the San Juan Agency at Shiprock soon after 1900. I have personal recollections of his pride in the registered rams of various breeds with which he was experimenting there. Another who has made important contributions of personal effort and experience along this line is Superintendent S. F. Stacher of Crown Point. Contary to its usual policy, the Indian Bureau has left him undisturbed at his post for a round twenty years—long enough to give some effect to his efforts; and great has been the consequent improvement in flocks in the eastern Navaho area.

Today the problem of the Navaho sheep is a serious concern of every agent for the tribe, and most of them are buying three or four hundred rams yearly for the improvement of the stock. The rams are sold to the Navaho at cost, the Government financing the operation. The system has one drawback, I have been told: purchase is by bid or contract, and the successful bidder may have the lowest prices rather than the best animals. Sheep men in New Mexico or one of the neighboring states generally get the contract.

THE BEST BREED

Talking with traders throughout the Navaho country, I have invariably been told that the Government's efforts at improvement of the sheep aim at producing an animal for the American market, and neglect utterly the market at home which consists in the native loom. It is desirable, to be sure, that Navaho sheep be prolific lambers, good meat

---

[15] A Government livestock expert told Mrs. Colton that in his opinion "the sheep sent in were a very mixed lot bought up cheap by the Government, undoubtedly English strains American bred."

animals, heavy wool producers, for each of these qualities is an economic factor of prime importance to tribal welfare; but a fourth desideratum exists and it has been utterly neglected, by the testimony of all my informants. I refer to the suitability of the wool of these improved strains to the native craft of weaving (pl. 96A). The Government officials concerned seem to have decided that the French merino strain, the Rambouillet, is the best for the purpose of selective improvement, and new Rambouillet blood is being brought in every year. It is a good stock for the purpose, being adapted to the peculiar range conditions of the country, a good meat producer, and a heavy shearer of wool of high quality. But the wool is short, fine, and closely curled, forming tight little knots that the Navaho woman with her simple cards and spindle cannot straighten out; it is excessively greasy too,[16] and almost beyond cleaning by hand washing alone. In consequence, the Navaho rug is becoming more and more a mass of knots, unevenly scoured and (being still greasy) unevenly dyed, with every passing year. So traders today are carefully saving out all the old straight, hair-like wool of the unimproved strains that is sold to them, and selling it back to the weavers; but of course it is not adequate to the demand, and it grows steadily more scarce.[17] Meanwhile the Government neglects its opportunity (if not its plain duty) to take the situation in hand and determine by study and controlled experiment the best breed for the economic and environmental problems involved.

Inevitably there is better agreement on the nature of the evil than on its solution; general acquiescence in the proposition that the Rambouillet strain favored by most Government agents is not the ideal, but wide divergence of opinion on what strain would best meet the situation. Mrs. Colton after careful inquiry and experiment (particularly among the Hopi and neighboring Navaho) thinks the Corriedale might please all hands;[18] but the Shiprock Agency tried that breed one year and the Navaho did not like it—said it was not hardy, not a good "rustler," al-

---

[16] A serious drawback from another angle, Mrs. Colton reminds me: sand and dirt adhere to the animal, loading him down to a point of actual interference with his foraging ability!

[17] With sufficient tariff protection against cheap foreign fleeces, notably from South Africa, Navaho wool might be in demand for tweeds, although too heavy for most suitings, in the opinion of a wool buyer as quoted in the Southwest Tourist News (Gallup, N. M.) of August 23, 1932.

[18] Colton: 1932. An excellent statement of the problem, with interesting illustrations of different wools and breeds. Two of her illustrations are reproduced in plate 96A. She would have the Government halt all introduction of new blood until by careful experiment the best strain has been found. Certainly the present hit-and-miss policy of indiscriminate cross-breeding has little in its favor.

PLATE 96

a

b

a, Four-horned sheep. Such sports, due apparently to inbreeding, were not uncommon a half-century ago, and a few may still still be seen. Photograph taken at
Farmington, N. M. about 1900, courtesy of Mr. R. C. Prewitt.

b, A Navaho flock, sheep and goats together. Courtesy of Mr. Philip Johnston.

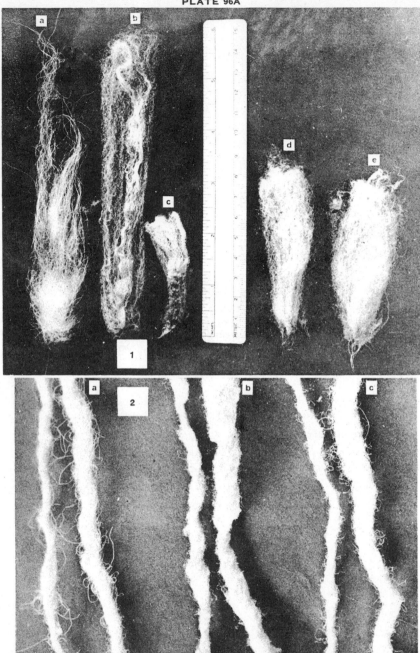

1, Fleeces of different breeds. **a** old Navaho; **b** Corriedale; **c** Rambouillet; **d** Corriedale-Navaho cross; **e** Corriedale-Rambouillet-Navaho cross. The 6-inch ruler gives a scale of lengths, whereby it will be seen that the old Navaho is there with the best of them in this respect. After Colton fig. 1.

2, Different fleeces in hand-spun yarn, warp and weft. **a** old Navaho; **b** Merino: notice its knottiness; **c** Corriedale. After Colton fig 4.

though satisfactory for the abundance of its long-staple wool. The Hampshire or black-face is well liked there for lambs and meat, but is a poor wool producer.[19] Mr. O. J. Carson of Farmington, a sheep man as well as Indian trader, concedes the Rambouillet best for herding and for lambs, but thinks no pure strain will solve the problem. He would distribute rams of different strains among the flocks in different years, varying the breed constantly with Rambouillet, Hampshire, Lincoln, Corriedale, to secure certain qualities of each without giving their weaknesses much chance for development.

I was told by Mr. E. Z. Vogt, Custodian of El Morro National Monument and a sheep man, that Mr. Ed. Sargent of Chama is said to have the largest sheep in New Mexico, his flocks being a mixture of Rambouillet and Cotswold strains. Mr. Vogt added that size has its drawbacks, ewes bred up to the production of eight or nine pounds of wool being poor rangers as a rule.

Mr. B. I. Staples in his constant striving for better Navaho craftsmanship has attacked the problem squarely in an interesting experiment. He took several Navaho to the Denver Stock Show in 1932 and let them choose a breed for the improvement of their flocks back in New Mexico. They agreed on the Dorset, and Mr. Staples in August, 1932, received a lamb from the prize-winning Dorset of the 1931 show. He plans to use both Dorset and Rambouillet strains, the former having the advantage of a very long-staple wool—more than four inches—with very little grease, and of being hardy, meaty, and a prolific breeder. His method of financing the experiment is of exceptional ingenuity. The Dorset ram was bought from a Boston fund called the Red Wing Fund; and in order not merely to reimburse but to increase the fund, the following plan has been devised. Each year Mr. Staples will select two Navaho men—conscientious, deserving sheep men, preferably from among those who lost most of their flocks in the severe winter of 1931-32—and have them choose ten ewes (from neighboring flocks, or wherever they can be bought) which the fund will buy. The service of the Dorset ram will be provided without cost, and the first crop of lambs will be divided between the fund and the owner of the ewes. The lambs owned by the fund will be apportioned to other men under the same conditions. All wool sheared from sheep thus provided may be kept by the owner, but must be woven into rugs or blankets. Thus its suitability will be thoroughly tested and the weaving industry encouraged, at one stroke.

[19] Information from Mr. Sam Drolet of the Shiprock Trading Company.

Another experiment of Mr. Staples is the mixture of mohair (Angora goat hair) with ordinary wool. They are carded together, then spun, the heavy straight hair offsetting the knotty tendency of the wool. A report on the success of the experiment is not yet forthcoming, but as this is an old Hopi trick (Mrs. Moris Burge has told me) it should prove practical.

So in the matter of wool we see another factor of change and uncertainty to becloud further the misty future of Navaho weaving. Economic advantage will carry the day, we may be sure; but will the friends of Navaho weaving find a soundly economic solution in time to avert the disaster which now threatens? It will be a pity if they do not; the world is full of fine sheep, but where shall we seek our Indian blankets when the Navaho no longer weave?

SAFEGUARDS AND STANDARDS

The present century has witnessed the industrialization of many more native Indian crafts than Navaho weaving. The silver-work of the same people, the pottery of several Pueblos, notably of the Rio Grande group, the basketry of various tribes—all have attained a market demand and a volume of output ranking them as manufactures in the ordinary commercial sense. As such they become subject to the benignity of Federal protection and to the active support of mercantile associations; but they become, alas, the object of jealous imitation, unfair competition, as well.

In 1930 a bill was before Congress to authorize the marking and official supervision of all authentic Indian goods for their protection in the open market. It failed despite the active support of various interested groups, notably the Eastern Association on Indian Affairs. Pending its renovation at a more favorable moment, the Federal Trade Commission has been invoked in the self-same cause, and with better success. The *Southwest Tourist News* of August 23, 1932, reported that the Commission had won its case against the Beacon Manufacturing Company, and on July 9 of that year had issued an order restraining that company from advertising and selling its machine-woven bed blankets as "Indian" blankets. It was said that displays featuring a cardboard Indian loom with a Beacon blanket issuing therefrom had been used in advertising; and if true, this case certainly was flagrant enough to warrant a curb. Another suit brought by the Commission was against the Maisel Trading Post, Inc., of Albuquerque, charged with misleading advertising of "Indian" silver jewelry made in a mechanized shop, although by Indian workmen.

PLATE 97

Trading store scenes, recent. The men are buying groceries, the woman selling a rug. Courtesy of Mr. Philip Johnston.

PLATE 98

Chief blankets, terraced style. **a** size 68 x 56 ins. colors black, white, indigo blue, bayeta red. Bought by H. F. Bond, agent to the Utes, on Ute reservation in Colorado about 1875. Wm. Claflin Jr. museum cat. 24795.

b size 78 x 63 ins., colors black, white, indigo blue, bayeta red. This is fig. 50 **a** in Matthews 1884, hence woven before that year but probably not before 1880 for it is like new today.

The defendant was enjoined to be more careful in his advertising, I am told.

UNITED INDIAN TRADERS ASSOCIATION

The growing prevalence of such abuses of the nascent demand for Indian goods led a number of traders among the Navaho to meet in Gallup immediately after the Intertribal Ceremonial in 1931 and organize for the protection of their Indian merchandise, of which the principal item is the Navaho rug. Mr. Berton I. Staples, president from the outset, has told me of the aims and progress of the Association, which was incorporated (in New Mexico) on a non-profit basis in the year following, with the approval of the Bureau of Indian Affairs. Briefly stated, the Association is pledged to maintain in its own dealings and to advocate as a Government policy and in trade generally, certain standards of workmanship and material in Indian goods. Its standard for textiles follows:

INDIAN HANDMADE BLANKETS OR RUGS:

Material used shall be virgin wool or virgin angora wool, the same shall be hand-washed, hand-carded and hand-dyed, the warp shall be all wool and hand-spun, the wool shall be all wool and hand-spun and the blanket shall be hand-woven by an Indian.

This definition of the modern standard of Navaho weaving from the trader's standpoint is full of interest. It excludes Germantown and cotton warp, forbids imported and machine-processed wools, but permits non-Indian dyeing provided it be done by hand. Nothing is said of color or pattern—no doubt wisely, for these are hard to rule upon empirically—but the failure to stipulate a native loom may prove eventually a point of weakness; for if Indians can make silver jewelry by machine, why can they not weave in the same way? Perhaps, though, the drafters of the standards thought Navaho weaving sufficiently protected by the fact that mechanical weaving cannot successfully imitate that done by hand.[20]

Individuals as well as dealers may be members of the Association, although in a more restricted class; but the directors, seven in number, must have had at least ten years' experience in direct Indian dealings. Any member may be dropped by the directors without explanation, for the

[20] Because weft color cannot be dropped in machine weaving as in the hand loom: every thread of weft must be carried wholly across the fabric on one side or the other; also because hand work produces irregularities not found in machine work.

Association is determined to uphold its aims and standards. To August, 1932, some 75 traders and dealers had joined the new body, with only a few of importance holding back. These were taking a skeptical attitude, predicting failure as with similar enterprises of the past. So, its leaders believe, if the Association can weather the first critical years it will become almost completely representative of Southwestern Indian dealers. Already it has accomplishments to its score. One was the exemption of reservation Indians from the 10% tax on jewelry, rugs, and furs in the Revenue Act of 1932. This impost would have borne especially heavily on the Navaho, for rugs and jewelry comprise a large source of revenue, while the tax on furs would have affected the tribes of Alaska in particular.

The most promising undertaking of the United Indian Traders in my opinion is the labeling of every Indian object sold with a tag or sticker bearing both the Association's guaranty of authenticity and the dealer's Association membership number. In case of fraud, poor quality, misrepresentation, or dissatisfaction from any cause whatsoever, the Association makes good to the buyer and comes back on the dealer whose number betrays him at once as the original seller and guarantor. If the Association can educate the buying public to the point of demanding its label on every Indian object it buys, then Beacon blankets and Maisel jewelry may go begging; but that will require much time and effort, great wisdom, and unity of purpose. Whatever the result, the aim is laudable and the means adopted seem entirely practical. At any rate the Association has acted wisely in not concerning itself with price scales, division of territory, or anything restrictive of fair competition, and one cannot but wish it well.

CHAPTER XIV

THE GROWTH OF DESIGN—1800-1920

INCE about 1800, date of the earliest Navaho textiles of authentic record known to me, a growth of design is plainly apparent. It is more of a growth than an evolution, for the styles comprising it change character rather abruptly, as if in response to new stimuli from without rather than logical progression within the craft. Withal there is increasing breadth and complexity, so the word growth is justified. Three of these changes are so obvious that they compel the recognition of four dominant styles or pattern types, each preeminent at a given period of time. They are by no means discontinuous or unrelated, for the strong Navaho characteristics of strength and clarity, achieved through strict adherence to a pattern of simple geometric elements evenly balanced, are dominant throughout. All Navaho weaving (except perhaps its earliest, simplest forms) bears the tribal stamp, though imprinted upon a graphic pattern of foreign origin. Always the Navaho are borrowing and adapting; we see it in every phase of this as in other of their tribal crafts and customs.[1]

FIRST STYLE: THE STRIPED—BEGINNING TO 1800

Navaho weaving enters the historic scene in patterns of horizontal stripes exclusively. All the Massacre Cave fragments dating from 1804-05, shown in plates 60 and 61 are of this type, and those in Peabody Museum (pls. 61 and 62) from White House ruin as well. So too is the blanket shown in plate 63a, found in a Navaho burial with a mummified body. Every chief's blanket antedating the year 1870 (pls. 48a, 64, 74, 75, except-ing 75a) bears an all-striped pattern. Stripes are prominent or predominant in every specimen antedating Bosque Redondo (pls. 37, 59, 68b, 72, 76, 77, 78 in addition to those already cited). If these specimens could be con-

---

[1] The reader is not expected to accept blindly the conclusions herein set forth. Let him rather judge for himself of their validity, for every specimen of Navaho weaving I have ever seen which had a history acceptable to me dating it prior to the year 1880, is figured in this book—with a few exceptions where photographs were not obtainable or the tribal origin was doubtful.

sidered truly representative of Navaho design of the late 18th and early 19th centuries, we should have an overwhelmingly consistent body of evidence to direct the conclusion that figured patterns were unknown at that epoch. I think this conclusion is well-nigh justified, even while admitting that our few surviving specimens are a ridiculously small percentage of the total output of the period. The Massacre Cave fragments, taken together with the White House fragments and the burial blanket, are especially significant, representing not the selective fruit of the collecting instinct but a cross-section of tribal dress of their period. They illustrate what the plain people, men and women, were wearing in those days; they are, in short, average and thoroughly characteristic. To me they are convincing evidence of the style of the times; but the evidence is slight, to be sure.

If stripes were not universal we at least must admit they were so strongly in vogue as to constitute a style in themselves. Contemporary references no less than the evidence of existing specimens prove the point clearly. Espejo in 1583 found the Rio Grande Pueblo people wearing cotton mantles striped blue and white (Bolton 174), so we may infer that the striped style came down from prehistoric times. The inference is strengthened on consideration of the fact that the Pueblo weavers of modern times, even the Hopi today, have produced little but striped patterns. Stripes are traditionally Pueblo, in all times, and it seems likely enough that the Navaho adopted them at the outset, only to abandon them as too cramped a repertory for their expanding genius, while the Pueblos remained true to the old fashion almost to the end of their career as weavers. The woman's dress of a century ago bore a pattern of plain stripes, as we saw in Chapter 7. Culin (pl. III*b*) reproduces an engraving of 1822 showing a group of Indians of the San Francisco Bay region with at least five blankets or serapes in evidence, all of them bearing striped patterns. Abert in 1846 found the people of Acoma generally wearing "the Navajoe blanket, marked with broad stripes, alternately black and white" (55): the chief blanket, evidently. Ives in 1858 (124) noticed a similar spectacle at Hopi, saying it reminded him of a stratified rock. Edwards, with Doniphan in 1846, said of the Indian villagers of Valencia, on the Rio Grande below Albuquerque (63): "They are dressed in tunics of the same material as the Mexican blanket, and wear what is called the Navajo Poncho; so named from being made by the Navajo Indians. It is of very fine texture, with both sides alike, and the pattern always in broad black and white stripes."

PLATE 99

Serape, late terraced style. The use of blocks instead of solid lines in terrace building is characteristic of the later examples of this style. Size 52 x 72 ins., colors: darkest figures indigo blue native yarn, light are white native, background a sort of "Moki pattern" of red and green stripes, red both bayeta and 3-ply yarn, green 3-ply yarn.

Obtained near Old Fort Wingate by Gov. W. F. M. Arny of New Mexico, who served in 1865-66 and given in 1874 to a relative of its present owner, Mr. C. B. Cosgrove.

PLATE 100

Serape, late terraced style, showing blocks instead of solid lines in terraced figures. Size 48 x 76 ins., colors: darker lines indigo blue native, lightest white; red ground (bayeta with possibly some machine-spun), with terrace blocks in blue, yellow, green, last two colors either machine-spun or a retwisted commercial fabric (my notes are not precise on the point).

Collected by H. F. Bond, agent to the Utes, on their reservation in the 1870's. Wm. Claflin Jr. museum cat. 24794.

There are at least three possible sources of this earliest style, with infinite degrees of combination among them. Most fundamental of them all is a technical factor which is so strong in the textile crafts, as we saw in the earliest chapters of this book: design is built up, not laid on. Every textile is akin to a brick wall in which each stitch is a brick, and it is natural to work in straight lines in the building. It is natural, too, to work in horizontal lines, for weaving proceeds in horizontal layers up the warp strings of the fabric. The inevitable, logical first step toward textile design in loom work is a simple change of weft color, and the result is a pattern of plain horizontal stripes. Textile figures antedate the loom, to be sure, but the beginner on the loom will take his first hesitant steps with the simplest of them; in this I speak from experience. The Navaho learned to weave in Spanish wool without previous loom experience, as we have seen; they learned in all probability after the Pueblo Rebellion of 1680, becoming known as weavers only well along in the following century. What then more natural than to find them working in simple striped patterns at the close of that century? The interval of time is not great for the establishment of an alien craft of complex technic in a tribe growing rapidly and moving always. So much for the theory of technological origin of the earliest known style in design. Whether or not we accept it wholly, we cannot entirely ignore it, for no people, civilized or other, attains immediate skill and sophistication in a pursuit utterly new and strange. There must be an apprenticeship, and to me the period of the plain stripe is the apprentice period of Navaho weaving.

With equal truth may we say that no handicraft seeks a new home without bringing along certain essential baggage, so when the Navaho learned to rig and manipulate a loom, they also certainly learned something of the designs their instructors were accustomed to weave upon it. Those instructors were the Pueblos, since the Navaho loom is purely a Pueblo device; but sheep are Spanish, and the Navaho wove only in wool. Our remaining two possible sources of the striped style are therefore these two peoples. For the Spanish theory it may be said that the Pueblos had sheep and many other things Spanish before these found a place in Navaho life; they presumably were weavers in wool before they taught the Navaho and they may have taken over a new style of design along with the new textile fiber.

An examination of the textile art of the two peoples concerned is the necessary next step in our inquiry into the origins of Navaho design. The sources of information are scanty in either case, yet from relatively few specimens of an art—even fragmentary—one may gauge the broad generalities of its character. If we had, for example, only a dozen fragments to represent our knowledge of Navaho weaving, we would reach the unmistakable and sound conclusion that it embodied a style of geometric patterning in bold simplicity. So from the small number of specimens of prehistoric Pueblo textile pattern a like judgment may be formulated— but we find nothing to suggest that the Navaho took up and carried on the elaborately figured style of their preceptors in weaving, as a glance at plates 35 and 108a will show. The general pattern is complex, elaborate, with much interlocking of angular lines, little segregation of figures, and a generally diagonal trend throughout. There is no single point in common with the simple horizontal lines of the early Navaho specimens. But thanks to Espejo we know that the Pueblos had at least two textile styles —perhaps not coetaneously—one of which may well have been transmitted to their pupils, the Navaho.

Going behind the prehistoric Pueblos to the Basketmakers we find this same fundamental pattern type of plain stripes, for all that it may be but the influence of textile structure and the limitations of technic acting independently upon each group. Figure 4, showing a typical pattern from a Basketmaker bag, does none the less accord closely with the pattern of the Massacre Cave and White House fragments shown in plates 60, 61, and 62. In each, it will be noted, the only departure from the straight line is the beaded line, simplest of variants, made by alternating weft colors at each course of fabric until a return to solid color breaks the pattern again into one of plain stripes. To assume a Basketmaker influence upon Navaho style is unnecessary, since stripes seemingly have always been in vogue in the Southwest. It would be more reasonable to conclude that here is a simple, fundamental style of textile patterning, used in ancient as in modern times; a style appealing in its simplicity to craftsmen of slight experience, or limited in their esthetic range by the coarseness of their material or the crudity of their methods. The Navaho were beginners at the loom. The Basketmakers had not attained to the loom. The Pueblos, in between, were loom experts; it is natural to find their textile design the most sophisticated of the three. Yet they too worked in plain stripes, as Espejo's chronicle testifies. So the Navaho obviously had a choice of styles and wisely chose the simplest at the outset of their loom career.

The possible Spanish influence remains to be weighed. Here again a decision is difficult. The weavers of Spain of course had progressed far beyond the stage of simple striped patterns. But so have our own weavers,

PLATE 101

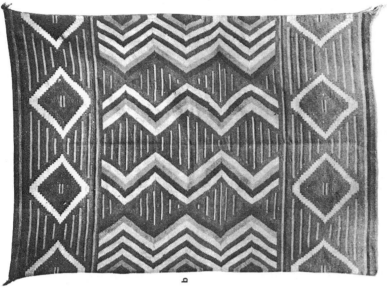

b

a

Two **serapes,** late terraced style. a native white and indigo blue, bayeta red, blue-green machine-spun yarn. Note small hole in center. Bought "before the Custer massacre" (1876) by Sergeant J. Crockett Givens of Company I, 9th Cavalry, from Chief Mariano (active in Navaho affairs in early reservation days). Givens in a letter in owner's possession dated 1911 says blanket then over 50 years old, hence all signs point to a weaving date in the sixties or seventies.

b has native white and indigo blue yarn with bayeta red and yellow and brown machine-spun yarn. Note that its lines run upward in the center panel. Both blankets about 55 x 70 ins. in size. Owner wishes his name withheld.

PLATE 102

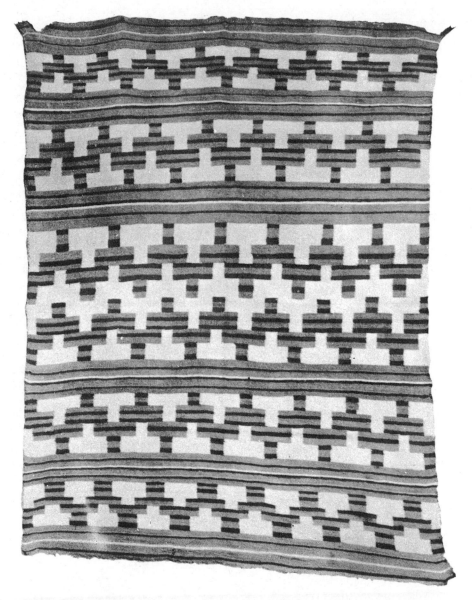

Serape, late terraced style, size 52 x 68 ins., colors indigo blue in two shades, white, red, the latter probably a late bayeta, rose-colored. Collected by H. F. Bond on Ute reservation in 1870's. Wm. Claflin Jr. museum cat. 24797. The breakdown of the flowing terraced figure into single units is an interesting feature of this specimen, and a sign of the times.

yet we see stripes everywhere. Doubtless there were striped as well as figured fabrics among those brought into the Southwest from Mexico and Spain in early times. If the stripe had the greater influence it had the more direct appeal to a people unskilled in the complexities of the esthetic no less than in the practical aspects of weaving. A child prefers his own execution of five-finger exercises on the piano to a virtuoso's interpretation of Liszt. My conclusion in this matter is that the Navaho had a-plenty of patterns and figures before their eyes, what with the pottery, basketry, and textiles of the Pueblos, the ritualistic or conventional representations of their own tribe, and the highly decorated gear and clothing of the Spanish. Of all this they chose the striped style for their first efforts at weaving because it fitted so snugly into their simple artistic concepts and their meager skill. They moved out of it fast enough, as we shall see: and that is another point in favor of their having adopted it from a choice based on necessity, as a stepping-stone to better things. That the historic Pueblos never go far beyond the phase of plain stripes is no impediment to this conclusion. From the moment of Coronado's entry into Hawikuh they were a conquered people, their peak of achievement passed. Navaho rise parallels Pueblo decline.

SECOND STYLE: THE TERRACED—1800-1863

Soon after the year 1800 a great change seems to have come upon Navaho design. How long it may have been in the making, one cannot say; doubtless if we had more abundant evidence of the character of design prior to 1800 the advent of the second style would be forecast well in advance of the event, for such changes invariably intermingle and overlap. Early references to Navaho weaving have little or nothing to say of style and color, so our evidence must again take the form of surviving examples. All such that I could find and accept as to history are shown in these pages, except for a few of which photographs were unobtainable. A glance over the older dated specimens of plates 1, 37, 59, 68b, 76, 78, 86, 93, 99-102, 104, reveals at once that here is a definite departure from the slavish adherence to plain stripes that characterizes the striped style. The stripes remain (every specimen has at least a few) but they are secondary to the pattern. The primary figures are zigzag lines running horizontally from edge to edge. Often, particularly in the center of the piece, their apices meet to form diamonds. Most characteristic touch of all, these diagonal or zigzag lines have stepped edges almost invariably: little right angles which are the hallmark of this style. One gets the impression that the Navaho weavers have just learned to make right angles, and are as pleased as children with the accomplishment. However that may be, here is freedom, expansion, rhythmic movement. Stripes lead monotonously back and forth, but steps lead upward, and upon them Navaho weaving is climbing toward a fuller expression of its advancing artistry and skill.

Best exponent of this terraced style is the bayeta serape usually woven in the three colors of indigo blue, natural white, and bayeta red. Indeed, I am sure that bayeta plays a large part in this sudden efflorescence of textile art. Yet I cannot define that part, much less prove it. Did some event of the early 19th century make bayeta more abundantly available, or bring the Navaho into closer contact with other artists in wool? Is it, on the other hand, merely that a bud long swelling has suddenly flowered? The only happening of great historic importance in this period is the revolt of Mexico from Spain; but that, as we saw, stirred a wave which sank to the smallest of ripples by the time it reached distant New Mexico. Little of its impetus could have carried to the Navaho, from all accounts of the local situation at this time.

These conjectures are perhaps building an impression that the terraced style is of Mexican or Spanish inspiration. True, it resembles much Mediterranean weaving, from Anatolia to Morocco,[2] and the Moorish influence was strong in Spanish art. Yet there is nothing comparable in the Spanish weaving of Mexico at this period, so far as I can learn. Mena figures a number of serapes dating back to the 18th century and later, and their design is not akin to this. Nowhere in them does one find a right angle, for example; nowhere that even distribution of the design over the whole surface, but rather a concentration upon a central figure, as in plate 108*b*.

Speculation on the source of this style would be idle; and much search I fear would prove fruitless. This for the reason that we are confronted with too much evidence instead of not enough. Like the striped, the terraced is one of those styles that evolve naturally from the inherent structural character of textile fabrics. All flat textiles grow in two directions at once, row upon row of weft reaching from side to side, climbing from end to end. Those made upon a foundation, as all loom-weaving is done, show a right-angular progression, the weft bearing that relation to the warp. This is true of coiled basketry and the radial-warp bag no less than of the blanket woven on the loom. In them the terraced style is found quite

---

[2] It is a favorite motive in Arab and Berber textiles of northern Africa, of which Mr. Homer E. Sargent of Pasadena has shown me some superb examples in his collection of hand-woven textiles.

PLATE 103

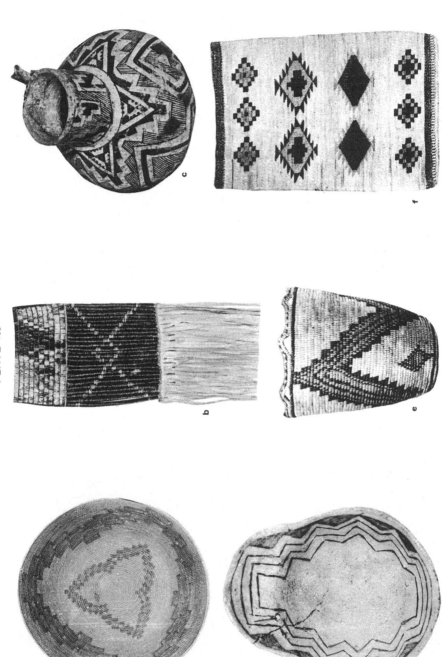

Ubiquity of the terraced style. By way of demonstrating that the terraced style is of no time or place but fundamental to geometric art, particularly textile, I chose these specimens at random in the Southwest Museum.
a Cahuilla basket cat. C. F. I. 10. b deerskin pipe bag, porcupine quill decoration, Sioux, cat. 577G74. c clay pitcher, prehistoric Pueblo, cat. 77G8. d clay ladle, Basketmaker, cat. Gates 872. e Klikitat basket, cat. 75L58. f corn husk bag, Nez Perce, cat. 75L17.

PLATE 104

Two child's **serapes**, often classed as double saddle blankets because of the similarity in size. The child's garment is likely to be light and fine with an elaborate pattern, the saddle cloth loose and heavy, with the simplest of patterns. **a** is Matthews 1884 fig. 52; of it and similar fabrics he says "made for child's wear but sometimes used as saddle blankets." Size 30 x 48 ins., colors indigo blue and white native, bayeta and machine-spun red, the latter in thin stripes only. Mrs. C. Matthews coll. U. S. National Museum cat. 281490.

b. size 33 x 50 ins., colors indigo blue and white native, bayeta red ground. This piece is an interesting study in the breakdown of the terraced style. Collected in 1873 by Major J. W. Powell Museum of the American Indian, Heye Foundation cat 15-7719.

as commonly as in loom products, for this style is but the graphic expression of that structural trend toward a dual progression, both across the warp and along it. Study of any example of it in the figures already cited soon reveals this fact: the characteristic steps of the design run horizontally for a space, then mount vertically (forming the right angle) and continue as before.

For the universality of this style, a glance at plate 103 should be convincing. Yet only a few examples therein appear, while scores of others could be given if the matter required further proof. The skeptical reader will find in any library books on primitive arts and simple handicrafts. In them examples of the terraced style are likely to be encountered, for it peeps out everywhere. If we yearn to find it a foreign importation, the evidence is at hand. If on the other hand we favor a local origin, it is easy to prove this style native to the Southwest from a time beyond our vision.

The terrace is the esthetic expression of the bayeta period. In those three categories of Navaho textiles generally embodying bayeta it is most often found: shoulder blankets, woman's dress, serape. Bayeta and the terraced style in the four colors of red, white, blue, black—those are the supreme expression of Navaho skill at the loom. A greater latitude in both color and pattern came in later times. Yet the fine texture of bayeta, the rich dignity of those four patrician colors, and the classic severity of the terraced style made a combination never equaled before or since. Still, I do not believe the terraced displaced the striped. We find it ubiquitous bcause we are dealing with selected specimens, "museum pieces." The humbler products of the loom bore patterns of plain stripes, but these have not survived. Like the prehistoric Pueblos, the Navaho surely used both stripes and figures; but that is only another way of saying that old styles persist, especially if they are simple, fundamental ones like the striped.[3]

THIRD STYLE: THE DIAMOND—1863-1900

The chastening, humbling experience of Bosque Redondo is probably the most important milestone in the history of the Navaho. It enthralled them body and soul to the white man and his ways, and it could not fail to cast a blight upon their outstanding esthetic expression. With Bosque

---

[3] Much as I dislike speculation, it seems almost justified here. Stripes never pass entirely out of use. That is as true in our own textiles as in Navaho weaving of later times. They are too simple and effective to suffer extinction, or even temporary eclipse; and we must remember that for every fine serape and chief blanket a hundred coarse, common fabrics were woven.

Redondo the era of fine weaving passed,[4] and with it passed the terraced
style. Thenceforth no style holds such undisputed sway as did the striped
and the terraced in their times. Something of them both lingers on, and
new elements come in. There is a sudden expansion, by accretion rather
than logical growth, with a variety of almost a heterogeneous character in
the whole range of expression. A new motif creeps in, becoming so common, as the novel ready-spun and pre-dyed weft known as Germantown
sweeps the reservation, that it attains to the dignity of exemplifying a third
style. The serrated or diamond-pointed line is this newcomer, shown in
plates 104*b*, 113, alongside the terraced line it so quickly displaced in popular favor. Its upward lines are diagonal instead of vertical, its angles therefore oblique instead of right-angular.[5] Its use at first is in much the same
fashion as its predecessor, in patterns of zigzag bands of color which sweep
across the blanket like mountain peaks against the sky.[6] Plates 88, 109,
110, 112*b*, 113 show the style in this use, while in plates 16, 24, 25, 34, 41*a*
52*a, b,* 68*a*, 78*a*, 92, 112*a, c,* it is modified. One readily sees the strong
affinity with that preceding it, for the diamond is but a squeezing down
of the terraced. The units composing the pattern have become larger,
however, the lines bolder, the whole fabric less refined in all details, it will
be noted. This is because the Navaho blanket is in process of becoming
a rug, consequently is heavier and coarser than of old. Gone are the days of
fine-lined bayeta work with its multitude of little blocks and right angles.
Something of their general character remains, however; the rhythm of
these grosser patterns is that of the old, the concept of a blanket as something to be embellished by horizontal zones of color remains for a time
little changed. Yet in every detail one reads careless haste, loss of the old
pride.

Germantown gave this dying flame new fuel, it must be said. Plates
16, 52*a, b,* 88, 89, 112 are of Germantown, and they show the old tenets of

---

[4] Traders and dealers today vaunt blankets "as fine as were ever woven." Ask
them to show you one counting fifteen warp strings and thirty-five or forty picks
of weft to the inch, as do many of the pre-Bosque specimens.

[5] Joyce (201) notes a similar change in prehistoric Peru, saying the diagonal
pattern is of later development than the vertical. Certainly diagonal lines are more
easily made in the loom because they permit the weaver to build up the pattern in
blocks. With vertical lines, the two adjacent colors must be woven simultaneously,
since they share the same warp string at the point of junction. Figures of diagonal
trend, however, require no overlap of color where they join their neighbors.

[6] Contemporary references on the diamond style: "Diamonds and parallels the
most prominent forms" (Drake I: 75). "The colors are woven in bands and diamonds.
We have never observed blankets with figures of a complicated pattern" (Letterman: 291).

Contemporary illustrations will be found in Wallace: 154, and Land of Sunshine, April 1895, pp. 83 and 85; also idem., February 1899, p. 117.

PLATE 105

Another small **serape.** The catalogue says "Moki woman's dress?", but the piece is Navaho in every particular, and Hopi women never wore such gaudy fabrics as this. Size 32 x 50 ins., colors native white, red, green—the last two suspected of being aniline colors, selvage indigo blue. Collected in Arizona probably by Frank H. Cushing in 1884, Peabody Museum (Harvard) cat. 37582.

PLATE 106

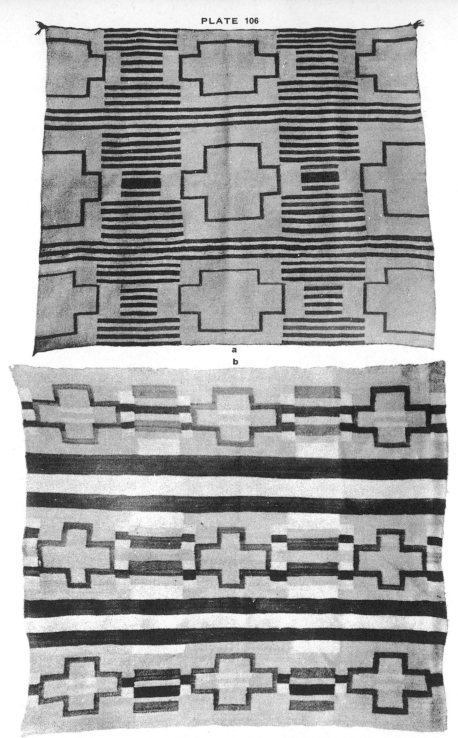

a

b

Decadence of the shoulder blanket. **a** size 60 x 51 ins., colors narrow stripes black and gray, crosses indigo blue on red (late bayeta?) ground. Woman's pattern, but large enough for a man's blanket. Bought by Frank Clark of Augusta, Georgia, on the Shoshone reservation in 1870. Wm. Claflin Jr. museum cat. 24793.

   b size 68 x 55 ins., colors black, white, red, orange, purple-blue, all native wool aniline-dyed. Woven about 1890. Denver Art Museum cat. RN10.

blanket patterning going down before the welter of new ideas, stimulated by an abundance of fine yarn in novel colorings. In some the meandering lines dominate the pattern, in others they are scarcely noticeable; but in all is the new line, the serrated, its constant series of diamonds or half-diamonds barbing every ridge and segment. As the terraced style was the characteristic expression of bayeta, so is the diamond of Germantown. "Diamonds, diamonds everywhere," describes most of the best Germantown weaving. Emphasizing them and setting them apart is frequently found a new device: outlining, or tracing a contour in a thin line of contrasting color, well shown in plates 52*b*, 110*a*, 112. It is highly characteristic of Germantown fabrics in this style, but I have never seen it used in the other.

TRANSITION

The beginnings of reservation life, of adjustment to American ways, Government supervision, trading-post business methods, mark a period of turmoil in the career of the Navaho. The seal of their long isolation was suddenly broken by their wholesale removal to a remote military reservation. Immediately afterward their country was opened up to American penetration. A decade later, hardly more, came the transcontinental railroad. Thus a tide set in which has never abated, a flood of new ideas, new materials, new things to do and new ways of doing old. All this is reflected in the weaving of the period, which breaks rapidly away from its traditional moorings. Blankets are still made in the old patterns, but so are rugs, in new patterns. An army officer wants "something fancy" and makes a sketch of his idea to guide the weaver. A trader's wife appears in a figured dress, or lays on her living-room floor a rug fresh from an eastern factory. The trader exhorts his weavers to take heed of the new market, and displays catalogues of the latest linoleum patterns by way of inspiration. Soldiers in gaudy uniform and impressive insignia ride briskly about. Railroad trains come puffing and screaming down the long slope of the continental divide. The whole world of the Navaho is born again. Can the people remain unchanged?

Graphic impressions of these novel sights and stirring events creep into the tribal looms and Navaho weaving comes to know a new mode of expression, the pictorial (pls. 114, 115). It is doubtful if any weaver ever attempted to draw a picture or tell a story upon her loom until after the American conquest. Now she launches forth ambitiously with flags and rampant eagles and square-wheeled railway cars. New figures and patterns make their impression on her fancy and another factor enters the expanding complex of Navaho design: it becomes imitative, impressionistic, heterogeneous. The canvas soon grows too small to hold so much new matter and another departure is made from the old traditional manner of orderly design: patterns become crowded, diffuse, filled with odds and ends of design with no sequential relation or common factor of harmony.

What matter? The white man is demanding blankets—big ones, little ones. The trader pays handsomely for everything brought in. Smart weavers are buying the new yarn, ready-spun, ready-dyed, and of such brilliant colorings! Fine, smooth warp string the trader sells too; of cotton, much thinner than home-spun wool, and much easier to use. Then there are the new dyes, a whole bucketful of brilliant color for the cost of a goatskin or a few pounds of raw wool. Everything is made easy for the weaver. It is her millennium. The white man's ways are best, after all!

Amid this welter of change and excitement the traditional styles struggle gamely on. The diamond finds its most brilliant expression in the florid Germantown weaving of the end of the century, often showing a truly lovely flower amid the rank weeds of the new-found freedom. A strange hybrid style comes to the fore, a combination of the striped and the diamond, in which these two outmoded fashions unite to repel the forces of change. The specimen shown in plate 37 is the earliest known of this type, dating it back into the 1860's, whence it continued popular until the end of the century. The dated illustrations of plates 66, 78, 116-118 prove its time range and amply reveal its character, a mixture of plain and blocked stripes, made up of the familiar diamond unit. It is the last stand of classicism, this diamond-striped mode, of pure geometric design in all its simple dignity and harmonious balance, its clarity and restraint. In it the best features of the two styles wed in complete unity, but its quiet charm is soon lost in the hectic shuffle of the reservation period.

The terraced and diamond styles themselves have another expression as they leave the crowded scene. The old horizontal zigzag lines suddenly rear themselves upright, and instead of running their undulating course from side to side of the blanket, they stretch from end to end in a very effective "lightning" pattern shown in plates 16, 24, 25, 101*b*, 111, 112*a* and *c*, 119, 120. Another new idea this, a fundamental departure from all previously held, for it makes the main structural lines of the pattern run vertically, whereas formerly and from time immemorial they had run

PLATE 107

BLACK   RED   BROWN

The diamond style in prehistoric times. **a**, prehistoric Peru.
  b to **f** are patterns in red, black and brown on Basketmaker sandals in the Latter Day Saints Museum, Salt Lake City, Utah.

PLATE 108

Diamond style, ancient and modern. This, like the terraced to which it is closely akin, is a fundamental style in geometric textile ornament.

a design on a basket, Pueblo I (prehistoric) after Kidder and Guernsey fig. 28.

b a modern Saltillo **serape**, Fred K. Hinchman coll. Southwest Museum cat. 202L13.

PLATE 109

Early diamond style, its main lines following those of the early terraced. Evidently a Germantown blanket, from its clean, even lines, and dated 1897 by the copyright notation on the photograph, otherwise unidentified, from the Munk Library, Southwest Museum. The blanket is not actually in the loom but stretched upon it. The weaver wears the velvet shirt, calico skirt, Oregon City blanket, of modern times, with the old-style deerskin moccasins.

PLATE 110

a

b

Later diamond style in native wool. a is a rug, about 5 x 7 feet, colors red, white, black, orange, yellow, on a gray and black striped ground; all but the red apparently native dyes. Woven about 1898. Owner, Mrs. A. M. Amsden, Farmington, New Mexico.

b, size 63 x 86 in., colors red, yellow, orange, purple, black, blue, white, most if not all of aniline dye on native wool. A good example of the color orgy of early aniline days (woven about 1890). Owner, Mr. J. Lloyd Ambrose, Thoreau, New Mexico.

horizontally. More of this will be seen in the new style, however, the one which brings Navaho design down to date.

FOURTH STYLE: THE BORDERED—1890 TO PRESENT

Mr. Robert C. Prewitt, of Prewitt, New Mexico—an old-time Indian trader—once gave a criterion of age in Navaho blankets which has proved the most valuable of all, the only one I have discovered with a really high degree of consistency. "When you see a blanket with a border," he said, "you may be sure it was made not earlier than 1890." That test has been applied to some scores of dated blankets and has never failed if we make a slightly limiting condition: the border must be one of straight lines. The meandered ("Greek fret") border goes back to the 1870's, as plate 82 proves. Matthews' (1884) figure 53 shows it again, in the decade following, and other evidence, such as old photographs and magazine illustrations, prove that this forerunner of the straight border had a great vogue in the early reservation period. First appearance in point of time seems to be in the 1860's, in the Chief White Antelope blanket shown in plate 1. But here it is used as a band of design, not a complete pattern closure.[7] The latter function clearly comes later.[8]

Blankets with borders (rugs, most of them are) unquestionably do mark a style, entirely consistent in both time and character. Having weathered the storms of the transition period, the Navaho weaver seems to have settled into a pattern type with heartfelt relief, for the bordered style quickly claimed a hold on her affections that nothing since the terraced has been able to rival. Of late years it has lost ground, to be sure, as a tendency to revive earlier styles has become manifest. But from 1900 to 1920 few rugs left the loom without at least one neat strip of color along each edge as a border or frame for the design within (pls. 16, 91*b*, 92, 94, 95, 97, 112*a*, 115).

The character of that design within is too motley to be described. Any device known to geometric patterning is likely to be found there. That phase of the bordered style will never be impaled on human pen. It has all the nondescript character of the American culture which fostered it, for this style is beyond much question a white man's imposition on the

---

[7] This device is the first definitely intrusive element I could recognize in Navaho weaving. It occurs often with the terraced style, of which it heralds the break-down.

[8] References and illustrations for the bordered style: Matthews (1884: 387) speaks of the border all around as "a very rare thing in Navajo blankets." Hollister (fig. 10, p. 59) shows 13 blankets in a Navaho home scene, with only one bordered—this in a work published in 1903.

nascent rug business, since all our pictures are framed and all our rugs bordered. It is a mania with us: everything graphic must have a top, a bottom, two sides. The Navaho abhorred the very idea, and a tell-tale little strip of color leading outward through the enclosing lines will generally be found in the earlier bordered specimens, to break the baleful charm of that complete enclosure.[9]

The significance of the border lies in the changed concept of her artistic problem it gives the weaver. It creates an area of blank space to be filled, and in so doing suggests the use of isolated geometric figures. That of course is a new thing. Traditional Navaho design, whatever the style, was continuous. Its rhythm was one of regular flow rather than of repetition and balance. Isolated figures were not prominently used. The old patterns were not space-fillings, they were rather alternations of horizontal decorative zones, succeeding one another in regular order as far as space permitted. Any old Navaho blanket might have been woven by the bolt and cut into individual pieces at regular intervals without damage to the pattern. Not so the bordered blanket. It is a frame, designed to receive a picture; and any other concept (such as conservative weavers often held, trying to wed the old and the new) does not eventuate happily. A prominent central figure, with perhaps smaller decorative units harmoniously subordinated, is best adapted to this pattern type. Many excellent designs have been worked out in the bordered style; but many more have resulted in a mere amorphous hodge-podge, not Navaho, not even Indian, nor anything characteristic or pleasing. This style somehow does not express the racial genius for dynamic rhythm so strongly marked in Indian art.

CONCLUSIONS

Someone better equipped for artistic appraisal and analysis than the present writer surely could draw conclusions of exceptional value from a study of Navaho textile expression. The problem is so compact and clean-cut, so brief and recent in its time span, that almost microscopic examination is possible. Within the space of a single century (the 19th) four distinct styles held sway.[10] The two latest are related to events of out-

---

[9] Another widespread practice, that of breaking the complete circle or enclosure, for reasons purely superstitious. The prehistoric potters of the Southwest did it often, like the Hopi and Zuñi today in their pottery and the Paiute in the "marriage basket" (pl. 4) they make for the Navaho.

[10] Spiegelberg (448), a pioneer dealer, recognized three "eras" described as: 1, "Old weaves," the native dye era; 2, "Go-between," part old weaves and part "Germantown, zephyr, Saxony and other yarns"—1875 to 1885; 3, Modern, 1885 onward, with Germantown, Saxony and "other yarns," with the addition of natural

PLATE 111

Late diamond style, size 58 x 80 in., colors black, white, orange figures on red ground, purple selvage; aniline colors on native wool. Woven in the nineties (it once belonged to D. M. Riordan, Navaho agent); author's coll. A typical rug of the careless "bigger and better" days, its thread count only 4 warp and 8 weft to the inch.

PLATE 112

Three small blankets in the Fred K. Hinchman coll., Southwest Museum. Woven in the nineties, they show the diamond style in typical complex pattern and many colors.

a size 36 x 52 ins., cotton warp, Germantown (4-ply) yarn in green, white, brown, purple, on red; cat. 202L65.

b size 33 x 49 ins., cotton warp, Germantown yarn in green, yellow, purple, white, on red; cat. 202L66.

c size 34 x 51 ins., native yarn aniline dyed in red (ground) black, white, orange, yellow, green; Germantown white, green, purple; cat. 202L64.

standing practical importance to the tribe: Bosque Redondo with the transition from terraced to diamond, then the reservation period with the adoption of the bordered. One thus is led to believe that external factors possibly determined the change from striped to terraced in the early years of the century (apparently), and to consider the possibility of some purely adventitious influence at the base of the earliest and simplest style of them all, the striped.

Yet this external theory must be applied with increasing reservations as we come down the years, for there is much of logical progression and development in the advance from the striped through the terraced to the diamond. All are linked by an increasing complexity upon the basic foundation of the horizontal line in repetitious rhythm. They are allied too by the common factor of pure design expressed in rectilinear geometric form. We feel strongly that these styles do truly and worthily express the Navaho artist in wool, just as they expressed her artistic Southwestern forebears in their basketry, their simple finger weaving, and their ceramic decoration. How the transition came, if indeed it did come down in unbroken line from them, will never be exactly known. One point should be emphasized: the most casual of contacts or associations might have struck a spark to fire the whole tribe of weavers. A basket traded in, an old sandal found in a Basketmaker cave, a buried clay vessel exposed by erosion, even a mere surface fragment of one—any of these may have fallen into the hands of a gifted weaver, giving her the formula (marvelous in its simplicity) of the terraced style, for example, and launched a tribal renaissance. The supposition is not preposterous when we consider that all the outstanding modern forms of esthetic expression are credited to a handful of men of genius who wrought virtually the whole fabric. The individual genius fills a large segment of the entire human horizon, and especially is this true in the arts.[11]

SYMBOLISM IN DESIGN AND COLOR

"If God did not exist we should have to invent him," Voltaire remarked, and some people feel the same way about symbolism in Navaho blankets. As the poet finds undercurrents of romantic expression in the song of the lark or the blush of a rose, so do they in the swastikas, stars,

---

wool colors and aniline dyes. In these classes the emphasis is on material, in mine it is on pattern.

[11] Kidder thinks (1924: 103) the extraordinary efflorescence of ceramic art among the prehistoric peoples of the Mimbres Valley, New Mexico, can be explained only on this theory.

and terraces of blanket patterns. It is not enough that the weaver be an artist; she must be a religious mystic as well. Weaving to them is not so much an industrial occupation as a votive act, and figures and patterns which in wall paper would be nothing more than pure design become esoteric expressions when they occur in Navaho wool.

Symbolism is a strong element in primitive art, beyond a doubt.[12] In the carving and painting of the Northwest Coast, the sculpture of the Maya, even portions of the ceramic design of the Pueblo Southwest and the textile art of prehistoric Peru, it may be considered a controlling factor. One limitation is soon apparent: symbolism is strongest in those media of expression that are least trammeled by the basic technic. Sculpture and painting are largely independent of technical limitation; weaving and basketry are highly restricted, as we have seen. The sand-painting of the Navaho is a perfectly fluid medium, not to be compared with the loom in expressive possibilities. Another restriction: symbolism waxes strongest in objects of non-utilitarian use. The sacred jars of Pueblo kivas, like sand-paintings and totem-poles, have no practical function. But the blanket has always been either a garment or a rug—a perfectly practical, everyday object of wear and use. Generally speaking, then, neither its structure nor its function would dispose the Navaho blanket (and how much less the trading-post rug!) to symbolic expression. Such expression inheres naturally in the vestments of the priest; we find relatively little in cooks' aprons and butchers' smocks. Function and symbolism are closely allied always. The Navaho blanket, as we have seen, never has had a ceremonial or sacred function: the sand-painting, the "marriage basket," the dance mask, yes—but not the blanket.

All of the allegedly symbolic figures of Navaho design are those which commonly stand alone: cross, star, swastika, terrace, zigzag. Most of these are of late introduction. The use of isolated figures is characteristic of the final style-period, and to a lesser extent of the transition period preceding it. Nobody ascribes symbolism to the earlier patterns: the plain stripes, the continuous rise and fall of the terraced style or the same pattern done in the barbed or diamond style. The element of pure geometric design is so strong here that it seems to deny the symbolic. Later, however, when the nuclear element of the terraced style is used alone it becomes to the symbolist a "clouds and rain" figure if inverted, a "mountain range"

---

[12] "It is remarkable that in the art of many tribes the world over, ornament that appears to us as purely formal, is associated with meanings, that it is interpreted" (Boas: 88). This author however attributes no symbolism to Navaho textile design.

PLATE 113

Three styles in one. Size 56 x 76 ins., colors red ground, black, white, and green zigzag figures, white terrace blocks, narrow stripes white, black, purple, orange. Striped, terraced and diamond are pleasingly combined in this large **serape** (or early rug). Weaving date unknown, but obviously an early aniline piece, probably 1880's. Mrs. Henry A. Everett coll. Southwest Museum cat. 591G2.

PLATE 114

The pictorial. Governor W. F. M. Arny, Navaho weaver, and the American flag. Photo taken in 1873; after Pepper 1923.

if upright. The zigzag unit of the diamond style becomes a bolt of lightning. The textiles embodying these figures are usually of such late date that they were beyond little doubt woven for sale to the white man. Hence an odd deduction, but an inescapable one: the Navaho woman, unimaginative when weaving fine bayeta shoulder blankets for husband or father, burst suddenly into enraptured poesy when it became her proud lot to weave coarse rugs for the Indian trader! Peering yet more deeply into this astounding birth of artistic piety, we cannot escape the conclusion that it is somehow bound up with the inspiring society of the soldier, the trader, and the Indian agent, or perhaps the benign influence of Arbuckle's coffee and Duke's Mixture tobacco. Why else should it flower during the reservation period? If the star and the swastika embody the immemorial legendry of the tribe, why do we not find them in use before the era of mail-order catalogues and rugs made to order? A pretty mess indeed, this symbolism, if it forces us to view Kit Carson as the artistic Messiah of the tribe and the early Indian traders as the apostles of the esoteric!

The subject is tempting, but we would better get down to facts and wind up a discussion which usually drags on fruitlessly. I have yet to find a serious student of the Navaho advocating the symbolic interpretation of Navaho design.[18] The pseudo-ceremonial rugs woven of late years are copies of symbolic figures, to be sure, and if they are correctly done may be interpreted by one who knows Navaho legend and ritual— as few people do. Some such ancient, widespread symbol as the cross, embodying an idea probably crudely expressed as "the four corners of the earth," "the four winds," or "the powers that dwell in the four cardinal points" may well have found its way into a shoulder blanket intended for a medicine-man. The same may be said of the barbed "lightning" figure in a later time. There may be weavers who indulge such pretty concepts as hour-glass figures representing the sands of time or colored borders the pathway of life round the earth. Anything is possible, nowadays, in Navaho weaving. But as for general symbolic meaning in Navaho textile figures, let the reader make a simple test for himself: choose a rug (they're always more symbolic than blankets) full of "symbolic" figures. Send its photograph to three good interpreters—Navaho or white, as you prefer—each in turn. Compare their readings, and draw your own conclusions.

The case of color symbolism is no less clear. Color does play an out-

_____

[18] By "serious student" I mean one who justifies his statements as he goes. None of us has a God-given knowledge of any subject, that our mere unsupported word should stand as gospel.

standing part in Navaho tradition and ceremonial. Each of the four
sacred mountains has its color, associated with the cardinal point it represents (Matthews 1897: 215 ff; Reichard: 10), and references to the color
of various worlds in Navaho cosmogony, or of their inhabitants, physical
features, etc., are abundant in the recorded legends. White, blue, black,
yellow are the principal colors, with red seemingly secondary, and sometimes substituted for black in certain usages (Reichard: 10). Black is
symbolic of male beings, blue of female (Matthews 1897: 236). I have
found no evidence of the application to blanketry of these color impli-
cations. Black and blue occur together in men's and women's garments
alike. Red, a secondary color in symbolism, is primary in weaving, while
yellow (probably the most successful of purely native colors) is very little
used. One may account for the dominance of these colors in Navaho
blankets on purely practical grounds. Black and white are natural colors
found in the sheep; obviously they would be used, particularly as they
contrast strongly. Blue is the color of the best dyestuff the Navaho country ever knew—indigo.[14] Red speaks for itself—richest, gaudiest, most
vivid of all colors. Only yellow remains, and here is a point of interest to
be noted: although a leading color symbolically it is of little importance
in weaving. Can this be because it is the only color of the five which the
Navaho had to make for themselves? At any rate, these non-symbolic
considerations are important. Whether they are all-powerful is not proved:
there may be a color symbolism in weaving which has escaped us, although this is greatly to be doubted. After all, there are only a half-dozen
colors (artists recognize only three). What else could the Navaho choose
for their color symbolism?

The Navaho woman was devout—more than we, in the days when
her native faith stood unshaken and serene. Her devotion did not seek
artistic expression on the loom. Neither does ours. She was an artist, making the most of her limited range of color, material, and pattern without
the slightest discoverable inhibition. Her work is self-explanatory. It has
won widespread acclaim without interpretation, on its own artistic merits.

Yet a question remains. Why should Navaho weaving be innocent
of symbolism when the artistry of most Indian tribes shows that influence
so strongly? Are the Navaho somehow different, more sophisticated, less
sensitive to the spiritual and the imaginative? The answer I think lies in
this, that Navaho weaving is not a native tribal craft. We have seen it
taken over bodily from the Pueblos, its basic material an innovation of

[14] The only colorant (not excepting cochineal) I have never seen fade.

PLATE 115

The pictorial. Size not specified (I never saw it), colors black, coral pink (probably faded aniline), and white, on evidently native wool. Collected presumably in the 1880's by Colonel Carmody, U. S. Army, whose relative Mr. John Condon brought it to Brooklyn Museum, by whose courtesy this photograph is used. Cat. not specified. Note the zigzag border.

PLATE 116

Diamond-striped style. Size 56 x 74 ins., colors indigo blue, native yellow-green, probably aniline red, white, gray bands, all native wool. Woven about 1887. Owner, Mr. Earl H. Morris. Made probably as a **serape,** used many years as a rug. Such pieces are just of a weight for good service in either function.

the Spaniards. Pueblo influence was paramount in its early years, Spanish influence was strong during its middle period, when the *serape Navajo* was widely sought and warmly praised; and the modern period has been completely industrialized by the American. Hence there is no valid basis of comparison between this craft and Pueblo ceramics or Maya sculpture, or that ancient widespread craft of basketry in which symbolism is so manifest.[15]

Symbolism is not spontaneous or personal; not the outflowing of genius or the sudden burst of a brilliant individual concept, but a conventional, almost ritual expression of ideas old and well established in their social group. It grows like a slow plant, and like a plant its flowers are of a set pattern, determined by natural factors that have been long at work. The turbulent career of Navaho weaving could brook no such quiet growths as this.

---

[15] Pueblo weaving affords an interesting parallel. The old traditional cotton garments have many little symbolic touches in their makeup and their embroidered ornament. But the woolen fabrics are severely plain and utilitarian, with the exception of those like the woman's shawl, which are simply copies in wool of the older types.

PLATE 117

Serape-rug in the diamond-striped style bought (probably new) in 1887. Size 52 x 70 ins., colors: stripes of white, indigo blue, black; diamonds blue, black, white, orange, green, on a ground varying in color from orange-yellow to orange-red. All native wool, probably aniline colors except indigo blue. The peculiar burnt red ground seems to be a mixture of red and orange dyes. Thrift might dictate such mixtures as a means of using left-over dye. F. K. Hinchman coll. Southwest Museum cat. 202L55.

PLATE 118

Another recent **serape**. It was bought new in the early nineties. Size 58 x 75 ins., colors: diamonds in black, white, faded orange, on faded red ground; natural tan-gray panels, all native wool. Certainly an early aniline piece; cat. 202L68, Fred K. Hinchman coll. Southwest Museum.

CHAPTER XV

THE REVIVAL—1920 TO PRESENT

E HAVE followed Navaho weaving through one complete cycle of being and into another. Each rested upon an economic basis and was molded by and to the needs of the time—for this is a craft, an industry, and like all such its existence depends on a human want. The first cycle was the purely intra-tribal or native period in which, coming as an alien craft without, it established itself in time as the principal source of clothing for the tribe. The second cycle began with the era of the reservation and the trading post, when the loom was diverted from its function of producing Navaho clothing and set to weaving American rugs. This phase is still in full vigor, yet there are signs of an impending readjustment to the changing times. The Navaho rug came into being because the American demanded a textile meeting his needs and satisfying his graphic concepts; that it retained something to the tribal flavor is not due to him but to the weaver who either could not or would not divest herself completely of her racial individuality. Now the American has come to a better understanding and appreciation of that racial heritage and is beginning to demand that the Indian be himself again. Specifically, he wants a larger Navaho ingredient in Navaho weaving and is encouraging a revival of the once-despised native styles.

The revival idea is not new. It has been tried before with scant success, for nothing is harder than to retrace pathways long abandoned. The Navaho, like the rest of us, will become anything in the world except his old self. Yet there may be sufficient impulse in the present movement to overcome this instinctive dread of looking backward, and temper the present with a moderate draft of the past. That is the essence of the revival idea, to modify present-day Navaho weaving along old-time lines; not, as some alarmists seem to believe, to attempt a sweeping ouster of the modern and a triumphant reinstatement of its precedent forms and methods.

Miss Mary Wheelwright, secretary of the Boston Branch of the Eastern Association on Indian Affairs and owner of an Indian art shop in that city, seems to have cast the first pebble to ripple the stagnant surface of the Navaho rug industry in the present revival movement. Her account of it follows as written for me:

In 1920 on a camping trip I stopped at Chin Lee, Cañon de Chelly, at the trading post of L. H. McSparron to see a Yebechai Ceremony nearby, and had a talk with Mr. Mc-Sparron about the colours and patterns of the Navaho blankets as produced by the Indians then. Mr. McSparron said he was discouraged at the poor markets, for the blankets, said that it was growing more difficult to sell them, and I told him that I was sure that there were many who felt as I did that the modern blankets were ugly and had lost their Indian quality in design. As to the colours, that had gone almost entirely, as after attempting to sell blankets dyed with commercial dyes the public preferred undyed wools to these colours, and so most of the best weaving was in brown, grey, black and white and made into regular floor rug types, as different from the old blankets as could be conceived. When the Indians were thus deprived of colours in their weaving they tried to make the rugs attractive to the traders who were their only buyers by elaborating the patterns after designs suggested often by linoleum and other rugs they saw in the stores.

I asked Mr. McSparron if any Indians knew how to use their old vegetable dyes; he said that a few still did, and I asked him if he would be willing to try and produce some old style blankets, if I would be willing to buy the inevitable first failures.

He agreed to do this and asked me to send him some patterns as he found that owing to the fact that antique dealers had bought up all the old blankets that the Indians had forgotten their old designs. I did this by a very primitive method, taking my old blankets and others I borrowed and printing out the pattern on a sheet of brown paper and then very roughly sketching in the colours. The first colours Mr. McSparron got were a greenish yellow from rabbit brush, a good black and a good brown, and a brownish red from cedar bark.

To my delight I found that my friends liked these new

blankets and readily bought them from me, and then Mr. McSparron reported that he could sell them as fast as he could get them, even though they were more expensive than those he had before as the vegetable dyeing took longer to do and he had to give the Indians more money for the blankets.

They had lost the art of dyeing either blue or red, for I sent out as an experiment indigo and cochineal but they could not use them. As time went on they made a fine clear yellow, a good green and turned out some lovely neutral tinted blankets and soon other traders began following Mr. McSparron's example.

The Indians were glad of the return of their organic patterns which meant something to them and glad of the return of colours, but always longed for blue and red for their work and I am so thankful that with the help of Mr. and Mrs. Burge and the Eastern Association on Indian Affairs, they can have the opportunity of making really beautiful coloured blankets, comparable to those their ancestors made, but much credit is due to the vision, enterprise and persistence of Mr. McSparron, who first tried the experiment.

THE NATIONAL ASSOCIATION ON INDIAN AFFAIRS

The reference to the Eastern Association on Indian Affairs in the conclusion of Miss Wheelwright's account is to another and later phase of the movement so courageously begun by her and Mr. McSparron at Chinle. This Association, the name of which has recently been changed to National Association on Indian Affairs, arose out of an emergency and remained to become a potent force for Indian welfare in the Southwest. Its history as sketched for me by Miss Amelia Elizabeth White, Secretary, begins with a visit by her to New Mexico, at about the time of Miss Wheelwright's fruitful call at Chin Le. Miss White, new to the Southwest, was astonished to find Indians still actively engaged in their traditional handicrafts; and forthwith she returned to New York and opened a shop for the sale of the worthy products of this activity.

In 1922 Senator H. O. Bursum of New Mexico introduced his now famous bill to clear up disputed land titles in which Indians were concerned. Miss White had a telegram from friends in New Mexico telling her the bill would dispossess many Pueblo Indians and kill their native crafts, and imploring her to arouse interest in the East against the measure. The result was the formation of the Eastern Association on Indian Affairs and the raising of a storm of protest, nation-wide, that defeated the Bursum bill in its objectionable form after two years of hard struggle.

The Association next gave its attention to the general health situation of Southwestern Indians; trachoma in particular was ravaging them. It was instrumental in having an officer of the U. S. Public Health Service detailed to the Indian Bureau, and it sent a Public Health nurse to Española, New Mexico, to study sanitary conditions among the Pueblos, in coöperation with Bureau officials. Soon it had nurses at Zuñi and Jemez, and among the Navaho. Here again it won its fight: the Government took over the work as a recognized obligation toward its Indian wards, and the Association turned to Indian arts and crafts for its next campaign of improvement. The first step was the draft of a plan for creating an Arts and Crafts section in the Indian Bureau, in charge of an official whose duties would comprise stimulation of native crafts and development of a market for their products. Nothing, as yet, has come of the plan; but the Association is not sitting with hands folded. Margaret McKittrick Burge, its active Field Investigator, here takes up the story to prove the point.[1]

At the last annual meeting it was decided that we should map out some project for improving Indian arts and crafts, which, if successful, would be as convincing a demonstration in that line, as our nursing projects have been in health matters. From an economic as well as an æsthetic standpoint, an effort to revive the former high standard of design and weave in Navajo rugs seemed to offer the most promising field for our work. Most modern rugs have degenerated to such an extent in design, color and weave that it is difficult to believe that they are made by the same people who wove the beautiful textiles collected a few decades ago, and now to be found in museums and private collections all over the country. Although over a million dollars' worth of rugs is sold from the reservation annually, because of the poor quality, the price per rug received by the weaver, considering the work involved, is ridiculously low.

The first problem was to give the weavers and traders an idea of the type of design found in the old blankets. We

---

1 From the 1932 report of the Association.

PLATE 119

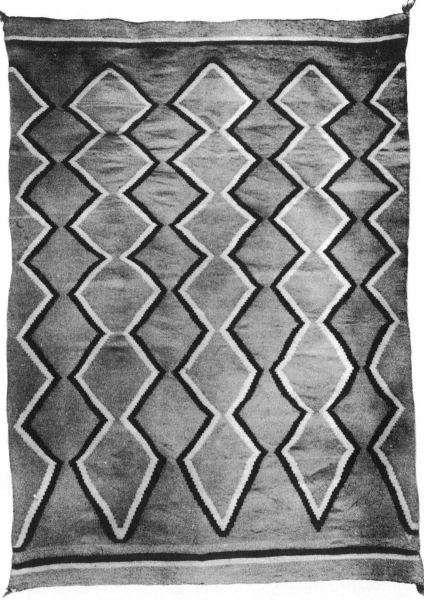

Last of the terraced style. Its lines have gone vertical. Size 46 x 64 ins., colors native white and indigo blue figures on red ground of mixed late bayeta (Manchester?) and machine-spun yarn.

Bought at Taos, N. M., in the early 1880's. Denver Art Museum cat. RN17.

PLATE 120

Last of the terraced style. Size 42 x 66 ins., colors black, white, green, on red (all apparently aniline). Its history goes back to the late eighties. Fred K. Hinchman coll. Southwest Museum cat. 202L.74.

decided the most practical way of doing this was to distribute photographs and sketches of the fine specimens of blankets taken from the best collections all over the country. We first tried mounting a photograph on a heavy card, and putting beside it an enlarged detail giving the colors used in the design. The result was that rugs were woven which in design were quarters of whole rugs. In other words, the weaver copied the colored detail without reference to the photograph. We then tried having the photographs enlarged to 8 x 10, and found that this larger photograph gave a much better idea of the whole design. Instead of presenting a detail to show the color, the photograph itself was filled in sufficiently to show the colors used throughout the design. So far this has been satisfactory as far as the weavers are concerned. Our problem has been to turn out these photographs in sufficient quantity to supply traders and the schools that we have interested in this movement. Through the coöperation of a number of people a system has been worked out which I believe will meet the situation. The owners of fine blankets have been most kind in permitting us to photograph their specimens. The actual photographing, which requires both time and patience, is done by Mr. C. Wickham Moore. A special hanger has been constructed from which to hang the blankets during the photographing. This was necessary because the traders are continually combatting a habit of the less skillful weavers of making their rugs crooked on the edges, so it is important that the rug in the photograph be as straight as possible, or the weavers may use the fact that the photograph is crooked as an excuse for careless weaving. After the photographs are secured, Mr. George Bloom makes four 8 x 10 enlargements. Of these, three prints are mounted on cards for distribution to the schools, weavers or traders, and one print is kept for the files as a record. The coloring of the photographs was a tremendous problem until the services of Mr. Moris Burge were secured. This was made possible by the Massachusetts Branch of the Eastern Association and the New Mexico Association.

Because of the wide variation in shades of color in the blankets, an exact reproduction would entail considerable

time and labor, besides being unnecessary. The actual purpose of these designs is to stimulate and revive the use of the
old and true Navaho blanket patterns and as soon as the
weavers are creating new designs, within the old tradition,
these photographs will have fulfilled their purpose and
their distribution will no longer be necessary. So in many of
the photographs colors are intensified to bring out the design
more clearly. Besides, it is hoped that the weavers will not
copy the exact colors and patterns, but rather use the colored
photographs merely as a suggestion for the new rugs. After
the prints are colored they are shellacked, labelled, bound and
catalogued, Mr. Deric Nusbaum and Mr. Robert Eckert doing this part of the work. They are then sent out in sets, a
careful record being kept of the designs included in each set
and its destination, so that when later requests for designs
are received there will be no duplication in sending them
out. Although each card is labelled as a "loan," cards are very
seldom returned to us. The field is so large that an incredible
number of designs are needed to make any impression
whatsoever.

As soon as we began distributing designs we were told
that it was impossible even to approach the colors indicated
in the photographs. The matter of dyes was then taken up
with Miss Lucy S. Cabot of Boston. Miss Cabot has studied
dyeing for years. At Mr. Bloom's suggestion last spring we
sent Miss Cabot some fragments of old blankets to give ideas
of the colors it would be necessary to match. She consulted
Mr. Walter Heintz of the DuPont Company, who recommended a series of dyes using 28% acetic acid as a mordant,
which is inexpensive and quite safe for the Indians to handle.
The colors are beautiful and the dyes are almost as easy to
mix as water colors. The dye comes in dry form and is very
highly concentrated. This powder is mixed up into what are
known as stock solutions, three tablespoons of color to a pint
bottle of water, and these solutions are used by the teaspoon-
ful in proportion to the amount of wool to be dyed. The
water is first heated very hot and color added. It is kept just
below boiling for half an hour, or as the Indians say for as
long as it takes to eat dinner. It then boils for half an hour.

Then two teaspoonfuls of acetic acid are added, and it boils for another half hour. It is also fairly easy with a little experience to obtain almost any desired shade, as the dyes are exceedingly flexible. If, for instance, a blue and yellow are being used to obtain a shade of green either blue or yellow may be added to modify the shade at any time during the process up to about the last five or ten minutes of boiling. The process is quite simple.

Mrs. Burge and Miss Cabot in 1932 made a tour of dye demonstration covering the whole Navaho territory, from the Santa Fe Indian School to remote Shonto in Arizona. Traders and Indians alike took kindly to the new colors and the almost-forgotten patterns. One old weaver remarked that the old-time vegetal dyes were mixed just like these new ones, by adding a little at a time until the desired shade was attained. The photographs were a revelation to many, for few indeed are the old blankets extant among the Navaho. One girl who had been to Santa Fe to see the marvelous old blankets in the Laboratory of Anthropology there, confided to Mrs. Burge that she had heard the old folks talk of the fine blankets of former days, but never really believed them until she went and saw for herself. The experience gave her a new respect for her people.

"I am convinced that just as beautiful rugs can be woven today as were in the past," continues Mrs. Burge in her report. "It is entirely a matter of education and appreciation. I am also convinced that the best results can be obtained by working intensively with small groups of weavers and traders who are most interested, and that it will be necessary to make repeated visits to these groups, and to put the traders in touch with markets for their better grade blankets."

Experiments with commercial as well as native colorants are proceeding apace, for these revivalists are practical reformers, holding no brief for any particular method but aiming directly at the desired result. The acetic acid dye Mrs. Burge described in her report just quoted has not been a success in Navaho hands, latest advices tell. The necessity of handling mordant and colorant separately and in right proportion has been a stumbling block, for the Navaho weaver is long accustomed to having them already combined in one package. Wells and Richardson of Diamond Dye fame were appealed to and furnished shreds of old blankets to show the desired colors. They have just responded with a package dye quite as simple as the old but with a greater color range and much more delicacy of hue. This improved dye has been given the name Old Navaho.

The revival stands today as an accomplished fact whatever its future destiny. Mr. McSparron, its pioneer, reports that sixty per centum of all blankets brought to him are of this type. Other traders who are backing the movement make perhaps a less impressive showing, yet the aggregate of output proves the new type a strong factor in the market. Miss Wheelwright since 1930 has offered an annual prize for the best blanket of vegetal dye and native pattern displayed at the International Indian Ceremonial at Gallup, and the prize winner for 1932 was bought straight from the judges' hands by the Denver Art Museum. It is shown in plate 121. Under the double stimulus of private encouragement and commercial demand, much of the old-time technic of native dyeing has been recalled to life. More interesting still, it has been increased—more than doubled in variety of materials used and shades of color produced—by a flurry of experimentation. The weavers have learned the important fact that almost any color in plants can be transferred to wool with little loss of value if the proper method be used. So in addition to the rabbit-brush yellow, canaigre orange, and mountain mahogany red of the old days, there are browns of black-walnut hull and red-browns of juniper and yucca-root bark, mauves of alder bark with a dash of aniline, purples of coyote berry, greens of yucca stalks, tumbleweed, even alfalfa. Boiling extracts the color and fixes it in the wool, with a mordant of crushed juniper berries or native alum, unless sufficient mordant quality inheres in the ingredients.

At Chinle in the summer of 1932 I was shown a blanket of bright scarlet color, with the assurance of the woman who did the dyeing and weaving that she used hackberries and nothing else in achieving the shade, pounding the raw berries into the wool. Mrs. B. I. Staples who has been experimenting in native dyeing for years at Crafts del Navajo, Coolidge, New Mexico, where her husband is doing much to foster the old-time Navaho crafts, gets a very pleasing buff-brown shade with the ground-lichen *Parmelia molliuscule,* used by the old-time dyers in making red colorant. She has worked with cochineal, too, getting many pleasing shades of purple and pink. Another purple, deep and brilliant, is produced by Mary Russell F. Colton of Flagstaff, Arizona—patroness of an interesting revival of Hopi crafts into which we cannot enter here—by boiling the distinctive blue corn of ancient Pueblo stock which the Hopi still cultivate. In short, the bars are down, and one may expect anything in color and colorant until the range of available plants has been exhaust-

PLATE 121

Blanket-rug in the revival style, size 54 x 76 ins. The dyes used are aniline, but of better quality than those the traders sell. Denver Art Museum cat. RN24. Colorist Jean Parker Dodge.

ed and their possibilities thoroughly explored.

The reader must not conclude that atrocities are being committed in the name of good old-fashioned methods—that Navaho coloring is running riot as in the early aniline days of the eighties and nineties. Three factors are keeping this interesting train of experiments in orderly control. First is the fact that native plants never (or seldom, at any rate) yield violent shades. On the contrary, their hues are almost invariably of a delicate pastel character which fits them readily into the color scheme. Second is the close supervision being exercised at all the centers of experimentation by Americans who realize the pitfalls of the inartistic and the over-gaudy. Third is the fact that the Navaho women producing the colors are experienced and intelligent beyond the average. They understand and respect the old-time traditions of Navaho weaving, they know that the new style was conceived and fostered in a spirit of reverence for this sound craftsmanship and artistry of former days; and they will not debauch it unless the trader insists.

Another question remains, that of the durability of the new colors. Mr. McSparron told me he would rather guarantee a native dye than an aniline. He showed me blankets ten or twelve years old, in use constantly, which held their colors almost pristine. Mrs. Staples and Mrs. Colton have conducted fading tests of various sorts and found the native dyes soundly resistant to fading, if not entirely proof. Mr. McSparron has a trick for determining whether doubtful colors are aniline or vegetal, when the weaver herself brings in the new blanket for sale to him. If she avers the colors are native, he proposes to throw the blanket into boiling water as a test, before buying it. If she consents, he is satisfied that there is no aniline dye present; so the native dyes have a local reputation, at least.

THE REVIVAL STYLE APPRAISED

The new-old style in Navaho weaving is meeting some active opposition and considerable passive ill-will. The opponents are mainly traders and dealers of long experience and conservative bent, who have long since formulated standards based on the bordered style in vivid colorings, and are determined, naturally enough, never to admit that they have been wrong all these years. Most of them are thoroughly honest in their views. They cite the undeniable fact that the public in general has a fairly definite idea of what a Navaho blanket or rug should be, and demands something to accord with its garish, barbaric concept; they hold that the revival type does not meet the public expectation, that it will be viewed with suspicion when offered as a genuine Navaho, and neglected for the other type with which people are more familiar.[2] They make the point, too, that the revival style is neither old nor new. Lacking the mellow touch of time and wear, it does not achieve the color tones of the type it imitates nor, generally, the freedom of style in design, the excellence of wool, or the fineness of spinning and weaving. It is, in short, an inferior imitation. Wherefore a number of traders and dealers decry the revival.

The passive resisters for the greater part are skeptics who have not really made up their minds on the point. They will be glad enough to see the revival style put new life into the rug business, which they know is not all it might be although they do not know clearly just why. A little practical demonstration of pecuniary advantage will make them enthusiastic supporters; but until it comes they will look askance on the new movement as something of a fad—an "arty" fad, backed by impractical, inexperienced Easterners who are just toying at a game in which they have no real stake. This resisting group comprises mainly the younger traders and dealers who were brought up in the bordered tradition but are not wedded to it beyond hope of change. They, like their elders, see the whole matter through the hard, cold eyes of business, as simply a problem in supply and demand; wherever the demand seems to lie, there will they be found.

The active supporters of the revival style are themselves a double group. First come the artists, the students of the Indian and his arts, and all those persons whose approach to the matter is artistic, benevolent, or sentimental—whereas the average trader's approach is commercial from first to last. Second in the group come those traders and dealers who take the broader view of Navaho weaving and its kindred activities, those who believe it is good business to bolster and maintain the artistic ingredient of these crafts as conducive to greater satisfaction to all concerned: weaver, trader, dealer, buyer. To the extremist's among them the product of the Navaho loom was originally a blanket and rightfully should be a blanket; they would wipe out of memory that painful interlude during which it was a good, serviceable rug, strong enough in its pattern and colors to jump off the floor and stand alone. The more moderate are content that the revival style should be used for rugs as well as blankets. All meet,

---

2 Mr. Cotton, who has sold many rugs of the new type, phrases it well. He says they do not sell themselves but have to be sold. When a dealer orders a consignment of rugs from his stock he does not include any of this type unless by request, as the consignee is likely to complain.

however, on the common ground of the artistic: there must be good taste, after the tenets generally accepted in such matters, in both color and pattern. Long relegated to the sun-porch and the den, the Navaho rug must be made worthy of the living room and the bedroom; it must harmonize with the French wallpaper, the Colonial furniture, the figured curtains. A certain degree of boldness may be allowed at times, that it may attune itself to the sharper note of aluminum and red leather in modernistic interiors; but whatever the situation, it must chime in with the prevailing harmony.

Now, to anyone not familiar with old Navaho weaving, it must seem that the revivalists would devitalize and conventionalize the modern output beyond all recognition. Yet the exact contrary is their aim, say they: the bordered style they would abandon has suffered these indignities already; its dull conventionalism of color, its unimaginative routine of pattern, however striking these may appear at fresh glance, are as foreign to Indian art as they are deadly to constant companionship. The pre-aniline blanket was simpler and better balanced in design, more harmonious in coloring, more artistic in its whole concept: a worthier piece than its modern successor. But it was no less Indian, it was in fact far more Navaho. Nature created the colors in the Navaho country and the patterns in which they were displayed bore the authentic tribal stamp. There is the true Navaho expression, not in the later rug which got its colors from a factory and its pattern from a catalogue. Far from wanting to change the Navaho, we would make him more Navaho, less white man; far from dictating his weaving, we would protect it from that dictation which has brought it, in both technic and artistry, already so low. Thus the revivalists and so the issue is joined.

To one who is no passionate partisan of either side, the revival movement seems to promise nothing but good. Nobody expects it to sweep the reservation like wildfire, dooming the bordered style to swift extinction. There are thousands of Navaho weavers today, most of them middle-aged or elderly women, all veterans in the use of aniline dyes and the patterns associated with them. Can anybody seriously believe that these women will suddenly alter the habits of a lifetime? If the newer style does displace the older it will do so gradually. The bordered displaced the other quickly enough, a half-century ago, yet it was a good twenty years in gaining complete ascendancy.[3] And aniline dyes were a novelty, a source

---

3 In the more remote corners of the reservation, native dyes were used until at least 1900, aniline dyes having been introduced (in the trading posts of the southern Navaho territory) about 1880.

of rich, abundant color, a great time and labor saver—a godsend in short; they will be abandoned far more slowly than they were adopted. The public will not be deprived of its Greek-bordered, highly colored rugs, if it really wants that rococo type, for many a year to come. Whether the revival style lives or dies, the other has promise of many more years of life— assuming of course that Navaho weaving continues as an important industry in the face of the many disturbing factors an ever-encroaching alien civilization is bringing to bear upon it.

Instead of a threat, most thoughtful observers see in the revival style a great promise for the future of the craft. It is different, undeniably— vastly different; and being so it broadens immeasurably the appeal of the Navaho textile. It wins a whole host of new friends whose esthetic sensibilities were offended by the blatant colors and insipid design of the prevailing type. It finds a score of new uses (and new uses mean new markets), being at once colorful enough for the summer cottage and the den, subdued enough for the boudoir, striking enough for the modernistic interior, and simple enough for the old-fashioned "period" setting. It is a rug, a couch cover, a wall hanging, as one may prefer; for like the old-time blanket, the new type has sufficient weight for service on the floor yet is not too stiff and heavy for more flexible uses.

Those are purely practical considerations. Alongside them the ardent revivalists place another factor, an imponderable and very uncertain one: the esthetic, in its effect upon the Navaho. They fondly hope for a great artistic renaissance, for a return to the days when weaving was (presumably) done with pride and joy and a complete, self-effacing devotion to the task of producing textiles both useful and beautiful. They expect the dyeing torch to flame forth again and shed its bright rays over a re-inspired nation of artists-in-wool. The miracle may come to pass: we know so little of the Indian and his ultimate artistic potentialities. But we know a great deal of the trader, the tourist, the legislator who conrols Indian destinies, the official who enforces legislative mandates, the price of Arbuckle's coffee, and the influence of the Government school, the automobile, the movie; and knowing these, how hard it is to believe that the thoroughly industrialized craft of Navaho weaving will throw off its shackles and emerge untrammeled as a joyous art.

The backers of the revival movement—those who are really doing something about it, as opposed to the frothing lecturers and writers— are not unduly swayed by exalted sentiment. They know that art in the mass must pay its way, even though an occasional genius may elect to

PLATE 122

Two small rugs in the revival style, both woven in 1932 at Chinle. Author's coll. a size 44 x 65 ins., colors black, white, brown stripes and blocks on a yellow-green ground. b size 39 x 60 ins., colors black, yellow, brown, on white. The colors are mainly if not wholly vegetal. To date neither has shown any sign of fading.

PLATE 123

Weavers of today. These women were assembled from all parts of the reservation to participate in a conference held February 13-16, 1933, at the government Indian school and the Laboratory of Anthropology, both in Santa Fe, New Mexico. The object of the gathering was to awaken an interest in the old styles and methods, as exemplified in the Laboratory's collections and the work done in the school.

Not a single product of the native loom is in evidence, with the possible exception of one woven belt; but some of the foot-gear and most of the jewelry is native. All of the older women wear the gaudy machine-woven shawl, and the voluminous calico skirts which are said to be a survival of American styles of the Civil War period. Courtesy of Laboratory of Anthropology.

perish for his principles; they admit that the market is the ultimate arbiter of the issue and avow that the market will respond to better Navaho blankets, at higher prices.[4] Patience, encouragement, appreciation, even some financial support will be needed for a time. But eventually the new style will take hold and then it will revitalize itself, cease to be merely imitative. The best weavers will practise it, for the benefit of an exacting clientèle. Better remuneration, greater pride in work, fuller independence of individual, tribal and racial expression—all will result, and Navaho weaving will have taken a new lease of life. This the sponsors of the revival confidently believe; and in their forefront is the National Association on Indian Affairs, which never lost a fight.

THE FUTURE OF NAVAHO WEAVING

This brief study of an aboriginal craft which became a modern industry cannot in full conscience close its pages without a glance ahead, for studies of the past have little value unless they serve in some measure to illumine the future. I see the immediate future of Navaho weaving as a race between two forces. One of these is the Americanization of the Navaho; the other is the education of the American to the Indian. They are mutually antagonistic, the first of them working against the future of our craft, the second for it. Let us examine them both as they appear today.

The Navaho weaving industry today is one the economist would call marginal, hence precarious. Like many mines, oil wells, farm lands, it requires favoring circumstances to assure profitable activity. With weaving, these circumstances are spare time and cheap wool. Traders long ago noticed that most of their rug purchases are made in the spring because most weaving is done during the long idle days of winter. When lambing and shearing time, harvesting time come, weaving virtually halts. During the summer it lags. Traders know, too, that cheap wool, hard times, stimulate weaving because wool in rug form brings a little more money (very little, as we shall see) than wool in raw form; but when the wool market is brisk and prices high, rug production dwindles. In fine, the Navaho woman weaves when she has nothing better to do or when the family wool crop cannot be sold to better advantage in the raw. The reader will have sensed the underlying reason for this perhaps surprising state of affairs: the price of rugs, which is the reward of the weaver's labor. Two instances will make this point abundantly clear.

---

4 Marshall Field and Company of Chicago saw great possibilities in the revival style for use in modernist interiors, Mr. Moris Burge has told me.

First: during the World War and for a time thereafter raw wool brought a higher price per pound than rugs of average quality have commanded during the present depression period. Second: Messrs. Bernard and Drolet of the Shiprock Trading Company recently made an interesting experiment in the economics of weaving. They hired one of their experienced weavers to come to the store and weave by the hour, making a rug 2½ by 5 feet in size, of simple pattern. One rug ended the experiment: appraised at a fair market value ($12.00) it was worth about thirty per cent of its cost to them ($40.80) at twenty cents an hour, the weaver's wage, for they had furnished the materials themselves. I saw the rug and I agreed that the trader's valuation was entirely fair as prices stood in the summer of 1932. In other words, this weaver (entirely typical of all) habitually wove rugs for the market at a wage of five cents an hour.

Here is the point at which our two forces clash. Remembering that many Navaho today attend school, work for Americans at good wages, drive automobiles, indulge in many of the conveniences and even luxuries of modern American life—how long will Navaho women consent to toil at the loom for a wage of five cents an hour?[15] So much for the force of Americanization. Now for the other. How far has our appreciation of the Indian's art and craft progressed—is it far enough to offset the pull of this force and keep the woman at her loom by paying her a fair price for her work?

I must confess that I am of two minds about it all. Not doubting the eventual extinction of this crude aboriginal device which struggles on so persistently against the tremendous resources of the power-driven loom, I still do not believe the end will come swiftly. The revival movement may raise the general standard of workmanship and increase the weaver's reward. Even if it does not, a diminishing supply of Navaho rugs will tend to raise prices and encourage continued production. But there are powerful factors on the other side of the contest. The tribe is getting royalties on oil produced on the reservation (discovered only in 1923), and if affluence comes the old ways will vanish like snow in spring. Oklahoma demonstrated that, years ago. The whole alluring picture of American life and ways is spread before the Navaho, urging him to "be a white man." Government teaches it in the schools, missionaries preach it,

---

[5] Dr. Gladys Reichard has in preparation a study of Navaho weaving from the subjective, i. e. the weaver's point of view, which may throw some valuable light on this point. I commend her work to my readers in any event, both for the high authority of Dr. Reichard and as covering a phase of the subject upon which I have not touched—weaving as the weaver sees it.

expediency and the line of least resistance echo the constant appeal on every hand. Even in our growing sympathy for the Indian a danger lurks, for America has ever assimilated most rapidly those alien groups to which the heartiest welcome was extended. Surely the end of it all is clearly enough in view. The only question remaining is: how long?

WORKS CITED
NAVAHO WEAVING

WORKS CITED

ABBOTT, F. H.
> 1914. The Navaho Indians and the public domain. *The Native American,* 15: 27-31. Phoenix, Ariz.

ABERT, J. W.
> 1848. Report of examination of New Mexico, 1846-47. Washington, D. C.

BACKUS, E.
> 1860. An account of the Navajoes of New Mexico. (In Schoolcraft, H. R., Archives of Aboriginal Knowledge, IV, 209-215.) Philadelphia.

BANCROFT, H. H.
> 1889. Arizona and New Mexico, 1530-1888. (Bancroft's Works, vol. XVII.) San Francisco.

BANDELIER, A. F.
> 1883. Historical introduction to studies among the sedentary Indians of New Mexico. *Papers of the Archaeological Institute of America, American Series,* no. I. Boston.
> 1890. Final report of investigations among the Indians of the Southwestern United States, carried on mainly in the years from 1880 to 1885. *Ibid.* no. III. Cambridge, Mass.
> 1890,a. Contributions to the history of the southwestern portion of the United States. *Ibid.,* no. V. Cambridge, Mass.

BARREIRO, Antonio
> 1928. A glance over New Mexico. (Ojeada sobre Nuevo-Mexico, 1832.) Translated by Lansing B. Bloom in *New Mexico Historical Society Publications in History,* vol. V. Santa Fe, N. M.

BARTLETT, John Russell
> 1854. Personal narrative of explorations and incidents in Texas, New Mexico, California, Sonora, and Chihuahua. New York.

BEADLE, J. H.
> 1879. Western wilds and the men who redeem them. San Francisco.

BENAVIDES, Fray Alonso de
> 1916. The Memorial of Fray Alonso de Benavides, 1630. Translated by Mrs. Edward E. Ayer. Chicago.

BLOOM, Lansing B.
> 1927. Early weaving in New Mexico. *New Mexico Historical Review,* II: 228-234. Santa Fe, N. M.

BOAS, Franz
    1927.   Primitive art. Oslo, Norway.
BOLTON, Herbert E., *editor*.
    1916.   Spanish exploration in the Southwest, 1542-1706. (Original narratives of early American history.) New York.
BROWNE, Peter
    1852.   Communication on Saxony wools. *Proceedings American Philosophical Society,* V: 259-261. Philadelphia.
CALHOUN, James S.
    1915.   The official correspondence of James S. Calhoun while Indian Agent at Santa Fe and Superintendent of Indian Affairs in New Mexico. Edited by Annie Heloise Abel. Washington.
CHEETHAM, Francis T.
    1926.   Kit Carson. *New Mexico Historical Review,* I: 375-399. Santa Fe, N. M.
COLTON, Mary Russell F.
    1932.   Wool for our Indian weavers—what shall it be? *Museum Notes* (Museum of Northern Arizona), vol. 4, no. 12. Flagstaff, Ariz.
COMMISSIONER OF INDIAN AFFAIRS
    1854-1914.   Annual reports (cited as R. C. I. A. followed by year of issue). Washington.
COUES, Elliott
    1900.   On the trail of a Franciscan pioneer. The diary and itinerary of Francisco Garcés, 1775-1776. New York.
CRAWFORD, M. D. C.
    1915.   Peruvian textiles. *Anthropological Papers American Museum of Natural History,* vol. XII, part III. New York.
    1916.   Peruvian fabrics. idem, vol. XII, part IV.
CULIN, Stewart
    1907.   Games of the North American Indians. *Twenty-fourth Annual Report of the Bureau of American Ethnology,* 3-846. Washton.
CURTIS, Edward S.
    1907-1930.   The North American Indian. 20 vols. Cambridge and Norwood, Mass.
DAVIS, W. W. H.
    1857.   El Gringo; or, New Mexico and her people. New York.

DOUGLASS, A. E.
> 1929. The secrets of the Southwest shown by talkative tree rings. *National Geographic Magazine,* LVI: 700-737. Washington.

DRAKE, Francis S., *editor.*
> 1891. The Indian tribes of the United States. Philadelphia

EDWARDS, Frank S.
> 1847. A campaign in New Mexico with Colonel Doniphan. Philadelphia.

EMMONS, George T.
> 1907. The Chilkat blanket. *Memoirs American Museum of Natural History,* vol. III, part IV. New York.

FRANCISCAN FATHERS
> 1910. An ethnologic dictionary of the Navaho language. St. Michaels, Arizona.
> 1912. A vocabulary of the Navaho language. St. Michaels, Ariz.

GALLEGOS, Hernán
> 1927. The Gallegos relation of the Rodríguez expedition to New Mexico. Translated and edited by George P. Hammond and Agapito Rey. *New Mexico Historical Review,* II: 239-268, 334-362. Santa Fe, N. M.

GODDARD, P. E.
> 1913. Indians of the Southwest. *American Museum of Natural History Handbook Series,* no. 2. New York.

GREGG, Josiah
> 1844. Commerce of the prairies. New York.

GUERNSEY, S. J.
> 1931. Explorations in northeastern Arizona 1920-1923. *Papers of the Peabody Museum of American Archæology and Ethnology,* vol. XII, no. 1. Cambridge, Mass.

HAMMOND, G. P.
> 1927. Don Juan de Oñate and the founding of New Mexico. *New Mexico Historical Review,* vol. I, no. 1 to vol. II, no. 2. Santa Fe.

HARRINGTON, M. R.
> 1933. Gypsum Cave, Nevada. *Southwest Museum Papers,* No. 8. Los Angeles.

HEWETT, Edgar L.
> 1906. Origin of the name Navaho. *American Anthropologist,* n. s. 8: 193. Lancaster, Pa.
> 1930. Ancient life in the American Southwest. Indianapolis.

HODGE, F. W.
>   1895. The early Navajo and Apache. *American Anthropologist*, 8: 223-240. Washington.

HOFFMAN, W. J.
>   1896. The Menomini Indians. *Fourteenth Annual Report of the Bureau of American Ethnology*, 3-328. Washington.

HOLLISTER, U. S.
>   1903. The Navajo and his blanket. Denver, Colo.

HOLMES, W. H.
>   1884. Prehistoric textile fabrics of the United States, derived from impressions on pottery. *Third Annual Report of the Bureau of Ethnology*, 393-425. Washington.
>   1896. Prehistoric textile art of the eastern United States. *Thirteenth Annual Report of the Bureau of Ethnology*, 3-46. Washington.

HOLT, Rosa Belle
>   1901. Rugs Oriental and Occidental. Chicago.

HOOPER, Luther
>   1915. The loom and spindle: past, present, and future. *Smithsonian Report* for 1914, 629-678. Washington.

HOUGH, Walter
>   1902. A collection of Hopi ceremonial pigments. *Report of the U. S. National Museum* for 1900, 463-471. Washington, D. C.
>   1914. Culture of the ancient pueblos of the upper Gila river region, Arizona and New Mexico. *Bulletin 87, U. S. National Museum*, Washington.
>   1919. The Hopi Indian collection in the United States National Museum. *Proceedings U. S. National Museum*, 54: 235-296. Washington.

HRDLICKA, Ales
>   1900. Physical and physiological observations on the Navaho. *American Anthropologist*, n. s. 2: 339-345. New York.

HUBBELL, John Lorenzo, *and* HOGG, John Edwin
>   1930. Fifty years an Indian trader. *Touring Topics*, December 1930. Los Angeles.

HUMMEL, J. J.
>   1885. The dyeing of textile fabrics. London.

IVES, J. C.
>   1861. Report upon the Colorado river of the west. Washington.

JAMES, George Wharton
   1920. Indian blankets and their makers. Chicago.
JOYCE, Thomas A.
   1912. South American archæology. New York.
JUDD, Neil M.
   1930. Excavation and repair of Betatakin. *Proceedings U. S. National Museum,* 77: 1-77. Washington.
KIDDER, A. V.
   1920. Ruins of the historic period in the upper San Juan valley, New Mexico. *American Anthropologist,* n. s. 22: 322-329. Lancaster, Pa.
   1924. An introduction to the study of Southwestern archæology. New Haven, Conn.
   1926. A sandal from northeastern Arizona. *American Anthropologist,* n. s. 28: 618-632. Menasha, Wis.
KIDDER, A. V., *and* GUERNSEY, S. J.
   1919. Archeological explorations in northeastern Arizona. *Bulletin 65, Bureau of American Ethnology.* Washington.
KISSELL, Mary Lois
   1916. A new type of spinning in North America. *American Anthropologist,* n. s. 18: 264-270. Lancaster, Pa.
LETTERMAN (Letherman), Jonathan.
   1856. Sketch of the Navajo tribe of Indians, Territory of New Mexico. *Tenth Annual Report of the Smithsonian Institution,* 283-297. Washington.
LINDQUIST, G. E. E.
   1923. The red man in the United States. New York.
LITTLE, James A.
   1881. Jacob Hamblin. Salt Lake City, Utah.
LOWERY, Woodbury
   1901. The Spanish settlements within the present limits of the United States. New York.
LUMMIS, Charles F.
   1893. The Spanish pioneers. Chicago.
   1896. The best blanket in the world. *Land of Sunshine,* 6: 8-11. Los Angeles.
LUXÁN, Diego Pérez de
   1929. Journal of the expedition into New Mexico made by Antonio de Espejo, 1582-1583. Translated by George Peter Hammond and Agapito Rey. Los Angeles.

MALLERY, Garrick
  1893. Picture writing of the American Indians. *Tenth Annual Report of the Bureau of Ethnology,* 4-822. Washington.
MASON, Otis T.
  1904. Indian basketry. New York.
MATTHEWS, Washington
  1884. Navajo weavers. *Third Annual Report of the Bureau of Ethnology,* 371-391. Washington.
  1897. Navaho legends. Boston.
  1900. A two-faced Navaho blanket. *American Anthropologist,* n. s. 2: 638-642. New York.
McGREGOR, John
  1929. The cotton industry among the ancients. *Progressive Arizona,* March, 1929. Phoenix, Ariz.
McGREGOR, J. C.
  1931. Prehistoric cotton fabrics of Arizona. *Museum Notes* (Museum of Northern Arizona), vol. 4, no. 2. Flagstaff, Ariz.
MEAD, Charles W.
  1924. Old civilizations of Inca land. *American Museum of Natural History, Handbook Series,* no. 11, New York.
MEANS, Philip Ainsworth
  1930. The origin of tapestry technique in pre-Spanish Peru. *Metropolitan Museum Studies,* vol. III, no. 1. New York.
  1931. Ancient civilizations of the Andes. New York.
  1932. A study of Peruvian textiles. Boston.
MENA, Ramón
  1925. El Zarape. *Anales del Museo Nacional de Arqueologia,* Epoca 5a, tomo I: 373-400. Mexico City.
MINDELEFF, Victor
  1891. A study of Pueblo architecture: Tusayan and Cibola. *Eighth Annual Report of the Bureau of Ethnology,* 3-228. Washington.
MONTELL, Gösta
  1929. Dress and ornaments in ancient Peru. Göteborg and London.
MORRIS, Earl H.
  1925. Exploring in the canyon of death. *National Geographic Magazine,* XLVIII: 263-300. Washington.
MUSEUM NOTES
  1930. The Hopi craftsman. *Museum Notes* (Museum of Northern Arizona), vol. 3, no. 1. Flagstaff, Ariz.

NORDENSKIÖLD, J.
1893.   The Cliff-dwellers of the Mesa Verde. Translated by D. Lloyd Morgan. Stockholm, Sweden.

NUSBAUM, Jesse L.
1922.   A Basket-Maker cave in Kane County, Utah. With notes on the artifacts by A. V. Kidder and S. J. Guernsey. *Indian Notes and Monographs,* Museum of the American Indian, Heye Foundation. New York.

O'NEALE, Lila M., *and* KROEBER, A. L.
1930.   Textile periods in ancient Peru. *University of California Publications in American Archæology and Ethnology,* 28: 23-56. Berkeley, Calif.

PEPPER, George H.
1902.   The making of a Navajo blanket. *Everybody's Magazine,* January, 1902. New York.
1903.   Native Navajo dyes. *The Papoose,* I: 1-11 (Feb. 1903). New York.
1923.   Navaho weaving. (Manuscript with illustrations, used by courtesy of the Museum of the American Indian, Heye Foundation.)

PINO, Pedro
1812.   Exposición del Nuevo Mexico. Cadiz, Spain.

PRINCE, L. Bradford
1883.   Historical sketches of New Mexico. Kansas City, Mo.

READ, Benjamin M.
1912.   Illustrated history of New Mexico. Santa Fe, N. M.

REICHARD, Gladys A.
1928.   Social life of the Navajo Indians. *Columbia University Contributions to Anthropology,* vol. VII. New York.

REPORT
1867.   Report of the Joint Special Committee on the condition of the Indian tribes. Washington.

REPORTS
1856.   Reports of explorations and surveys to ascertain the most practicable and economical route for a railroad from the Mississippi river to the Pacific ocean. *32d Congress, 2d Session. Ex. Doc. No. 78.* Washington.

ROBERTS, Frank H. H., Jr.
1932.   The village of the great kivas on the Zuñi reservation in New

Mexico. *Bulletin 2, Bureau of American Ethnology.* Washington.

RUDO ENSAYO
1863. Rudo Ensayo de la Provincia de Sonora (anonymous, 1761-62). St. Augustine, Florida.

RUSSELL, Frank
1908. The Pima Indians. *Twenty-sixth Annual Report of the Bureau of American Ethnology,* 1-390. Washington.

SABIN, Edwin L.
1914. Kit Carson days. Chicago.

SCHOOLCRAFT, H. R. *See* Backus, E.

SHUFELDT, R. W.
1891. The Navajo belt-weaver. *Proceedings U. S. National Museum,* XIV: 391-394. Washington.

SPIEGELBERG, A. F.
1904. Navajo blankets. *Out West,* XX: 447-449. Los Angeles.

SPIER, Leslie
1924. Zuñi weaving technique. *American Anthropologist,* n. s. 26: 64. Menasha, Wis.
1928. Havasupai ethnography. *American Museum of Natural History, Anthropological Papers,* vol. XXIX, part III. New York.

STEVENSON, James
1891. The ceremonial of Hasjelti Dailjis and mythical sand painting of the Navajo Indians. *Eighth Annual Report of the Bureau of Ethnology,* 229-285. Washington.

THOMAS, A. B.
1932. Forgotten frontiers. Norman, Okla.

THORNDIKE, Rachel Sherman, *editor.*
1894. The Sherman letters. Correspondence between General and Senator Sherman from 1837 to 1891. New York.

TWITCHELL, Ralph Emerson
1914. The Spanish archives of New Mexico. Cedar Rapids, Iowa.

VILLAGRÁ, Gaspar Pérez de. Historia de Nueva Mexico. Alcala, Spain, 1610. (Translation by Gilberto Espinosa to be published by the Quivira Society, Los Angeles, 1933.)

WALLACE, Susan E.
1888. Land of the Pueblos. New York.

WELSH, Herbert
1885. Report of a visit to the Navajo, Pueblo, and Hualapais Indians. Philadelphia.

WELTFISH, Gene

1930. Prehistoric North American basketry techniques and modern distributions. *American Anthropologist,* n. s. 32: 454-495.

WINSHIP, George Parker

1896. The Coronado expedition, 1540-1542. *Fourteenth Annual Report of the Bureau of American Ethnology,* 329-613. Washington.

WISSLER, Clark

1922. The American Indian. (2d edition.) New York.

WOOTON, E. O., *and* STANDLEY, Paul C.

1915. Flora of New Mexico. *Contributions from the United States National Herbarium,* vol. 19, *Smithsonian Institution, U. S. National Museum.* Washington.

ZÁRATE-SALMERÓN, *Fray* Gerónimo

1899-1900. Relaciones de todas las cosas que en el Nuevo-Mexico se han visto y savido, así por mar como por tierra, desde el año 1538 hasta él de 1626. Translation by Charles F. Lummis in *Land of Sunshine,* vols. XI-XII. Los Angeles.

INDEX
NAVAHO WEAVING

INDEX *

Abbott, F. H., cited, 182
Abert, J. W., cited, 147, 206
Acoma, 113, 116, 121, 206
Alder (Alnus incana), 81
Aldrich, S. E., 174-178
Aleutian Islands, 30
Algonkian weaving, 2, 9, 16
Arizona State Museum, 64, 98, 103
Alnus incana, see Alder
Alum, see Alunogen
Alunogen, 69, 73
Alvarado, Hernando de, 113
Ambrose, J. L., 97
American Museum of Natural History, 11, 25, 71, 194; pls. 7, 74
Apache, 72, 97, 121, 122, 124, 127, 131, 157, 179, 181, 192; Mescalero Apache, 158-160, 166
Atkinson, Spencer R., 149
Atlantic and Pacific Railroad, 34, 61, 177
Aztec ruin, 3
Aztec weaving, 23

Backus, E., cited, 157
Baisley, Mrs. C. F., 95
Baize, see Bayeta
Bancroft, H. H., cited, 129, 130, 155, 156
Bandelier, A. F., cited, 112
Barreiro, A., cited, 147
Bartlett, J. R., cited, 20, 141, 156
Bartlett, Katherine, 4
Basketmakers, age, 3; dyes, 69-71; weaving, 2, 3, 4, 7, 8, 12, 17, 30; figs. 4, 8, pl. 107

Baskets, Basketmakers, 125; coiled, 5; Hopi, 3, pl. 2; Navaho, 6, 83, 125, pl. 4; Northwest coast, 16; Paiute, 5, 83, 125, pl. 4; Ute, 83, 125, pl. 4
Basket weave, 12, 13
Bassett, A., 79
Batten, 21, figs. 5, 12; pl. 16
Bayeta, 97, 102-103, 135-151
Beadle, J. H., cited, 183
Benavides, A. de, cited, 73, 121, 126, 128-129
Benham Indian Trading Co., 194
Bennett, J. W., 175
Bernard, Bruce, 196
Betatakin, 25
Bigelovia, see Rabbit brush
Bloom, L. B., cited, 132, 133
Boas, F., cited, 218
Bohn, John, 177
Bolton, H. E., 117, 118, 127, 206
Bosque Redondo, 164-169, 183
Boyce Thompson Southwestern Arboretum, 79
Braiding, 2-3, pl. 7
Brazil wood, 88, 89, 143
Brocade, 57
Brooklyn Museum, 23, 140; pls. 60, 115
Browne, P., cited, 198
Burbank, E. A., 189
Burge, Moris, 225, 227, 235
Burge, (Margaret McKittrick) Mrs. Moris, 202, 226-229
Bursum, H. O., 225
Burt, W. H., 32